Palgrave Studies in the History of Economic Thought

Palgrave Studies in the History of Economic Thought publishes contributions by leading scholars, illuminating key events, theories and individuals that have had a lasting impact on the development of modern-day economics. The topics covered include the development of economies, institutions and theories.

More information about this series at
http://www.palgrave.com/gp/series/14585

Tengda Hua

Merchants, Market and Monarchy

Economic Thought and History in Early Modern China

palgrave
macmillan

Tengda Hua
Department of Economics
Shanghai University of Political Science and Law
Shanghai, China

ISSN 2662-6578 ISSN 2662-6586 (electronic)
Palgrave Studies in the History of Economic Thought
ISBN 978-3-030-77188-1 ISBN 978-3-030-77189-8 (eBook)
https://doi.org/10.1007/978-3-030-77189-8

Cover illustration: ©DuKai photographer/GettyImages

This Palgrave Macmillan imprint is published by the registered company Springer Nature Switzerland AG
The registered company address is: Gewerbestrasse 11, 6330 Cham, Switzerland

Dedicated to
my dear parents, Mrs. Zheng Jingwen, and Mr. Hua Yiwei,
my dear Doctoral supervisor Prof. Dr. Dres. h.c. Bertram Schefold,
my dear Master supervisor Prof. Michael Haliassos,
and
the younger version of me who spent his golden time in Frankfurt am Main, Germany (2013–2020)

Foreword

I.

This book is an outgrowth of the project 'Chinese and European History of Economic Thought in Comparison', which I pursue together with the Sinologist Prof. Iwo Amelung at the Forschungskolleg Humanwissenschaften in Bad Homburg. Economic history emphasizes the importance of scientific knowledge for the explanation of success in economic development. By contrast, the relevance of economic knowledge for the creation of institutions and policies favouring growth receives much less attention. The project investigates this problematic, confronting Chinese and European experiences, from Antiquity to the present. The comparison might help to explain the divergence of Chinese and European paths in the eighteenth century. The texts, mainly by philosophers and statesmen, express the development of culturally characteristic concepts for frameworks that remain relevant for the understanding of the Chinese and European economies in their specific contexts. Even though modern liberalism and the emergence of Chinese Marxism appear to have rendered traditional economic thought irrelevant, a closer examination reveals that it offers intellectual resources, which are tapped consciously or unconsciously, and it thus continues to play an important role up to today.

One of the questions often raised in economic history and in history of economic thought concerns the status of merchants. They were deprecated in Antiquity according to both traditions but began to play a more significant role in the West from the period of mercantilism onwards.

A specific critique, that of usury, was, in a sense, then turned on its head, insofar as the popular, philosophical and theological critique of usury was revised, and reasons, which scholastic thought had found for regarding interest taking as licit, were transformed into early propositions of economic theory and thus contributed to the emergence of rational capitalism. This specific critique of usury did not exist in ancient China. Unlike the European kingdoms, the Chinese state was a lender rather than a borrower. A certain disdain for the merchants remained even in the latest phase of pre-modern China, but the critique of usury played no particular role in that. Tengda Hua, confronted with this problematic, has chosen to concentrate on Ming China as a period that started with reforms aiming at restoring the primacy of agriculture with greater equality, and which was inward-looking, insofar as maritime trade was restricted, but then prosperity advanced, foreign trade, especially with Southeast Asia, grew, and the role of the merchants became visibly more important, yet the attitudes did not change much. It was a time at which discussions flourished and the book trade expanded, hence there was much debate about economic matters that involved the role of merchants. It would have to be analysed in the context of this big economic transformation. How was it interpreted in fact by the thinkers of this period, what did they propose to the imperial authority, in short: what kind of economic thought prospered under the circumstances?

The problem could be approached from different angles. The most important history of Chinese economic thought available in the West by Hu Jichuang (1988) follows the model of Western histories of economic thought. The book is organized chronologically and discusses the different schools and authors, who were primarily philosophers and statesmen or bureaucrats. Their texts are read in the endeavour to discover systematic economic ideas on value, price, commerce, taxation, and welfare in an economy dominated by the state. The advantage is that the positions of influential authors like Confucius as a philosopher or of Wang Anshi as an influential minister appear as coherent; one can get a view of how they saw the interaction of state and economy. An alternative to Hu's approach consists of writing an economic history, in which occasionally the ideas of thinkers help to interpret the facts, as in von Glahn's Economic History of China (2016). Hua has chosen a compromise: he looks at the status of merchants in relation to economic problems such as those of monopoly, taxation, or foreign trade; he assembles the views of different authors on the matter, trying to distinguish between different positions like for or against maritime trade, and he reports on the economic facts as a background to these voices. The sociological point of view thus prevails. The focus is not on the coherence of individual conceptions, but on ideological expressions of a given social formation, and there is a very little analytical reconstruction of economic theory. Hua's book uses both Hu's and Glahn's approaches. He imposes fewer Western concepts than Hu does in order to start from the Chinese conceptions of economic phenomena, where that is possible, and there is more emphasis on the thinking of individuals and of schools than in Glahn.

II.

The book is divided into eight chapters. After an introduction on the historical background and methodological considerations, the second chapter deals with the political system of the Ming dynasty and the origin of economic thought regarding the 'suppression of merchants' and 'egalitarianism'. The systematic part begins with Chapter 3 on the status of merchants in view of the state monopolies that were still strong in Ming China. The fourth chapter is concerned with merchants and commercial taxes and Chapter 5 with merchants and foreign trade. Chapter 6 deals with two originally philosophical oppositions: 'righteousness versus profits' and 'luxury versus frugality'. These are old and, in Chinese philosophy, fundamental distinctions. Chapter 7 discusses the status of merchants relative to scholars, peasants, and craftsmen in Ming China, that is, in relation to the traditional division of economic society into four classes: another old distinction. The final point is that the traditional hierarchy was not really superseded, despite the fundamental economic transformation. Chapter 8 states this, together with a summary of other conclusions. The stratification according to which the merchants rank below not only the ruling class, but also below agriculture and handicraft is traced back in the main to Guanzi; that the ruling class is dominated by the literati who become officials is traced back to the Sui dynasty. The aim is to explain what image of the functioning of the economy could be compatible with this persistent subordination of merchants, which, seen from today, appears to be nothing but a nasty prejudice.

For better understanding, it may be useful here to start with a comparison with European economic thought in Antiquity and the Middle Ages. The key concept there is that of the just price. It is thought that each commodity has its just price; it can be determined by the experts in the market. The difficulty of the merchant is that he cannot buy cheap and sell dear without violating the command to observe the just price at least once, at least as long as he is an intermediate trader and does not provide a tangible service such as transporting the merchandise. So, it was not clear how the merchant could remain virtuous; it could only be said that it was a venial sin, if he did not charge much in buying cheap and selling dear—Luther still maintained this traditional point of view. If the nobility did not respect merchants, they probably acted from a feeling of superiority based on martial pride or cultural distinction, but the rationalisation of their judgement on the basis of the theory of the just price was of great consequence for the history of economic thought, for it took a long time to find out what the contribution of the merchant really was, which could justify his profit. The way that led from the notion of just price to that of natural and, eventually, normal price was, from the point of view of historical sociology, a process of rationalisation similar to that which lead from interest as usury to interest as a compensation for deferred consumption. The Weberian term rationalisation contains a bias. It seems to say that the earlier conception was irrational, but it looks so only from the modern point of view. The older conception is rational in its specific context. The just price appears in classical Antiquity as the fair price, which decent vendors charge, who renounce to the extra-profit, which might perhaps be obtained by higgling in the market. Interest was denounced as usury, if the rich took advantage of the misery of the poor and demanded full repayment with an extra charge for a loan in an emergency, instead of providing unconditional or at least generous support.

So, what was the economic rationalisation for a low status of the merchant in China? A systematic theory of value did never really emerge, although Hu (1988) tried to delineate a theory of prices in Pre-Qin-thought, especially in Mohist philosophy. Hua does not really confront this basic question, but he concentrates on the nexus, which undoubtedly is fundamental in Chinese economic history and in the ideologies in all of what we know of Chinese history: the merchant stands in opposition to the state, in that he reallocates goods for his profit and the benefit of his family, which helps big merchants to build up a trading network, while the state has from the start a responsibility, not only to tax, but to distribute for the benefit of the people, and this was done not only by means of keeping law and order, by means of redistributing land, but also by means of state trade, the maintenance of state granaries, and by replacing the rich merchants with their virtual monopolies by state agencies, so that the scope left for the private trader tended to get minimized, at least repeatedly in theory, while the state monopoly operated in practice only in limited domains. Hua develops this position in its economic context. Future extensions will distinguish between the economic, the sociological, and the philosophical aspects of the underlying doctrines. It is not trivial to identify the aspects of the rich philosophical tradition of China, which could be regarded as economic. In order to concentrate on his main theme, Hua simplifies and speaks of Confucians, Legalists, and Daoists as 'schools of ancient Chinese economic thought'.

Chapter 2 begins with the mutual dependence of merchants and state, the merchants being subject to monarchic control, while their strengths often depend on their extended family relationships. The formation of state monopolies is dated to the early Han period (iron, salt, wine—a tea monopoly becomes important in the Tang dynasty). On the one hand, the state controls trade, the cities define locations where trade may take place, on the other, the state also disturbs trade, by fixing prices or by letting it happen that corrupt state officials confiscate merchandise. Hua discusses the politics of Wang Anshi, who started by encouraging strong state trade, based on bureaucratic entrepreneurship, but it ended in confiscatory taxation. Continuities and discontinuities of the state-merchant relationship have often been described, and Hua summarizes: 'The suppression of merchants in ancient China has always been based on none other than political requirements'. As it turns out, there are economic ideas behind the critique of ideology.

Hua observes that the deprecation of merchants gradually diminished in the West, but it increased in China over the millenia. There was a need to fight inequality, and thoughts on egalitarianism came up in all philosophical schools. By repressing traders, inequality could be reduced, or so it seemed. The merchants therefore were under pressure not only from above, but also from below, as is proved by the uprisings of the peasants. This is his general picture, and the question then is: What became of such intellectual traditions in the Ming period?

III.

This is the core of the book. Chapter 3 addresses the question whether the state-operated commerce during the Ming dynasty should be extended or reduced, and Hua fittingly begins with the thoughts of Qiu Jun, whom

Hu Jichuang regards as 'the broadest among Chinese scholars before the mid-19th century', as far as the history of economic thought is concerned. He was a Confucian and opposed the monopolies advocated by Sang Hongyang during the Salt and Iron Debate in the first-century B.C. He favoured private trade but did not go so far as to demand the abolition of all the monopolies. As Grand Secretary, he also had fiscal aims in view. Hua presents a number of other authors who were critical of state monopolies and then turn to supporters. Li Zhi, among the latter, advised to continue the policy of the Han dynasty to establish monopolies in order to prevent rich merchants from getting too much political power.

Hua then explains the policies to maintain the salt monopoly during the Ming dynasty in the form of salt licenses sold to the merchants. The matter is complicated; it involved different factions on the part of officials as well as mercantile interests. As economic history, it is well explained in von Glahn (2016, p. 288). The state, by selling too many licenses, undermined his source of revenue. The reflections on this complicated story with several ups and downs in the history of economic thought consisted in attempts to understand the logic of the power relationships; the discussions are evidence that 'the state's control over state run commerce had weakened during the Ming dynasty' (p. 94). Hua concludes that the bureaucracy exploited the merchants instead of helping them to expand their trade, and emperors, who, on occasion, tried to protect the merchants, were not able to control the state operators sufficiently. The final consumers had to bear the burden of inefficient arrangements.

The designation of the system of distribution based on the salt licenses as 'monopoly' seems to suggest that the chapter belongs to the theory of imperfect competition, so that one might try to isolate the understanding of market relationships by the different authors on the matter. I have tried to point to some elements of such understanding in my analysis of the Salt and Iron Debate (Schefold, 2019). Hua, in his account of the salt monopoly under the Ming, is mainly concerned with the power relationships in politics and the formation of interest groups, based on geographical origin, on the part of the merchants. The main explanatory variable is the income that the state derives from providing privileges.

Fittingly, the next chapter is concerned with taxation. It begins with the harsh policies by the founder of the dynasty, Emperor Hongwu. On the one hand, there was grace: commercial tax rates were lowered. On the other, there was oppression: the emperor would relocate thousands of merchants and confiscate property. Tax evasion was severely punished.

The taxes were defended as the mean to finance defence, and it was argued that the burden on farmers could be reduced in line with these reforms. The obvious question to be asked here is what the diverse authors thought about the incidence of taxation. On the whole, the contributions to economic thought are difficult to identify in a flood of summaries of political viewpoints, which were diverse in the face of a complex situation. An interesting instance of economic argumentation is given by Wang Fuzhi, who believed that the taxes to be paid by merchants could not be passed on to peasants or landowners. The reasons for this belief are worth analysing. What one misses in the texts—or has it not yet been found?—is the concept of a surplus.

The next chapter concerns the status of merchants and foreign trade. Foreign trade had been closely controlled and would be exposed to the influence of foreign merchants during the Ming period. Hua begins with thought on foreign trade in Chinese Antiquity, with Sang Hongyang as an example of an early author praising the advantages. There was an embargo on foreign trade in the beginning of the Ming dynasty; only the state would maintain the tributary trade with foreign powers that were regarded as Chinese vassals. This was detrimental to the interests of people living near the coast. The doctrine was that the imported goods were unnecessary luxuries and that the maritime contacts would invite invasions by pirates, while in fact the inhabitants of the coast maintained trading ships and colluded with the foreigners. The opponents of the sea ban pointed out that it involved lost employment opportunities and that the state could obtain fiscal revenue from tariffs as in earlier generations. Qiu Jun here reappears, now considered as the first author in the ideological trend of abolishing the sea ban in the Ming dynasty. He conceded that the trade with the Japanese was problematic because he thought that they would plunder the coast, but he devised a scheme for how private trade might be inspected and controlled. Later authors continued in this vein: 'Pirates become merchants when trade is smooth, and merchants become pirates when trade is banned'; Hua notes that Sombart had made a similar observation. He then describes how the merchants gradually built trading networks, first making use of the tributary trade, and how these Chinese initiatives became interwoven with the growing trade with the West, led by the Portuguese. The story helps to understand the extent and the importance of Chinese trading networks and Chinese communities in Southeast Asia.

IV.

The account returns to the philosophical discussions, by dealing with the oppositions of righteousness and profit, and frugality and luxury. This in line with the modern Chinese method to interpret economic thoughts primarily as ideological reflections of economic structures and not as leading ideas that help to lay the foundation for new institutions. Qiu Jun was consistent in his Confucianism; he thought that merchants should strive to be righteous and subordinate their interest in profits. From here, Hua goes back to Confucius himself and to Xunzi, who was more open, regarding 'desire' as a licit motive for commercial action. The evolution of thought then is traced up to the Ming dynasty, when authors like Li Zhi attempted to reconcile righteousness and profit; the pursuit of riches and of precious objects became a natural phenomenon. Li Zhi was popular when he defended the life styles of merchants. Hence it became possible that a famous scholar would write the epitaph of a merchant, in which he directly confronted the two views, that of an opposition, and that of a fruitful combination, of righteousness and profit. But even this author, Gu Xiancheng, still saw the clash between truth and the material interest.

There follows an interesting section on usury in Ming China. Chinese discussions on interest taking never denounced it as generally usurious as sometimes was done in the West. There were ceilings on interest rates. The principle that a loan had to be paid back was not questioned, but there was a debate on whether the state should provide loans or whether this activity could be left to private persons. Qiu Jun was, in contrast to Sang Hongyang, in favour of lending by private merchants and against government lending. Other thinkers feared that lending might induce borrowers to become lazy, and yet another position demanded that rich merchants should lend without asking for interest; the counter-argument was that this would mean 'robbing the rich and helping the poor.' Hua sees private merchants and the state as rivals in lending, and the merchants have an advantage, insofar as their networks reach out into remote areas of the countryside. One would like to know more about the principles guiding these policies.

The next section concerns thrift and luxury. There are the passages from Guanzi relating luxury consumption and employment, and there is awareness of external effects. As in ancient Rome, officials would proclaim frugality and live luxuriantly. In the comparison with historical facts, a section on the merchant's consumption of arts and books stands out; we here find the Chinese counterpart of Molière's Bourgeois gentilhomme. The Ming period saw a spectacular extension of the book trade, and merchants could gain prestige as book collectors.

V.

Chapter 7 places the merchants relative to the classes of scholars, peasants, and craftsmen and contains the main conclusions of the research. Did the economic transformation with the associated extensive discussions about economic matters lead to a transformation of the traditional hierarchy of the four classes? Hua finds many modifications, thinkers grant that all classes work diligently and deserve respect; but, when all is said and done, the traditional theory of the four occupational groups is not really overturned. There remains the weight of the Confucian tradition, there is the severity of the system of examinations, in which the chance of getting to higher ranks is very slim. Yet the salaries of bureaucrats were low, and Confucian thought provided a compensation for this. On-going criticism of luxury meant that merchants providing luxury goods through their trade were superfluous. On the other hand, it was said that, if a merchant was to be regarded as honourable, he should at least be rich. It was noted that merchants provided for charity, for temples and works of art, but this was to be ascribed to their wealth and not to a meritorious profession. Hua extends these comparisons systematically to the other classes, going through the text of many authors and their value judgements, which vary to some extent. For instance, some remark that peasants may be narrow-minded and merchants need more abilities. Scholars appreciate the artistic talents of craftsmen, but, in the end, the weight of the tradition remains. The final chapter then leads back to the discussion of the great divergence and hence to the comparative status of merchants in China and the West.

The book is important; it fills a lacuna in the Western literature on China, which abounds with works on economic history, but the history of Chinese economic thought has been neglected. It might be argued that economic thought in pre-modern Chinese history never is analytical, because it always emphasises philosophical, ethical, and political considerations so that the attempt to look for elements of economic reasoning that are capable of analytic reconstruction is vain, especially if the understanding of the role of merchants is to be investigated, which one might regard as a sociological question. But such an opinion would stand in contrast to the emerging discipline of history of economic thought in

China, within which parallels with the Western history continue to be sought, as in Hu (1988). It hardly seems possible to evaluate past 'economic' policies without asking what their economic implications were, even though it is certainly important to understand their political and ethical motivations. And it is not plausible that such policies were ever proposed without at least some consideration of their likely consequences, but this means that proponents of economic actions must have formed at least rudimentary hypotheses about economic causality.

Then it may again be said that these elements of causal economic thought are in the Chinese case less interesting than the far more extended philosophical, ethical, and political discourse. Some classical texts are commonly discussed in the perspective of the history of economic thought, such as Guanzi or the Debate on Salt and Iron, or, in this book, the work of Qiu Jun. How can we approach these works as economists and in the context of HET? We can classify and contextualize the ideas and evaluate them in relation to philosophical systems and political ideals. If we recognize the originality and the creativity of the authors, we discover that they are more than mere ideological reflections the conditions of the time; we can seek a hermeneutical understanding and portray the historical individuals with their conflictual choices. This, I believe, is where research in the history of Chinese economic thought will have to move in the future.

Frankfurt, Germany
December 2020

Bertram Schefold

References

Hu, J. (1988). *A concise history of chinese economic thought*. Foreign Languages Press.

Schefold, B. (2019). A western perspective on the Yantie lun. In L. Cheng, T. Peach, & F. Wang (Eds.), *The political economy of the Han dynasty and its legacy* (pp. 153–174). Routledge.

Von Glahn, R. (2016). *An economic history of China: From antiquity to the nineteenth century*. Cambridge University Press.

Preface

This is my first published monograph in English. As a young scholar who just reached his 30, it is my great honour that Palgrave Macmillan agrees to publish my book. I can still remember that the first English book I finished reading was the seventh book of Harry Potter series in 2007, when I was still a Grade 11 senior middle school student. I would never expect my own manuscript being published by a world-famous European press at the time. And no matter what kind of achievements I will make in my future academic career, and no matter how unsophisticated this book might look when looking back after years, this monograph will always occupy a dominant position in my life.

Here, I will succinctly explain why this book is innovative in the realm of economics and economic thought, why this book is interesting, how this book stays objective, and why this book is of some consequence and worth reading.

WHY INNOVATIVE. Regarding the commerce history of early modern China, there existed numerous books. However, in history of economic thought, the research of this period is nearly a vacuum. Previous scholars usually concentrated on the pre-Qin period. This is quite understandable since that is the source of almost everything of Chinese culture and society, including thoughts in miscellaneous subfields. However, after thousands years' evolving, the economic thought during early modern China must have changed quite a lot despite its unchanged origin. The thought in this period is also fertile and worth researching on, while the related material in English is quite deficient. As one of my greatest advantage, I may consult rich literatures in both English and classical Chinese, even some in German. After all, I stayed in Germany for seven years and communicated in German daily, although my German is far from proficiency. Moreover, since I received higher education in Germany, western economic thought is also within my expertise. While this book is discussing economic thought in early modern China, some western thoughts also appear as a brief comparison and frame of reference.

WHY INTERESTING. While western readers might not be unfamiliar with the commerce development and merchants in early modern China, it must be their first time to look closely into so many interesting thoughts of the scholars and officials in that period. Also, this book involves detailed history presenting the relations between Chinese merchants and European merchants at the time. While some existing literature might record it according to the journals and records of European merchants, travellers, and missionaries at the time, it will be equally interesting to see the same period of history from the perspective of Ming individuals. Finally, for those who dabbled in history of western economic thought, they might find it interesting and surprising that those famous western economic thinkers may find their echo in the Ming Empire.

WHY IMPARTIAL. Presenting the real history and decoding objectively has always been, and should be, the priority of all scholars, especially historians. In the research of economic history and economic thought, two types of bias might exist. First is different kinds of 'centrism', including eurocentrism, asiacentrism, etc. The second type of bias is at least equally severe. In many history books written in Chinese, or at a typical history class, the readers (or the students) were often taught that Emperor A was a '***mingjun***' (a wise emperor who was often described as capable and virtuous), while Emperor B was a '***hunjun***' (a fatuous emperor who was often described as barbarous and incompetent). It sounds like that a wise emperor never eliminates his opponent, and a fatuous emperor only knows how to enjoy a life of luxury and dissipation. In most situations, it is absolutely untrue, although we shall not rule out those specific cases. As well-trained scholars, we all know that such kind of rough categorising is quite naïve. Thus, it is of my great interest (also my duty) to reveal the real history in this specific subfield, by staying neutral from cover to cover, although some bias might still exist. As a young Chinese scholar, I have the good fortune to read the primary sources, while I was trained in Germany in one of the centres of excellence in the history of economic thought. The primary sources were often much more reliable than second-hand materials, although they were also often at least a bit biased knuckling under the will of the rulers at the time (naturally not all official historians were people of integrity). Nonetheless, they were so far the most reliable material that we may find.

WHY IMPORTANT. While western economic thoughts during early modern period has been fully researched, the blank of Ming Empire in this field really looks awkward. This book is, with no doubt, a valuable addition to the literature of history of economic thought, and meanwhile within the scope of popular topics regarding merchants and trade. In addition, this is a professional book in history of economic thought and economic history, yes, but it's more than that. The essence of culture, geographical elements, way of thinking, policy making, etc. all of these has not really changed much during the past centuries. While pre-Qin period and the Han Empire were quite remote, Ming China, as the latest empire ruled by the Han race, really provides essential reference for today. Not only the Chinese history lovers, historians, and other scholars in the West (especially those engaged in Chinese and European economic history and history of economic thought) might find this book necessary and interesting, but all people who are interested in current global issues and contemporary China may also find this book inspiring and timely. Even some very recent economic policies such as 'dual circulation' can find their parallel in early modern China as well.

This book, of course, still has a few deficiencies. I am looking forward to hearing more suggestions from my readers and colleagues, which will surely provide me more inspiration for perfecting this book and my future research as well. For communication and questions, please send emails to the following email address: tengda830@gmail.com.

Shanghai, China
November 2020

Tengda Hua

Acknowledgments

Here are some important individuals (and institutes) that I would like to express my specific gratitude. They accompanied and supported me along the way when I wrote this book. First of all, I would like to express my sincere gratitude to my parents, Mrs. Zheng Jingwen and Mr. Hua Yiwei. Their nurture and patience are the prerequisite for everything I accomplished and will accomplish, naturally including this book. Second, I would like to express my sincere gratitude to my dear doctoral supervisor, Prof. Bertram Schefold, for his superb, patient and kind instruction. For me, he is not merely a world well-known prestigious scholar in our speciality, but also like my grandpa. I would also like to thank Prof. Kent Deng and Prof. Joseph McDermott for the endorsement, Prof. Michael Haliassos, Prof. Rainer Klump and Prof. Guido Friebel for the assessment, and Mrs. Heidrun Schneider for the miscellaneous arrangements and paperwork. Then, I would like to thank Palgrave Macmillan for publishing my book, and also great help from the editors, Mr. Wyndham Hacket Pain and Ms. Hemapriya Eswanth. I would also like to thank Goethe University Frankfurt, my dear alma mater, where I spent my golden time (23 to 29 years old). Frankfurt is with no doubt my second hometown. In addition, I would like to thank my buddies, other family members and all my former professors and teachers. As one of the only child generation, my close friends are just like my brothers and sisters. Their company is quite essential for me. Finally, I would like to cherish the memory of my dear Grandma Bao Ruiqing, Grandpa Zheng Yuanxiang, Grandma Mao

Manzhu. They all love me so much, and it is huge pity that I cannot share this book with them. May the peace be with them!

Contents

About the Author

华腾达 **Tengda HUA** born in Shanghai in August 1990, currently works as an Assistant Professor in Shanghai University of Political Science and Law. He obtained his Doctoral degree and Master degree from Goethe University Frankfurt, Germany (Doctoral supervisor: Prof. Bertram Schefold). He spent 7 years in Frankfurt, where strong trace of Schopenhauer and Goethe may still be found. Before that he got his Bachelor degree from Tongji University in Shanghai, during which he spent an overseas semester in TU Darmstadt.

His current research interest mainly lies in history of economic thought, trade history, and other related topics. He is also a member of the European Society for the History of Economic Thought (ESHET). He was one of the winners of the Young Scholar Seminar at ESHET 2020 annual conference. He has, so far, visited 23 countries around the world with his parents and good friends. Witnessing different culture corresponds with his belief of 'crossing the borders of prejudice' inspired by Montaigne, which is also widely reflected in his academic research.

List of Figures

Major Chronological Period

The Mongolian-ruled Yuan China (1271–1368)
The Ming China (1368–1644)
Emperor Hongwu 1368–1398
Emperor Jianwen 1398–1402
Emperor Yongle 1402–1424
Emperor Hongxi 1424–1425
Emperor Xuande 1425–1435
Emperor Zhengtong 1435–1449
Emperor Jingtai 1449–1457
Emperor Tianshun 1457–1464
Emperor Chenghua 1464–1487
Emperor Hongzhi 1487–1505
Emperor Zhengde 1505–1521
Emperor Jiajing 1521–1567
Emperor Longqing 1567–1572
Emperor Wanli 1572–1620
Emperor Taichang 1620–1620
Emperor Tianqi 1620–1627
Emperor Chongzhen 1627–1644
The Manchu-ruled Qing China (1644–1912)

CHAPTER 1

Introduction

August 1552, two months before Matteo Ricci[1] was born. Francis Xavier, a Navarrese Catholic missionary and saint, wrote to his friend Gaspar, at Goa,

> I am on my way to the Chinese islands which are near Canton, denuded of all earthly, but surrounded, as I hope, with heavenly defences. I have imbibed the hope that heathen men in the continent of China will open to me the entrance.[2]

Late that month, the Santa Cruz reached the island of Shangchuan, only fourteen kilometres away from the southern coast of mainland China.

Although he has learnt that 'any attempt of the Chinese to smuggle an European into the country would be visited with the death of themselves and of their families',[3] around mid-November he bribed to a merchant who was willing to run this risk of life taking him, which cost Xavier

[1] Matteo Ricci (1552–1610) was an Italian Jesuit missionary. He lived in China for almost 30 years and died in Peking. He was renowned for introducing Christian teaching to the Ming empire and prompt cultural exchange between the East and the West. He enjoyed a high reputation among the high-level officials in Peking at the time.

[2] Venn (2009, p. 241).

[3] Venn (2009, p. 245).

T. Hua, *Merchants, Market and Monarchy*,
Palgrave Studies in the History of Economic Thought,
https://doi.org/10.1007/978-3-030-77189-8_1

'twenty pies of pepper, valued at 200 moidores'.[4] Unfortunately, he still failed to enter China with this risky attempt. He remained alone with António, his interpreter. He died at Shangchuan island on December 3, 1552, while waiting for a boat that may take him to mainland China. It is said that before he died, he shouted in the direction of mainland China, 'rocks, when can you crack open'? Decades after, Matteo Ricci met similar problems and suffered from other difficulties, despite the fact that he was admitted to China and even enjoyed some reputation at the court.

Closed boundary, strict sea ban, hardness to approach, hostility to outsiders including merchants... These are the impression that almost all European missionaries and merchants may have on the commercial activities of Ming Empire at that time. At the time, the merchants in the West has begun to play essential roles in economic affairs and world trade. They must be curious, behind those 'rocks' and under the seemingly harsh sea ban, what are the roles of the merchants? How do they engage in trade and survive? What do other Chinese people think of trade and merchants?... These are the questions we might also be curious about.

1.1 Merchants in Early Modern China

The striking contrast between the rise of the West and the stagnation of the rest of the world has remained among the most interesting and popular topics for research related to economics and economic history. Regarding the differences between the historical development of the West and China, we may recall the famous Needham's Grand Question that asked why China was overtaken by the West in science and technology despite the fact that 'medieval Europe was largely on a level with ancient Persia, India, or China',[5] or even, China being on a 'higher level of development precisely in the Middle Ages'[6]? It is widely acknowledged that the Chinese economy was not 'severely impoverished, at least in relative terms' until 'the rise of the opium trade in the early nineteenth century'.[7] In Needham's exact words, 'Why did modern science, as opposed to

[4] Venn (2009, p. 245).

[5] Polanyi (1944, pp. 47–48).

[6] Schefold (2014a, p. 13).

[7] Deng (2000, p. 1).

ancient and medieval science, develop only in the Western world but not in the Chinese or Indian civilisations?'[8] He asserted,

> The institution of the mandarinate had the effect of creaming off the best brains of the nation for more than 2000 years into the civil service. Merchants might acquire great wealth yet they were never secure, they were subjected to sumptuary laws, and they could be mulcted of their wealth by inordinate taxation and every other kind of governmental interference. Moreover they never achieved a mystique of their own.[9]

The 'Great Divergence', coined by Samuel Huntington[10] and popularised by scholars such as Kenneth Pomeranz,[11] is a related concept that has become familiar to most economic historians in the past two decades. It refers to the different growth paths and developmental pace adopted by civilisations, with Western Europe surpassing several glorious Eastern civilisations that have since lagged behind. The scholars have tried to identify various factors to explain this great divergence between East and West. For instance, traditional explanation 'for European success in contrast to China is competition amongst political units... but clearly it is not the whole story'.[12] Pomeranz, from another point of view, stated that 'China and Asia did participate in trading, but colonization brought a distinct advantage to the West'.[13]

The great divergence was obviously not the result of only a few variables; nevertheless, the role of merchants was undoubtedly very important. The status, behaviour, and role of merchants obviously reflected and epitomised the economic systems and characteristics of each country. In this regard, Weber and Sombart proposed the concept of an economic style:

> An economic style is characterized by an economic spirit, one might also say by the prevailing ethic and the mentalities of the people (1); it is based on natural and technical endowments (the technology being associated

[8] Needham (2005 [1969], p. 11).

[9] Needham (2005 [1969], p. 39).

[10] Andre (2001, pp. 180–182).

[11] See Pomeranz (2000).

[12] North (1990, p. 130).

[13] Pomeranz (2000, pp. 242–243).

> with a certain dynamic of its development) (2), an economic constitution (the question of property rights) (3), a social constitution (4) and a dynamic of accumulation (5).[14]

Moreover, factors related to the role of merchants, such as Western mercantilism and China's self-imposed isolation from external relations, are key explanatory variables as well to explain the Great Divergence. The Western merchants not only had free trade rights but were also recruited to play pivotal roles in their respective nations' overseas expansion, resulting in colonization bringing 'a distinct advantage to the West', as stated above. On the contrary, Chinese merchants were generally regarded as holding lower social status in both domestic and overseas trade, despite the 'virtual absence of effective legal and social barrier to the movement of individuals and families from one status to another'.[15] Accordingly, commerce in ancient China was long considered as complementary rather than central to the economy. As Needham pointed out,

> This situation prevailing, it was evidently impossible for the mercantile classes of Chinese culture to acquire anything like the positions of power and influence in the State which they attained during the Renaissance in Europe. In other words, not to put too fine a point upon the matter, whoever would explain the failure of Chinese society to develop modern science had better begin by explaining the failure of Chinese society to develop mercantile.[16]

No wonder why Fairbank pointed out that 'in Chinese history one urgent question is why the Chinese merchant class failed to break away from its dependence upon officialdom and create an independent entrepreneurial power'.[17]

This is an appropriate time to introduce one of the most commonly discussed concepts of economic thought, namely, the idea of *zhong nong yi shang* (emphasising agriculture and peasants while suppressing private commerce and merchants) that is intrinsically associated with the status of ancient Chinese merchants. Most scholars conclude that this idea

[14] Schefold (2000, p. 27).

[15] Ho (1962, p. xii).

[16] Needham (2005 [1969], pp. 39–40).

[17] Fairbank (1983, pp. 46–47).

remained predominant throughout the history of ancient China. *Nong* and *shang* can be interpreted in two ways, namely, 'agriculture or peasants' and 'commerce or merchants'. Based on the unified system of centralised power that began during the Qin Dynasty,[18] commerce in ancient Chinese society has usually been divided into two distinct camps, state-run businesses and private commerce.

Autocratic courts were willing to support and cultivate state-run commerce at any cost. Therefore, the so-called *yi shang* referred only to the 'suppression of private commerce', or more specifically, 'suppressing private merchants'. This idea was regarded as a pillar of economic thought and related policies in ancient China. A detailed analysis is provided in Sect. 2.2.

Another theory related to these discussions was social stratification. Ancient Chinese societies maintained the division of occupational labour for long periods. In *Zhouli*,[19] people's work was divided into nine categories, with merchants naturally comprising one of them: 'The sixth occupation was "merchant", those who were responsible for the circulation of goods and wealth'.[20] One broader classification was the theory of four occupational groups proposed by the author of *Guanzi*[21] that became the benchmark for the subsequent dynasty. It divided different professions by class strata, thereby providing the best evidence of widespread contempt for merchants.

Guanzi and Zhouli were the earliest works in ancient China that 'dealt among other things with economic issues'.[22] The author of *Guanzi* was

[18] The Qin dynasty was the first dynasty of Imperial China lasting for only 15 years, from 221 to 206 BC. The Qin dynasty was founded by Qin Shi Huang, the First Emperor of Qin (and the first emperor of Imperial China as well).

[19] *Zhouli*, also known as *The Rites of Zhou*, is a Confucian classic on bureaucracy and organizational theory, which first appeared in the middle of the second-century BC. It was written by Zhou GongDan, a famous politician and thinker in the Western Zhou Dynasty.

[20] Zhou (2004 [c. 400–100 BC], pp. 21–22).

[21] *Guanzi* is an ancient Chinese political and philosophical work that is named for and traditionally attributed to Guan Zhong, a well-known philosopher and statesman who in his later career served as Prime Minister to Duke Huan of Qi. *Guanzi*, with over 135,000 characters long, is one of the longest early Chinese philosophical texts.

[22] Roncaglia (2006, p. 23).

once thought to be Guan Zhong[23] Actually, most sections of *Guanzi* were not written by Guan Zhong himself. Instead, they were compiled over time by later generations. The author of *Guanzi* was the first to put forth the famous theory of four occupational groups, that is, 'Scholars, peasants, artisans, together with merchants, constitute the four occupations in society … The descendants of scholars should also be scholars, the descendants of peasants should also be peasants, the descendants of artisans should also be artisans, and the descendants of merchants should also be merchants'[24].

Most scholars thereafter conformed to two main interpretations of the original classification (see Fig. 1.1). The first indicated that merchants were considered the most inferior group, while the second suggested that merchants were juxtaposed with the other three occupational groups and ranked in no particular order. Supporters of the first interpretation often validated its legitimacy based on the longstanding tradition of emphasising agriculture and suppressing commerce in ancient China (especially after the Qin period). Additional evidence involved Guan Zhong—a renowned figure in the Legalist school—who was considered the creator of early theories related to state monopolies in Chinese history. Likewise, supporters of the second interpretation found their validation in *Guanzi* that made it clear that 'scholars, peasants, craftsmen, and merchants were all pillars of the country'.[25] The purpose of separating the occupations was to 'allow sons to inherit their fathers' occupation'.[26] In this sense, there was clearly no intention to specifically belittle the merchants.

It is worth noting that the meaning of *shi* in Guan Zhong's era and *shi* during the Ming period differed substantially. Guan Zhong lived during the Spring and Autumn period when *shi* referred to warriors, retainers, or advisers to princes. After the Qin period, and especially after the Sui dynasty, *shi* gradually became synonymous with scholars or even government officials. Whether they were court or local officials was of little importance. They came primarily from the scholar-gentry class who had

[23] Guan Zhong (720–645 BC), the chancellor and reformer of the State of Qi during the Spring and Autumn period under the rule of Duke Huan of Qi.

[24] Guan (1965 [c. 400–100 BC], Vol. 8, p. 47).

[25] Guan (1965 [c. 400–100 BC], Vol. 8, p. 45).

[26] Guan (1965 [c. 400–100 BC], Vol. 8, p. 45).

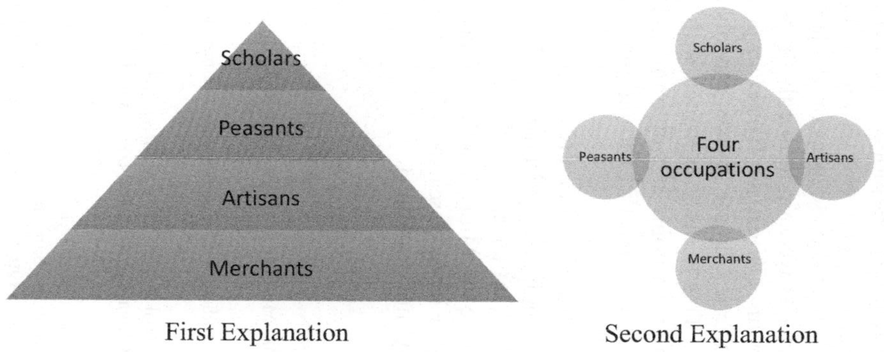

Fig. 1.1 Two main interpretations of the renowned theory of four occupational groups (*Source* Depicted by the author)

earned academic degrees (e.g. *xiucai*,[27] *juren*,[28] *or jinshi*[29]) by passing the imperial examinations established during the Sui dynasty.[30]

Nevertheless, regardless of whether the author of *Guanzi* ranked the four occupational groups side by side or placed them in a specific order, the rulers of the dynasties from Qin China forward confirmed that there was indeed a sequence of the four professions. 'The first two classes were seen as the necessary roots, the latter two as the essentially redundant extremities, or even as parasitical excrescences on the labour of the peasantry'.[31] Of the four, merchants were undoubtedly the most despised. As Richard Wilhelm stated in his *Chinesische Wirtschaftspsychologie*, 'of the four estates into which ancient Chinese society was divided, commerce occupied the lowest plane. This is easily explained with the far-reaching autarky of the agrarian family economy'[32] (my transl.). This seems to be the reflection of some 'collective mind'[33] throughout the whole ancient China.

The core questions that this book intends to answer are whether the preference and policies to emphasise agriculture and restrain commerce was continued in Ming China either among the scholars or at the court, and how the status and role of Ming merchants was correspondingly affected. First to be clarified is the research objective, i.e. the role and status of merchants in early modern China.

[27] *Xiucai* refers to scholars in Ming China who passed the imperial examination at county level.

[28] *Juren* refers to successful candidates in the imperial examinations at the provincial level in Ming China.

[29] *Jinshi* was the highest and final degree the candidates could get in the highest-level imperial examination in Ming China (held at the court and hosted by the emperor in person).

[30] The imperial examination, also called *keju* system, was a system of selecting officials by examination in ancient China. It is generally believed that the imperial examination system began in 607, the third year of Emperor Yangdi of the Sui Dynasty, which initiated awarding the *Jinshi* title which can be obtained after being examined by the emperor himself at the court (although many scholars have different views on it). The *Xiucai* and *Juren* mentioned above were lower titles awarded after passing the examination at county and provincial level respectively. Before keju system, the most popular systems of selecting officials were *Jiancha* system started in Han dynasty and *Jiupin-zhongzheng* system started in Wei. For details of imperial exam, please refer to Chapter 2, Sect. 2.1.

[31] Clunas (1991, p. 141).

[32] Wilhelm (1930, p. 67).

[33] Le Bon (1896, p. 6).

1.1.1 Merchants: Status and Role

The status of merchants in early modern China (mainly Ming merchants) is the core throughout this book. According to the *Oxford Dictionary of English*, the word 'status' can have three meanings: social position, legal position, and level of importance. This book focuses primarily on the first and third meanings. For instance, the relative position of merchants among the four occupational groups in Ming China was reflected as their social position, while the merchants' role in foreign trade and international conquests signified their level of importance to the state.

Some scholars may criticise the decision to choose merchants as a research object that they consider overly broad. I realized that there are many classifications of merchants, and previous studies related to merchants have tended to focus on smaller subsets. For example, in terms of wealth accumulation, they can be divided into three main categories: wealthy, midsized, and small merchants. Based on their respective expertise, small merchants can be further divided into travelling traders, vendors, shopkeepers, intermediary merchants, etc. Nevertheless, at least two-thirds of my book involves research from the perspective of the history of economic thought, and studies by other scholars had usually not subdivided the merchant groups in a similar method. At most, two categories may be discussed, respectively, namely, 'rich merchants'[34] and 'ordinary merchants', the latter usually referring to midsized and small merchants. My research objective focused mainly on ordinary merchants. As 'rich merchants' were frequently discussed in economic thought, their status and role was naturally within the realm of my research as well, especially when it concerns with the court's top design.

1.1.2 Market: Domestic and Foreign

Domestically, 'the Ming became a commercial world, not only despite the restoration of agrarian order that the Hongwu emperor put in place at the start of the dynasty, but as well because of it'.[35] At least in Jiangnan region, where 'most cities developed quite rapidly since

[34] 'Rich merchants', or *fumin*, appears frequently in ancient Chinese literature, meaning literally 'rich people'.

[35] Brook (1999, p. 12).

Emperor Zhengde and Emperor Jiajing periods',[36] 'markets of different sizes existed'.[37] The development of commerce was not confined only to state controlled markets (as we will see in Chapter 3). Private markets were also so flourished that the commercial taxation and tax evasion were among the most popular topics in scholars' debate (as we will see in Chapter 4). Their new dressing trend and consumption in arts and books surely interacted with the market and even the whole society taste (as we will see in Chapter 6). And ultimately, their successful business in the market somehow changed their relative status to the other occupations (as we will see in Chapter 7).

Regarding foreign trade, we may extract the records of Alvaro Semedo, a Portuguese missionary staying in China at that time,

> The most and best commodities [of Canton] are brought thither, because it is the most open and free seat of trade in that nation. And to say nothing of the fix neighbouring kingdoms, from whence all sorts of merchandise is brought thither, as well by natives as strangers: only that which the Portugueses take in for India, Giappone (Japan) and Manila, cometh one year with another to five thousand three hundred chests of several silk stuffs; each chest including 100 pieces of the most substantial silks, as velvet damask and satin; as half-damasks, painted and single 250 pieces of gold 2200 Ingots of 12 ounces weight a piece... Besides small pearl; sugar; porcelain dishes; China wood; rhubarb... it being hard to name them all even in a longer relation.[38]

We might get an impression from this that despite the official sea ban policy occupies the majority period of the Ming empire, the foreign trade did not really stagnate at all. The merchants engaged in overseas market and their role and status will be elaborated in Chapter 5.

1.1.3 Monarchy: Early Modern China

The state, or the monarchy, is distinctly a key element when we discuss the role and status of merchants. In this book, the relations between the merchants and the monarchy are covered by Chapters 2–5. While Chapters 6 or 7 discuss the relative position of merchants among the four occupations from the perspective of economic thought, we may still

[36] Fu (2007, p. 318).

[37] Fan (1998, p. 130).

[38] Semedo (1655 [1636], pp. 9–10).

catch a glimpse of the monarchy behind the merchants, scholars, and other occupations.

I would like to clarify that the 'early modern China' in my book refers mainly to the period between fourteenth century and seventeenth century. It roughly corresponds with Ming China (1368–1644), although not limited to Ming China. For instance, for some economic thinkers under late Mongolian's rule, such as Lu Shirong[39] and some other thinkers who spent their major lifetime in early Qing China (1644–1912), such as Huang Zongxi[40] Gu Yanwu[41] Wang Fuzhi[42] etc. their economic thought were also in the realm of this book. Nonetheless, for simplicity, I replace 'early modern China' with 'Ming China' in many parts of this book, since most of the thought and issues indeed happened during the Ming period.

There should be no dissent among scholars that medieval China ended long before, or at least before, Ming China. For instance, Xiong (2000) considers Sui and Tang China as 'late medieval China'.[43] Hansen (1990) considers the Southern Song's ruling period (1127–1276) as medieval China. However, regarding the beginning point of modern China, there exists no exact answer to this question. Immanuel C.Y. Hsü pointed out that many 'western historians and political scientists takes the Opium War of 1839–1842 as the point of departure'.[44] An alternative view considers 'the arrival of European explorers and missionaries during the transitional period from the Ming to the Ch'ing as a more justifiable starting point'.[45] My view is kind of leaning to the second, although still different. I am more following the classification of Clunas (1991, 1997), which

[39] Lu Shirong (?–1285) was a well-known economic thinker and finance official in Yuan China. Working under Kublai Khan (reigns from 1260 to 1294) was in great peril. Lu, together with his predecessors Wang Wentong (?–1262) and Ahmad Fanakati (?–1282), his successor Sengge (?–1291) were all killed by Kublai Khan when they were still in charge of state finance. For details, please refer to Shi (2017, pp. 236–240).

[40] Huang Zongxi (1610–1695) was a famous Chinese naturalist, political theorist, philosopher, and soldier during the latter part of the Ming dynasty.

[41] Gu Yanwu (1613–1682) was a Chinese philologist and geographer.

[42] Wang Fuzhi (1619–1692) was a famous Chinese essayist, historian, and philosopher of the late Ming.

[43] See Xiong (2000).

[44] Hsü (2000, p. 4).

[45] Hsü (2000, p. 4).

considers 'China of the Ming Dynasty'[46] as early modern China. Some other scholars such as Baldanza (2016) also considers Ming China as part of 'early modern Asia'.[47]

Many previous scholars focus only on a specific period of Ming China. While this might be more suitable in their case, in the realm of history of economic thought, this seems inappropriate. As we will see in this book, the economic thoughts obviously have their inner coherence throughout the whole three centuries involving Ming China. This kind of coherence exists not only in expression of economic thought, but also in many other fields as well, such as the commerce development, the taxation policy, the state's vacillation over international trade, etc. Lack of research on the transitional period bears the risk of developing some one-sided solution to our problems. Thus, if we want to investigate a specific question (for this book, mainly the status and role of merchants) in early modern China, we need to start from the very beginning of Ming China.

I chose to study Early Modern China, or mainly Ming China, for several reasons. First, from an academic perspective, an objective understanding of whether the status of Ming dynasty merchants synchronised with the degree of commercial development during the dynasty is urgently required, as is a clearer picture of the merchants' status among the four occupational groups. Although Ming China was still generally considered as a predominantly small peasant economy, 'the absolute levels of Ming and Ch'ing commerce were extremely large'.[48] In fact, the degree of commercial development in the latter stages was much higher than any previous dynasty, even surpassing the Tang[49] and Song[50] dynasties that were often considered the apex in ancient China. Moreover, 'a process of urbanization had been under way in China at least

[46] Clunas (1997, p. 9).

[47] See Baldanza (2016).

[48] Skinner and Elvin (1974, p. 23).

[49] The Tang dynasty, or the Tang Empire, was an imperial dynasty of China that ruled from 618 to 907, with an interregnum between 690 and 705 (Empress Wu Zetian, who was previously Empress of Emperor Gaozong of Tang Dynasty, change the name of her dynasty to Zhou during this period). It was preceded by the Sui dynasty (581–618) and followed by the Five Dynasties (907–960) and Ten Kingdoms (902–979) period.

[50] The Song dynasty was an imperial dynasty of China that began in 960 and lasted until 1279.

since the later Ming',[51] or even much earlier. In other words, based on commercial development, there was at least a reasonable possibility that the role of merchants during the Ming dynasty may have been substantially different than all preceding dynasties. Likewise, economic thought related to commerce, merchants, and mercantilism (if it exists in Ming China) among the intellectual classes may have differed significantly from those before the Ming Dynasty.

However, the economic thought in this period were poorly investigated so far. Quite a few scholars in this area believe that only thoughts before Qin and Han, i.e. first century, are worth researching on. For instance, Wittfogel asserted that 'virtually all great Chinese ideas on society, government, human relations, warfare and historiography, crystallized during the classical period of the territorial states and at the beginning of the imperial period'.[52] Interestingly, this situation also applies to Western economic thought, where the economic thoughts in 'Dark Middle Ages' were often neglected. However, increasing recent research shows that 'no matter in the early or late stage of Middle Ages, there exist rich economic thought'.[53] This applies to ancient China as well. Therefore, it is worth researching the Ming dynasty merchants to determine whether the status of Chinese merchants was transformed during the latter period of ancient China.

Second, my decision to search more profoundly into the Ming's commercial development arose primarily from personal interest. Qian Mu,[54] a renowned Chinese scholar, once suggested that 'modern China may generally trace its origin back to the Ming dynasty',[55] the last imperial dynasty ruled by Han nationals (Ming seized its power from Mongol, and the succeeding Qing was ruled by Manchu). Not only did it epitomise the evolution of imperial China for two thousand years, it was also an important period of history that can serve as a mirror for contemporary

[51] Skinner and Elvin (1974, p. 3).

[52] Wittfogel (1957, p. 421).

[53] Liang (2019, pp. 9–10).

[54] Qian Mu (1895.07.30–1990.08.30) was a Chinese historian, philosopher and writer. He is widely considered to be one of the greatest historians and philosophers of twentieth-century China.

[55] Qian (2012 [1952], p. 102).

China. Therefore, I am particularly interested in the history of commercial development during Ming China and the roles played by merchants at the time.

Many scholars, especially the Chinese researchers, prefer to study the Ming and Qing dynasties[56] together, which is often collectively referred to as the Ming-Qing period. It may be an irresponsible approach, after all, 'although the Qing Dynasty seemed to learn considerably from the Han Chinese,[57] the actual degree to which they were influenced by Central Plains[58] culture was very low'.[59] Regardless of the dominance of the highest levels of the courts by Manchu ministers coupled with the military power that was firmly controlled by the Eight Banners,[60] the country's ruling style alone cannot be compared with the Ming dynasty nor several previous dynasties, such as Han China[61] and Tang China. In terms of policy, it also 'absorbed the worthless parts of the Ming Dynasty and eliminated its essence'.[62] The policies of the late Qing government after the First Opium War[63] were criticised even more, and this led directly to the demise of their dynasty and the tragic history of modern China. Therefore, it is more meaningful to study the status of merchants in the Ming dynasty separately as a period when the characteristics of traditional China remained intact.

[56] Qing dynasty was officially established in 1636, and ruled China proper from 1644 to 1911. It was preceded by the Ming dynasty and succeeded by the Republic of China.

[57] Han Chinese are an East Asian ethnic group and nation native to China, making up over 90 percent of the total population. This is still the case for today.

[58] Central Plains is the area on the lower reaches of the Yellow River that formed the cradle of Chinese civilization. It forms part of the North China Plain.

[59] Wittfogel (1949, p. 13).

[60] 'Eight Banners': The Manchu administrative, social and military system established in 1601 by the Manchu leader Nurhachi. Named after eight coloured flags, banner companies became instrumental in the establishment of the Qing Dynasty in 1644. However, at the end of the Qing Dynasty the banners declined as an effective fighting force, with the next generation degenerating into privileged good for nothing.

[61] The Han dynasty was the second imperial dynasty of China (206 BC–220 AD), preceded by the Qin dynasty (221–206 BC) and succeeded by the Three Kingdoms period (220–280 AD).

[62] Wan (2004, pp. 28–29).

[63] The First Opium War (1839–1842) was a series of military engagements fought between Great Britain and Qing China.

To digress a little bit, I would like to emphasize my personal despisal against the court and the culture in Qing China. At the court, the officials used *nucai* (slave) as self-reference when addressing the emperor.[64] Targeting the scholars, literary punishment[65] was rampant, and many scholars were therefore killed. And among the people, all individuals were forced to plait their hair. These types of backwardness and insults were never seen in Ming China, which is obviously a kind of cultural retrogression and a tragedy for the Chinese civilization.

Third, the period during which the Ming Authority ruled China (1368–1644) coincided roughly with the Age of Discovery[66] in Europe (fifteenth–seventeenth centuries). While the history of economic thought in Ming China might be a grand new area to almost all Western scholars, from the perspective of economic history, Ming China is not unfamiliar to scholars in the West. Quite a few prestigious Western scholars such as Brook, Fairbank, Huang, Loewe, Lufrano, McDermott, von Glahn, etc. have written a number of important books in the commerce history in Ming dynasty, or at least a few chapters. I quote their major works in this book. And my main task is, of course, on the side of history of economic thought.

1.2 Methodology

1.2.1 Hermeneutical Approach: Combining Thought with History

For this book, I conducted an in-depth analysis of commercial development and the status of merchants during the Ming dynasty within the context of the history of economic thought and economic history (with focus on prevailing economic thought). To my knowledge and prior to

64 In Ming China *nucai* was only used by eunuchs, while in Qing China *nucai* was widely used among officials.

65 Literary punishment, or *wenziyu* in Chinese, refers to the situation when an author wrote something deemed to be offensive to the rulers.

66 The Age of Discovery stands for the period when European fleets appeared in almost all the major oceans all over the world during the fifteenth century to the seventeenth century, looking for new trade routes and trading partners to fuel the newly arising capitalism. With the opening of the new maritime route, cultural and trade exchanges between the East and the West began to increase, and colonialism and free trade also began to appear. The rapid development of Europe in this period laid the foundation for its surpassing Asian. And the discovery of the new route has a long-term impact on the development of the world during the past hundreds of years.

this book, no works have discussed the development of commerce in ancient China from the perspective of the history of economic thought,[67] nor has there been research that exclusively targeted merchants either in a specific period or in a more general sense from the perspective of economic thought. Up to this point, my book is ground-breaking in this sub-field.

To my best knowledge, only five books in English discuss the history of ancient Chinese economic thought. Schefold (2016) involves half a chapter combing through the ancient Chinese economic classics and thought. Hu (1984) created his two books based on his own three-volume work written in Chinese (from which I also quote quite a few in my book), providing a general picture of history of ancient Chinese economic thought throughout the dynasties, mainly pre-Qin period. Cheng et al. (2014) compiled twelve papers regarding ancient Chinese economic thought, which were written originally in Chinese. Cheng et al. (2019) involves ten papers discussing economic thought in Han dynasty. Nevertheless, none of the above books pay enough emphasis on commerce- or trade-related thoughts, not to mention the merchants. Moreover, none of these books talks about Ming China (only Hu [1988] involves one chapter on Ming China).

In my book, the history of economic thought is without doubt my primary concern.[68] One major advantage for me was the ability to read and quote texts in their original Chinese language, thereby allowing me to convey more accurate information compared with translated versions. As far as economic history is concerned, I relied primarily on secondary sources to quote the works of historians, sociologists, and other observers of Ming China.

In ancient China, 'since capitalist industry and commerce developed at a slow pace, economic thought had long not been able to break free from the feudalism-based framework with its focus on natural economy'.[69] Moreover, 'reflections on economic development were mostly

[67] Almost all the existing works discussing the development of commerce and the status of merchants in ancient China are from the perspective of economic history.

[68] Before I hand over this book, some scholars suggested to me that I should put some data into my work. I really appreciate their suggestion. However, analyzing data is the work in the realm of economic history. And I would like to emphasize here again, that the history of economic thought is the primary subject and the core of this book.

[69] Cheng et al. (2014, p. 48).

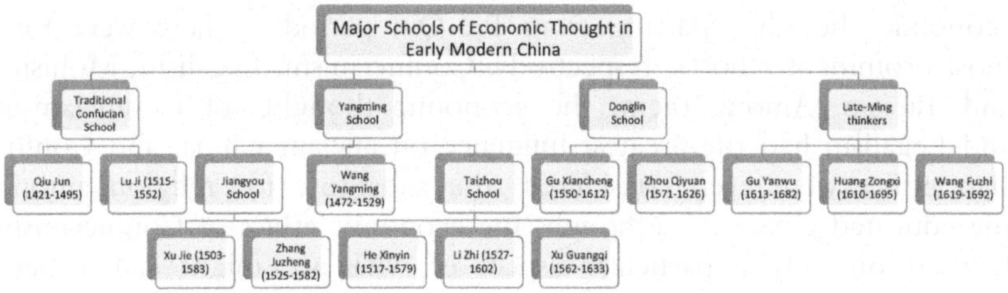

Fig. 1.2 Major schools of economic thought in early modern China (fifteenth to seventeenth centuries) (*Source* Depicted by the author)

embedded in more general philosophical and political treatises'.[70] Thus, it is not hard to understand why Rothbard asserted that 'ancient Chinese thought had virtually no impact outside the isolated Chinese Empire in later centuries'.[71]

Thus, the major methods I use here in this book is critique of ideology. In Chinese accounts of the history of economic thought, motives often seem more important than the logic of the argument, and this method is evidently the most efficient way to prevent our interpretation from distorting the original meaning.

1.2.2 *Contextualisation: Major Schools of Economic Thought in Early Modern China*

Plenty of existing literature discussed the thoughts in Ming China. Nonetheless, to my best knowledge, no existing books or papers discuss specifically the major schools of economic thought in ancient China of any period. I thus first present my summary of major schools of economic thought in early modern China (see Fig. 1.2). Most of them live their whole life in Ming China, while some late Ming prestigious thinkers spent their major career in Qing China.

For those who are not familiar with the history of Chinese economic thought, let's first briefly summarize the major schools of ancient Chinese

[70] Ma and Trautwein (2013, p. 2).

[71] Rothbard (2006, p. 23).

economic thought. Starting from Pre-Qin period,[72] there were four most prominent schools, respectively, Confucianism, Legalism, Mohism, and Taoism. Among them, the economic thoughts of Confucianism and Legalism had the greatest influence on ancient China, and Confucian ethics were even considered 'the substitute for religion among the educated classes',[73] although 'the economic ethics of Confucianism focused on only a particular aspect of what we might call ancient Chinese economic thought'.[74] Confucian economic thought was represented by Confucius,[75] Mencius,[76] and Xunzi,[77] while legalist economic thought was represented by Guan Zhong, Han Fei,[78] and Shang Yang.[79] Although Taoism was also a renowned school, its thoughts were relatively negative and its influence was generally limited to certain Huang-Lao[80] thoughts during the early Han Dynasty, after which it had little to no influence in the field of economic thought.

However, even thinkers within the same schools often did not adhere to exactly the same economic theories, and the core issues they discussed

[72] Pre-Qin period refers to the period before Qin dynasty, which mainly stands for Spring and Autumn period and Warring States Period (770–221 BC).

[73] Russell (1922, p. 34).

[74] Schefold (2014b, p. 623).

[75] Confucius (551–479 BC) was a Chinese philosopher and politician of the Spring and Autumn period. The philosophy of Confucius, also known as Confucianism, emphasized personal and governmental morality, correctness of social relationships, justice, kindness, and sincerity.

[76] Mencius (372–289 BC or 385–303 BC) was a Chinese Confucian philosopher who has often been described as the 'second Sage', that is after only Confucius himself. He is part of Confucius's fourth generation of disciples. Mencius inherited Confucius' thinking and developed them further.

[77] Xunzi (Xun Kuang, 310–c. 235 BC), was a Chinese Confucian philosopher and writer who lived during the Warring States period.

[78] Han Fei (280–233 BC), also known as Han Feizi, was a Chinese philosopher or statesman of the Legalist school during the Warring States period, and a prince of the state of Han.

[79] Shang Yang (390–338 BC) was an ancient Chinese philosopher, politician and a prominent legalist scholar.

[80] Huang-Lao was the most influential Chinese school of thought in the early second-century BC Han dynasty, having its origins in a broader political-philosophical drive looking for solutions to strengthen the feudal order as depicted in Zhou propaganda. It is generally interpreted as a school of syncretism, developing into a major religion—the beginnings of religious Taoism.

varied to some extent. For example, Xunzi, one of the representative Confucians, attached great importance to foreign trade, and most of his arguments regarding commerce were not previously considered by Confucius and Mencius.

The economic thought of the pre-Qin obviously had a profound influence on subsequent economic theories and policies, including those enacted during the Ming dynasty. Therefore, while elaborating the Ming dynasty's economic thoughts in this book, their 'pre-Qin origin' will be either briefly mentioned or discussed in detail when necessary.

When we elaborate the economic thoughts of the Ming thinkers, we must put enough emphasis on the specific historical and individual contexts,[81] just like when we study the economic thoughts of Western economic thinkers such as Adam Smith[82] (who grew up in Scotland and was thus quite different from other contemporary thinkers like Hume) and Ricardo[83] (who was first and foremost a banker and only wrote his economics masterpieces in his leisure time).

[81] Liang (2019, pp. 7–8).

[82] Adam Smith (1723–1790), Scottish economist, philosopher, and author who is widely considered the father of modern economics. Smith argued against mercantilism and was a major proponent of laissez-faire economic policies. His most well-known contribution to the field of economics was his book, *An Inquiry into the Nature and Causes of the Wealth of Nations* (1776). Another famous work of him is *The Theory of Moral Sentiments*.

[83] David Ricardo (1772–1823), English economist who gave systematized, classical form to the rising science of economics in the nineteenth century. His most notable book is *the Principles of Political Economy and Taxation* (1817).

Some economic thinkers still follow the traditional Confucianism. Qiu Jun[84] was the representative figure. He served as one of the Grand Secretaries[85] during Emperor Hongzhi era.[86] Emperor Hongzhi was famous for his benevolence and diligence (most emperors in Ming China were quite smart and good at controlling the officials, but slack about their duty as well). This is certainly a positive factor that Qiu was more likely to express his thought following the traditional Confucianism and could expect that the emperor would accept most of his suggestions.

The Yangming School was one of the most dominant schools in Ming China. Wang Yangming, the founder of the Yangming School, was a great Confucian scholar. After his death, the Yangming school was divided into two branches, the Jiangyou School and the Taizhou School. The philosophers of the Jiangyou School were mainly senior officials and mainstream thinkers (yet this kind of division is not absolutely reliable, which we will see in the following chapters), such as Zhang Juzheng[87] the Grand Secretary[88] during the Wanli period and Huang Zongxi during the Chongzhen[89] period. The Jiangyou School's ideas were thus relatively 'orthodox' since its disciples entered the court as officials, just as

[84] Qiu Jun (1421–1495), a Ming China politician and famous thinker, member of the Hanlin Academy, and once served in the Grand Secretariat during Emperor Hongzhi (r. 1487–1505) era.

[85] The Grand Secretariat (similar to cabinet, *neige* in Chinese) was only a coordinating agency nominally in the administration but de facto the highest ruling institution in Ming China. It often includes 3 or 4 secretaries (In some special occasions, there were only 2 secretaries or more than 5 secretaries. These situations were seen most likely due to a fierce political conflict, or sudden decease of some aged secretaries). The dominant secretary was addressed respectfully as 'the Grand Secretary' (*neige shoufu*). It first took shape after Emperor Hongwu abolished the position of Chancellor (similar to prime minister) in 1380.

[86] Emperor Hongzhi of Ming reigned from 1487 to 1505.

[87] Zhang Juzheng (1525–1582) was a Chinese politician who served as Grand Secretary in the late Ming dynasty during first ten years of the reigns of the Wanli emperors (r. 1572–1620).

[88] The Grand Secretary was de facto the Chancellor (similar to prime minister) in the administration in Ming China. His status was only below the emperor and higher than all the other officials. He led the daily work in the Grand Secretariat. Usually he seized the greatest power among all the officials. Only in some rare occasions his power was stripped away from his colleagues. For instance, Li Chunfang, the Grand Secretary served from 1568 to 1571 during Emperor Longqing era, often had to share his power with his deputy, the Vice Grand Secretary Gao Gong, who later became Li's successor in 1571.

[89] Emperor Chongzhen reigned from 1627 to 1644.

Wang Yangming had. The Taizhou School was represented by Li Zhi and many other 'grass-root' thinkers. They spent most of their time with ordinary people and some of them were even born from the lowest rung. Thus their thoughts, as we will see, showed plenty of sympathy for the well-being of ordinary people and did not care too much about the benefit of the state. Xu Guangqi[90] maybe surprisingly, also belongs to Taizhou School. He once served as the Vice Grand Secretary. Despite his frequent contact with Italian missionaries and his great emphasis on modern science, we still see a great deal of emphasis on agriculture and care for peasants in his thought.

Donglin School[91] was restored by Gu Xiancheng[92] and Gao Panlong[93] who taught at the Wuxi Donglin Academy (see Fig. 1.3), and was therefore named after. Improving the treatment of merchants and opposing the imposition of heavy commercial taxes on them were among the group's main platforms. However, in fact, the views expressed by members of the Donglin School reflected their own interests. The leaders and prominent members of this faction were inextricably linked to commerce. They either came from merchant families or were closely connected to them. Roughly one-third of the members of the Donglin School hailed from Southern Zhili[94] and Zhejiang, and around one-fifth hailed from Shanxi and Shaanxi. At the time, these regions were the areas where commerce

[90] Xu Guangqi (1562–1633) was a Chinese agronomist, astronomer, mathematician, politician, and writer during the Ming dynasty. He was a senior court official and once served as the Vice Grand Secretary. Xu was a Shanghai local and used to study in Longhua Temple (near Xujiahui). He was the major collaborator of the Italian Jesuits Matteo Ricci and Sabatino de Ursis, and assisted their translation of several classic Western texts into Chinese, including part of Euclid's Elements. Xujiahui, the most modern commercial center in current Shanghai, was named after him as a memorial. His tomb was buried in today's Guangqi park, which is near Xujiahui. Please refer to Wen et al. (2001, pp. 166–167).

[91] The Donglin School was established in 1604, during the Wanli era of Ming, when Gu Xiancheng (1550–1612), the then Grand Secretary, and Gao Panlong (1562–1626), a famous scholar, restored the Donglin Academy in Wuxi with the financial backing of local gentry and officials.

[92] Gu Xiancheng (1550–1612) once served as Grand Secretary, and was one of the major leaders of the Donglin School.

[93] Gao Panlong (1562–1626), a famous scholar, and served as one of the major leaders of the Donglin School.

[94] Southern Zhili (*Nanzhili*) includes today's Shanghai (municipality), Jiangsu province and Anhui province.

Fig. 1.3 The Entrance of Donglin Academy, the base of Donglin School (*Source* Photographed by the author in October, 2019 in Wuxi City)

was the most developed and the commercial community was the most active.[95] We will see how their thoughts are different compared with other schools in this book.

Regarding late Ming thinkers, Huang Zongxi and Gu Yanwu are the most representative. They spent most period of their life under the rule of Manchu. However, their youth, the most essential forming period of individual's outlook on life and world, were still within the rule of Ming empire. Moreover, although they were not eliminated by the succeeding Manchu (considering the fact that Qing rulers wiped out so many scholars who were loyal to Ming), they kept their thought independent of Qing's despotic power. Thus, we may not only include their thought in the realm of early modern period, but the thought during Ming as well.

The final point I would like to emphasize here is that although economic thinkers belonging to different schools must hold various opinions, in many cases, their thoughts were not necessarily dichotomy between each other, as we will see in this book.

[95] Wu (2004, Vol. 3, pp. 860–861).

1.2.3 *Comparison and Reconstruction: Attempt on Chinese Economic Thought*

Despite the deficiencies of ancient Chinese economic thought stated above, on the other hand, 'core economic institutions like state monopolies of trade' has been 'the subject of discussion in China on the basis of a solid, sometimes implicit understanding of the logic of economic processes'.[96] Schumpeter also once said,

> More than anywhere else we might expect to find such traces of analytic effort in ancient China, the home of the oldest literary culture of which we know. We find in fact a highly developed public administration that deal currently with agrarian, commercial, and financial problems... Moreover, there were methods of monetary management and of exchange control that seem to presuppose a certain amount of analysis. The phenomenon incident to the recurrent inflations were no doubt observed and discussed by men much superior to us in cultural refinement.[97]

And even though modern liberalism appears to have rendered traditional economic thought irrelevant, a closer examination reveals that it offers intellectual resources, which are tapped consciously or unconsciously, and it thus continues to play an important role up to today.[98] Thus, it is still worthwhile studying the status of merchants from the perspective of economic thought with 'analytic effort', despite the defects and gaps in ancient Chinese economic thought. In this book, we will see some thought analytically reconstructed. Although not much, it will provide some insights regarding what the thought looks like after being embedded into the existing analytical system.

In this book, as we will see, I also conduct some brief comparative study of economic thought borne by Ming economic thinkers and their European colleagues, for instance, the Taizhou School vs. Sir Thomas

[96] Schefold (2016, p. 351).

[97] Schumpeter (1954, p. 55).

[98] For details, please refer to the outline of the research project at the Forschungskolleg Humanwissenschaften: 'Chinese and European History of Economic Thought in Comparison' led by Prof. Bertram Schefold and Prof. Iwo Amelung.

More[99] Lu Ji vs. Mandeville[100] Qiu Jun vs. Adam Smith, Huang Zongxi vs. Bentham[101] Xu Guangqi vs. Malthus[102] etc. As Prof. Schefold pointed out, 'None of the economic theories, either in antiquity or in their later development such as mercantilism or the classical economic period, really have a parallel in China, because of a failure to develop a theory of value'.[103] It is indeed the case. Nevertheless, a brief comparison may still help the readers have a better understanding of the thought in Ming China, especially those who were not so familiar with ancient China and its early modern history.

This book evidently creates an essential foundation for my follow-up studies. Conditions permitting, I will further develop this book and compare Ming merchants with their European contemporaries in details.[104]

1.3 Structure of the Book

This book is structured as follows in Fig. 1.4.

In Chapter 2, the two major factors that set the tone for the relationship between the state and merchants as well as the status of merchants

[99] Sir Thomas More (1478–1535), English humanist and statesman, chancellor of England (1529–1532). His *Utopia* was written in Latin in 1516, which had a great influence on the development of socialist thought. In 1535, he was executed for opposing Henry VIII to be the head of the Church of England.

[100] Bernard de Mandeville (1670–1733), Dutch prose writer and philosopher who won European fame with *The Fable of the Bees*.

[101] Jeremy Bentham (1748–1832), English philosopher, economist, and theoretical jurist, the earliest and chief expounder of utilitarianism.

[102] Thomas Robert Malthus (1766–1834), English economist and demographer who is best known for his theory that population growth will always tend to outrun the food supply.

[103] Schefold (2016, p. 351).

[104] The comparison of economic thought born by Ming thinkers and Western thinkers at the time can be quite worthwhile, and interesting as well. My doctoral supervisor, Prof. Bertram Schefold, was leading the project 'Chinese and European History of Economic Thought in Comparison' (with Prof. Iwo Amelung) during the past couple of years at Goethe University Frankfurt. The merchants in Ming China and in Europe at the time are definitely among my current prior research topics.

Fig. 1.4 Main structure of this book (*Source* Depicted by the author)

in Ming China are analysed, namely, the cultural and institutional framework, and the origin of its prevalent economic thought. The latter was influenced primarily by two dominant theories, the emphasis on agriculture and suppression of commerce coupled with a belief in egalitarianism. First, the relationship between the state and merchants during the Ming dynasty was determined by centralisation in ancient China after the Qin Dynasty and the dependent state-merchant relationship formed therefrom. This unique state-centric system was monopolistic and featured strict market control and state encroachment on private commerce. In addition, the relationship between the system's restraints on merchants and the unification of the centralised monarchy are analysed. I then discuss ideas that led to the valorisation of agriculture and the suppression of commerce together with the theory of four occupational groups, after which the characteristics of the leading theories related to commerce and merchants in ancient China (including Ming China) are analysed. The final discussion in Chapter 2 relates to the concept of egalitarianism in ancient China.

Chapters 3–7 discuss the merchant's status in two parts. The role of merchants in the aforementioned state-merchant relationship is explained in Chapters 3–5, while Chapters 6 and 7 explore the position of merchants relative to scholars, farmers, and craftsmen based on the theory of four occupational groups.

Chapter 3 focuses on the status of merchants during the Ming dynasty under the state monopoly system based on conflicting economic thoughts that either supported or opposed state-owned commerce. Similar to previous dynasties, there were two clearly divided factions regarding state control of important products in Ming China, one favouring the 'enrichment of the country first' while the other preferred to 'make the people rich first'. Senior court officials represented by Qiu Jun and Zhang Juzheng expressed their opposition to state-owned commerce. For example, Qiu Jun proposed that the commoners should be left alone to conduct their own business. He made numerous statements in support of private merchants that had seldom been presented in previous dynasties. However, for extremely important commodities like salt[105] the leaders'

[105] In ancient China, state monopoly of salt was practiced during most of the time. The main reason is that due to the limitation of productivity, the salt output were far from good as now. However, the ancient people were mainly engaged in physical work and could not survive without salt. The status of salt is thus higher than that of all

thoughts revealed less opposition to state intervention. On the other side, scholars such as Li Wen[106] Lin Xiyuan[107] and Wang Fuzhi expressed clear support for state-owned business in their economic propositions. After discussing the state-owned business models of the two opposing camps in detail, I use the merchants' cooperation with the state-operated salt business to identify how these thoughts were applied in practice. In addition, specific economic thoughts of scholars related to administration of the salt business and the merchants' role are explored.

In Chapter 4, the position of Ming merchants related to the collection of commercial taxes by the state are explained from the perspective of economic thoughts regarding commercial taxation and the situations encountered by the merchants. The chapter is divided into three parts in chronological order: the early, middle, and late Ming dynasty. This division is generally based on the significant differences in the manner in which the commercial taxes were collected by the Ming dynasty government in each period. During the early Ming period, commercial taxation was relatively light, primarily because of the emperor's contempt for merchants and his scorn and marginalisation of any fiscal revenue collected from commerce. In the middle period, the state increased the categories of goods that were subject to commercial taxation and repeatedly levied those taxes. During the late Ming period, the repeated levies of commercial taxes became more critical for merchants. In one particularly notable event, Emperor Wanli's aggressive collection of mineral taxes exemplified blatant exploitation as the livelihoods of ordinary merchants were plundered. During these three distinct periods, dissimilar economic thoughts were born. These are discussed separately in detail to shape an understanding of the evolving status of merchants under the state's commercial tax system.

commodities. If people do not take in enough salt, it will harm the health. Moreover, salt was often used as a voucher for overseas trade. Thus, the value of salt to agricultural society is no less than that of oil to industrial society. And any individual merchant who privately sell salt more than 3 *dan* will be captured and executed in most of the times. For details, please refer to Qian (2009).

[106] Li Wen (1608–1647) was the leader of Fushe alliance and a senior official in late Ming.

[107] Lin Xiyuan (1481–1565) once served as the governor of Nanjing.

In Chapter 5, the role and status of merchants in foreign trade and international conquests as another important manifestation of state-merchant relations in Ming China are discussed. Before Emperor Longqing[108] abolished the sea ban policy in 1567, private Ming merchants were strictly prohibited from engaging in overseas trade. Only neighbouring countries' tributes to Beijing and Zheng He[109]'s voyages to foreign countries (sent by Emperor Yongle[110]) were approved as official international commercial activities. Two opposing economic thoughts existed in Ming China, on that supported the sea ban and one that supported a plan to open sea travel to allow private merchants to engage freely in foreign trade. Those supporting the sea ban adopted familiar perspectives, including 'calls to avoid violating ancestral law', 'claims that the supplemental state revenue would be minimal', and 'fears that overseas trade would lead to harassment and theft by pirates', among others, all of which demonstrated the obvious continentalist tendencies of Ming China. Those who promoted the opening of the sea to commercial trade (especially Qiu Jun and several thinkers during the middle and late Ming periods) expressed support for allowing private merchants to engage in foreign trade. Among other theories, they believed that 'the state and commoners shared same interests' and that 'pirates would become legitimate merchants once trading was allowed'. From the perspective of economic history, this book is focused on determining whether maritime merchants contributed to the commercial development of Ming China, whether their contribution was important to the country, and whether they benefitted by gaining corresponding social and economic status. The entire dynasty is divided into three periods: The first covers the beginning of the dynasty to around the end of the fifteenth century when the merchants struggled to survive under the tributary system. The second period covers the period up to 1567, including the role of merchants

[108] Emperor Longqing reigned from 1567 to 1572.

[109] Zheng He (1371–1433 or 1435) was a Chinese mariner, explorer, diplomat, fleet admiral, and court eunuch during China's early Ming dynasty. He was adopted the surname Zheng conferred by Emperor Yongle. Zheng commanded expeditionary treasure voyages to Southeast Asia, South Asia, Western Asia, and East Africa from 1405 to 1433. According to legend, his larger ships carried hundreds of sailors on four decks and were almost twice as long as any wooden ship ever recorded.

[110] Emperor Yongle, the fourth son of Emperor Hongwu, named Zhu Di, reigned from 1402 to 1424.

in the booming smuggling trade. The final period covers the role of maritime merchant groups and the fate of scattered merchants.

Three aspects of state monopolisation are revealed through detailed analysis: commercial taxation, foreign trade, and the status of merchants in state-merchant relations. In order to discuss the relative status of merchants among the four occupations, of utmost importance are critical debates about two pairs of core issues in the history of ancient Chinese economic thought: righteousness and profits, and thrift and luxury.

Thoughts related to righteousness and profits in Ming China are discussed in Chapter 6. At this point, we can identify the views of Ming economic thinkers regarding the necessity of merchants, for example, whether agriculture was sufficient to sustain the country going forward or whether commerce and merchants were necessary to augment income. Leading scholars like Qiu Jun, Han Bangqi[111] Li Mengyang[112] and scholars from Donglin School and the Yangming School[113] all posited that righteousness and profits could work in tandem, and Huang Zongxi and Gu Yanwu advocated a system wherein people could pursue self-interests. Moreover, the dispute between righteousness and profits raised an important issue in the history of economic thought regarding the merchants' views on usury (i.e. lending at exorbitant interest rates). As a small supplement to the main themes, the position of merchants and the economic thoughts of scholars regarding usury during the Ming dynasty are briefly discussed.

Issues of luxury versus frugality relate to the rationale of luxury lifestyles of some merchants. Debates involving the opinions of scholars and others were particularly prominent in the mid-to-late period of the Ming dynasty when commerce was booming. Merchants had been demonstrating their opulent wealth through the consumption of clothing, art, and books. When approached about this issue, Ming thinkers supported their preferences from among three main trains of thought:

[111] Han Bangqi (1479–1556) was a politician and a thinker in Ming China.

[112] Li Mengyang (1473–1530) was a well-known scholar, poet and politician. He once served as governor of Jiangxi Province.

[113] Yangmingism, also known Yangming School, is one of the major philosophical schools of Neo-Confucianism, based on the ideas of the idealist Neo-Confucian philosopher Wang Yangming (1472–1529).

anti-luxury bans presented by Lu Ji[114] and Yu Shenxing[115] equal emphasis on thrift and luxury, and the rejection of luxury proposed by scholars like Xu Jie[116] and Lü Kun[117] Discussions of these two pairs of economic thoughts are prerequisites in order to determine whether the traditional order of four occupations still applied during the Ming dynasty.

Chapter 7 builds on Chapter 6. The relative positions of merchants among the four occupations are studied, starting with the status of merchants relative to scholars. Traditionally, the economic ideology of Ming dynasty merchants, including theories presented by Wang Yang-ming[118] was interpreted as a signal that the traditional theory of four occupational groups was irreparably broken and ineffective. However, according to my research, while these can be used to explain the improving status of merchants during the Ming dynasty, they are not evidence that merchants had surpassed scholars in any form. In addition, several signs suggested that merchants were still marginalised in Ming. For instance, scholars thought that merchants still needed to become officials, their appreciation of merchants was conditional, and there were appeals from high-level scholars and officials to treat merchants well. In general, as reflected in the economic thoughts, the status of merchants remained lower than that of scholars even while the predominance of traditional agriculture-based thoughts was being challenged by proposals to place equal emphasis on agriculture and commerce. In practice, an agricultural decline parallel to major commercial development in the middle and late periods of the Ming dynasty elevated the status of merchants compared to the peasants. This commercial boom also elevated the status of artisans whose work had historically been ill-regarded as a lowly profession. Although merchants were traditionally placed below artisans because of their constant movement and the difficulty of controlling such a wayward

[114] Lu Ji (1515–1552), a famous economic thinker in Ming China.

[115] Yu Shenxing (1545–1608), a Ming politician.

[116] Xu Jie (1503–1583) was a famous politician of the Ming dynasty. He spent over 20 years in the Grand Secretariat and held the position of the Grand Secretary about 6 years. He was born in Songjiang (part of current Shanghai).

[117] Lü Kun (1536–1618) was a famous scholar and once served as Vice Minister of Justice.

[118] Wang Yangming (1472–1529) was a well-known calligrapher, military general, philosopher, politician, and writer during the Ming dynasty. He was the founder of the famous Yangming School.

group, their increasingly important role in Ming commerce garnered additional status that placed them on par with artisans. Chapter 8 serves as the conclusion.

References

Reference in German

Wilhelm, R. (1930). *Chinesische Wirtschaftspsychologie.* Deutsche Wissenschaftliche Buchhandlung.

Reference in English

Andre, F. (2001). Review of the great divergence. *Journal of Asian Studies, 60*(1), 180–182. https://doi.org/10.2307/2659525.

Baldanza, K. (2016). *Ming China and Vietnam negotiating borders in early modern Asia*. Cambridge University Press.

Brook, T. (1999). *The confusions of pleasure: Commerce and culture in Ming China*. University of California Press.

Cheng, L., Peach, T., & Wang, F. (2014). *The history of ancient Chinese economic thought*. Routledge.

Cheng, L., Peach, T., & Wang, F. (2019). *The political economy of the Han dynasty and its legacy.* Routledge.

Clunas, C. (1991). *Superfluous things: Material culture and social status in early modern China*. Polity Press.

Clunas, C. (1997). *Pictures and visuality in early modern China*. Reaktion Books.

Deng, K. G. (2000). A critical survey of recent research in Chinese economic history. *Economic History Review, 53,* 1–28.

Fairbank, J. K. (1983). *The United States and China*. Harvard University Press.

Hansen, V. (1990). *Changing gods in medieval China, 1127–1276.* Princeton University Press.

Ho, P. (1962). *The ladder of success in imperial China: Aspects of social mobility, 1368–1911.* Columbia University Press.

Hsü, I. C. Y. (2000). *The rise of modern China.* Oxford University Press.

Hu, J. (1984). *Chinese economic thought before the seventeenth century.* Foreign Language Press.

Hu, J. (1988). *A concise history of Chinese economic thought*. Foreign Languages Press.

Le Bon, G. (1896). *The crowd: A study of the popular mind.* The Macmillan.

Ma, Y., & Trautwein, H. (2013). *Thoughts on economic development in China.* Routledge.

Needham, J. (2005 [1969]). *The grand titration: Science and society in East and West* (Vol. 1). Routledge.
North, D. C. (1990). *Institutions, Institutional change and economic performance*. Cambridge University Press.
Polanyi, K. (1944). *The great transformation*. Boston: Beacon Press.
Pomeranz, K. (2000). *The great divergence: China, Europe, and the making of the modern world economy*. Princeton University Press.
Roncaglia, A. (2006). *The wealth of ideas: A history of economic thought*. Cambridge University Press.
Rothbard, M. N. (2006). *Economic thought before Adam Smith*. Edward Elgar.
Russell, B. (1922). *The problem of China*. George Allen and Unwin Ltd.
Schefold, B. (2000). *Economic interests and cultural determinants in European integration: Conference Proceedings of the 1998 Summer School, Brixen/Bressanone, 31 August-10 September 1998* (No. 21). Europäische Akademie.
Schefold, B. (2014a). Marx, Sombart, Weber and the debate about the genesis of modern capitalism. *Journal of Institutional Studies, 6*(2), 10–26.
Schefold, B. (2014b). Economics without political economy: Is the discipline undergoing another revolution. *Social Research, 81*(3), 613–636.
Schefold, B. (2016). *Great economic thinkers from antiquity to the historical school: Historical school, old and young*. Routledge.
Schumpeter, J. A. (1954). *A history of economic analysis*. George Allen & Unwin.
Skinner, G. W., & Elvin, M. (1974). *The Chinese city between two worlds*. Stanford University Press.
Venn, H. (2009). *The missionary life and labours of Francis Xavier taken from his own correspondence: With a sketch of the general results of Roman Catholic missions among the heathen*. Cambridge University Press.
Wittfogel, K. (1949). *History of Chinese society: Liao (907–1125)*. Lancaster Press.
Wittfogel, K. (1957). *Oriental despotism: A comparative study of total power*. Yale University Press.
Xiong, V. (2000). *Sui-Tang Chang'an: A study in the urban history of late medieval China*. The University of Michigan Press.

Reference in Chinese

Fan, J. (1998). *The development of commerce in Jiangnan region during Ming-Qing period*. Nanjing University Press.
Fu, Y. (2007). *The social economy of rural area during Ming-Qing period*. Zhonghua Publishing House.
Guan, Z., et al. (1965 [c. 400–100 BC]). *Guanzi*. Taiwan Commercial Press.
Liang, J. (2019). *Lectures on history of Western economic thought*. Fudan University Press.

Qian, Y. (2009). *Shentan Di Renjie*. China Social Science Press.
Qian, M. (2012 [1952]). *The political gains and losses in Chinese history*. Jiuzhou Press.
Semedo, A. (1655 [1636]). *The history of that great and renowned monarchy of China*. Translated by a person of quality. E. Tyler for John Crook.
Shi, J. (2017). *Robbing the people: Eight officials famous for accumulating wealth in Chinese history*. Zhongxin Press.
Wan, Y. (2004). *Court history of the Qing dynasty*. Baihua Wenyi Press.
Wen, G., et al. (2001). *The local history of Shanghai*. Shanghai Education Press.
Wu, H. (2004). *Chinese commerce history*. The Finance and Economics Press.
Zhou, G. (2004 [c. 400–100 BC]). *Zhouli*. Shanghai Ancient Books Publishing House.

CHAPTER 2

Institution: Designed System Faced by Ming Merchants

In ancient China, the regime, commerce, officials, and merchants were always intertwined. Thus, before discussing the Ming scholars' thoughts related to commerce and merchants, a separate chapter is necessary to identify and explain the surroundings faced by Ming merchants. To be more specific, this chapter first introduced fundamental elements in Chinese culture and society, i.e. Confucianism, kinship, the imperial exams, state monopoly, market control, etc. Their more ancient origin and their Ming status quo will both be elaborated. Then, this chapter moves on to the traditional characteristics of ancient Chinese economic thought that were typically reflected in theories that emphasised peasants and despised merchants. Equally important are the prevailing thoughts regarding egalitarianism.

2.1 System Origin: Continuation and Change

As Wittfogel pointed out, 'It may be possible, although not ideal, to write an economic history of feudal Europe without giving much consideration to its political institutions. For the complex bureaucratic societies of China, a purely economic history cannot produce satisfactory results'.[1]

[1] Wittfogel (1949, p. 25).

T. Hua, *Merchants, Market and Monarchy*,
Palgrave Studies in the History of Economic Thought,
https://doi.org/10.1007/978-3-030-77189-8_2

Political control centred on the autocratic imperial power that dominated all social and economic development, and there were 'no clear boundaries between the state and merchants'.[2] From the political perspective, this represented a typical form of dependency, albeit between the state and merchants instead of between nations. As Wang pointed out, 'The obedience of Chinese people to the internal authority is not only academic, but also personal, just like the relationship between mentors and apprentices'.[3] Here, the relationship between 'the state and merchants' is very much like that between mentors and apprentices.

Evidently this kind of dependency 'can only be grown from within'.[4] Thus, the mechanism that guided its formation was hidden behind cultural frameworks, institutional arrangements, and policy designs. We will now see their origin, and how they remained or evolved in Ming China.

2.1.1 Cultural Framework: Confucianism, Kinship, and Prefecture-County System

Let's start with Confucianism, which is not only the cultural framework of the political system, but the source of quite a few ancient Chinese economic thought as well. Confucianism is a cultural mainstream thought, philosophical and religious system that originated in China and influenced and spread to other countries in East Asia. It was revitalized but not originated by Confucius in the fifth-century BC. Confucianism was born out of the ritual and music tradition during Pre-Qin period, with the core values of benevolence, forgiveness, sincerity and filial piety, paying attention to the moral cultivation of the gentleman, emphasizing that the benevolence and the ritual complement each other, attaching importance to family ethics, promoting education and benevolent politics, and attacking tyranny.

Confucianism was, by using Weber's word, 'the rational ethic that reduced to an absolute minimum the tension towards the world, the religious devaluation of the world, and the practical rejection of the

[2] Guan (1995, pp. 77–78).

[3] Wang (2015, p. 36).

[4] McCloskey and DeMartino (2016, p. 534).

world'.[5] The traditional Confucians practice Confucianism by performing traditional duties. Every well-educated Chinese is strongly opposed to the need to continuously bearing the 'sin' concept, and everyone in the intellectual class believes that this idea is 'embarrassing and lacking in dignity'.[6] However, the ordinary Chinese people affected by Confucianism are still completely under the control of Confucianism. Well-educated senior officials tend to maintain awe of Confucianism as well.

Weber asserted that 'the power that exerted by far the strongest influence on the conduct of life was family piety, which was based on the belief in spirits'.[7] And it was the power of family piety that 'enabled and controlled the ever strong cohesion of the clan associations'.[8] Just like Li pointed out, 'the major social foundation of early China's intellectual tradition was the hierarchical clan kinship tradition, and the powerful and enduring customs that it bequeathed'.[9]

Kinship, 'which in Western medieval society had virtually lost all significance, remained important in China both for the local administration of the smallest units and for the character of economic association'.[10] The patrimonial government from above 'clashed with the kinship organisations from below, which were firmly structured as a counterweight to it'.[11] In ancient China, the patriarchal power 'survived and grew stronger until it became a force equal to the political power'.[12]

The imperial court remained, in fact, 'an administration of urban districts and subdistricts'.[13] However, 'beyond the city walls, its power ceased very quickly to be genuinely effective',[14] because in the village areas, both the power of the kinship groups and the organised self-government of the village were in charge, despite the fact that 'the power of the kinship groups and the administration of the village temple often

[5] Weber and Whimster (2004, p. 36).

[6] Weber and Whimster (2004, p. 37).

[7] Weber and Whimster (2004, p. 42).

[8] Weber and Whimster (2004, p. 42).

[9] Li (2019, p. 311).

[10] Weber et al. (1978, pp. 316–317).

[11] Weber et al. (1978, p. 317).

[12] Weber et al. (1978, p. 319).

[13] Weber et al. (1978, p. 321).

[14] Weber et al. (1978, p. 321).

failed to provide any sort of effective protection for property, especially the property of the better off'.[15] This leads to Emperor Qin Shihuang's patrimonial absolutism and his strong doubt about city inhabitants, including merchants.

Thus, as mentioned in Chapter 1, after Emperor Qin Shihuang[16] defined *zhongnong yishang* as the basic state policy, restraining of merchants became more 'orthodox' in the succeeding dynasties. The government's bureaucratic control, interference, and exploitation of commerce and merchants continued almost unabated, and it exhibited resolute and profound power over all commercial development.[17] The merchant class had never been instrumental in the mainstream of social development, instead merchants served at the mercy of various political forces and were unable to control their own destinies. After Sima Qian[18] wrote a biography for merchants in *Records of the Grand Historian*, rarely could anyone find another thorough description of the merchant class in any official history.[19] Even though a few words were occasionally mentioned about certain noteworthy individuals, it was impossible to trace the entire history of the merchants' image in ancient China.

Behind the systems implemented to suppress merchants during most dynasties were fairly comprehensive arrangements of power, that is, a unified central system with autocratic power at its core. At the same time, 'the stability of her order was the reason for the permanent existence of China'[20] as one country over a very long period that spanned multiple dynasties.

[15] Weber et al. (1978, p. 324).

[16] Qin Shi Huang ('First Emperor of Qin'; 259–210 BC) was the founder of the Qin dynasty and was the first emperor of a unified China. He was born Ying Zheng, a prince of the state of Qin. He became Zheng, the King of Qin when he was thirteen, then China's first emperor when he was 38 after the Qin had conquered all of the other Warring States and unified all of China in 221 BC.

[17] Li (2004, p. 114).

[18] Sima Qian (145–c.86 BC) was a Chinese historian of the early Han dynasty (206 BC–AD 220). He is considered the father of Chinese historiography for his *Records of the Grand Historian*, a general history of China in the Jizhuanti style covering more than two thousand years beginning from the rise of the legendary Yellow Emperor and the formation of the first Chinese polity to the reigning sovereign of Sima Qian's time, Emperor Wu of Han.

[19] Wu (2012, p. 55).

[20] Schefold (2016, p. 342).

Although there were periods of turbulence and even divisions, including famine, financial crisis, etc. each turmoil was resolved with a return to some form of unified order that was much longer than the separation period. A major feature of the Chinese Empire was its ability to continuously regenerate its empire system. For thousands of years, China not only maintained the image of a unified empire but also continuously recreated a unified empire that is essential to 'support the state solving the financial crisis'[21] and other catastrophes. The emperor integrated the most noble status of 'the whole world' with overwhelming absolute power'. He was the highest political leader and the only master, whose 'constant activities' were 'shepherding all the people, governing the realm, and supervising the various officials'.[22]

In ancient China, the emperor had absolute control and ownership, and 'promoted growth and enjoyed its benefits to support their patrimonial elites under authoritarian rule'.[23] All resources of national interest, the property of the people, and even all households ultimately belonged to the emperor. And throughout the longstanding preponderance of farming with its typical low productivity, in order to maintain the unification of imperial power over a vast empire like China, a complete infrastructure and set of systems was constructed to match its dimensions.

This first included central and local power distribution, to be more specific, the prefecture and county (*junxian* in Chinese) system[24] and the vertical bureaucratic organisation that cooperated with each other maximised the emperor's absolute control in order to stymie the potential

[21] Sun and Sun (2002, p. 221).

[22] Rickett (1998, p. 62).

[23] Mosca (2018, p. 44).

[24] The system of *junxian* was a two-level local administrative system in ancient China, where the prefecture administers its counties. It was almost prevalent throughout the feudal period of ancient China. Under this system, the central government administers the local government vertically, and the local officials are directly appointed and removed by the emperor, so that the local government is under the jurisdiction of the central government, which is conducive to the strengthening of centralization and national unity. This system marks the replacement of consanguinity politics by bureaucratic politics, and it is a sign of China's transition from aristocratic system to autocratic system. The system of *junxian* originated in the Spring and Autumn period and the Warring States period. After the reform of First Emperor of Qin, it remained dominant until the first year of Emperor Suzong of Tang Dynasty (758), when the system of *junxian* was replaced by another system called *zhouxian*.

covert development of local separatist forces.[25] And a typical characteristic of the county system in ancient China was its support from the clans. Kinship, 'which in Western medieval society had virtually lost all significance, remained important in China both for the local administration of the smallest units and for the character of economic association'.[26] Thus, due to the deep-rooted emphasis on 'family' in Chinese culture, it was 'the power of family piety that enabled and controlled the ever strong cohesion of the clan associations, which could operate as extended family businesses with a division of labour'.[27]

The above cultural framework still plays its vital role in Ming China. The merchant class in Ming itself is one type of kinship. The merchants who went out for business together either came from the same family, or came from the same patriarchal clan. They share the same dialect and thus more likely to build a close relationship and trust, which is quite essential for doing business. It may also provide some clues why the Donglin school members were unstinting in their efforts to fight for the merchants' benefit, even to some excessive extent, as we will see. They were not only colleagues. They form a kind of 'clan' as well.

2.1.2 *Institutional Arrangement: The Imperial Examination and Merchant Class*

The imperial examination is another essential prerequisite for controlling the national ideology and the social elite. 'Normal administration throughout the Ming period was dominated by civil service officials',[28] and there existed solemn respect for Confucianism and the imperial examination system based on Confucian culture, which 'was the main instrument for imposing social and political order in a unitary state over a huge area'[29] by attracting outstanding talent into the system who could be then used by the king.

[25] Xu (2011, p. 135).

[26] Weber et al. (1978, pp. 316–317).

[27] Weber and Whimster (2004, p. 42).

[28] Hucker (1958, p. 11).

[29] Maddison (2007, p. 15).

Going into details about imperial exams is obviously not among the tasks of this book. Instead, I only want to emphasize some related and interesting characteristics of the imperial exams in Ming China.

First, officials selected by the imperial exams played a more vital role than their predecessors in previous dynasties. Contrary to Emperor Qin Shihuang or Emperor Han Wudi[30] who maintained firm grasps throughout their periods of rule, several Ming emperors, especially during the middle and late periods, either lacked total control of 'governments led by literati chosen by examination rather than by hereditary aristocracy'[31] (e.g. Emperor Longqing and Emperor Chongzhen[32]) or they had minimal interest in governing the country (e.g. Emperor Zhengde,[33] who was obsessed with many forms of entertainment; Emperor Jiajing,[34] who was obsessed with the elixir of life; and Emperor Wanli,[35] who did not hold traditional biweekly courts for almost 20 years). Therefore, control over the empire often fell into the hands of powerful senior bureaucrats. And as Weber pointed out, 'as always in a patrimonial state, it was the official, both in that capacity and as tax-farmer, who had the best opportunities for accumulating wealth'.[36] This did not change much in Ming China. Nevertheless, although these bureaucrats might have sought personal gains for their families, their more essential role was still to serve as the 'agent' of the royal family and the state.

How can this happen? Despite various explanations, this phenomenon can at least partly attribute to the high-level maturity of imperial examination in Ming China, more than 700 hundred years after its establishment in Sui China. And most Ming emperors seem to be quite intelligent (but lazy as well). The emperor often just pull strings behind the scenes, and

[30] Emperor Han Wudi of Han (157–87 BC) was the seventh emperor of the Han dynasty of China, ruling from 141 to 87 BC. His reign lasted 54 years. His reign resulted in a vast territorial expansion and the development of a strong and centralized state resulting from his governmental reorganization, including his promotion of Confucian doctrines.

[31] Russell (1922, p. 34).

[32] Emperor Chongzhen reigned from 1627 to 1644.

[33] Emperor Zhengde reigned from 1505 to 1521.

[34] Emperor Jiajing reigned from 1521 to 1567.

[35] Emperor Wanli reigned from 1572 to 1620.

[36] Weber et al. (1978, p. 316).

the qualified 'agents' selected will follow his mind and guard the interest of the royal family and the state. Following the examples above, although Emperor Jiajing was busy with searching pills of immortality, he appointed some really capable officials to act on his behalf. For Emperor Wanli, since he did not hold traditional biweekly courts for almost 20 years, it is not uncommon that quite a few officials never see the emperor in a decade. However, Emperor Wanli still met with his Grand Secretariat at least twice a week to discuss the government affairs.

The second worth-mentioning characteristics of the imperial examination in Ming China is its increasing eight-legged style[37]: 'since the adoption of the eight-legged style in the examination, ancient learning has been discarded'.[38] Considering the fact that the majority of the economic thinkers showing up in this book were the ones who passed these 'Ming-style' imperial examination, their thought, as we will see, indeed showed a confined pragmatism predisposition instead of those open-minded metaphysics which more frequently appeared in those antiquity books. This kind of pragmatism often 'came from certain national confidence',[39] which was also reflected in the economic thought such as Continentalist orientation, as we will see.

Third, Ming China is the first period ever that the merchant class benefited a lot from the imperial exams, which may foreshadow the rise to prominence of merchant class's spokesmen, such as the Donglin School. Unlike the former dynasties, the merchants of the Ming Dynasty were not discriminated against or suppressed by the government from the very beginning. In the third year of Emperor Hongwu (1370) the state opened up the imperial examination, and clearly stated:

> The officials who [had] already been offered official ranks and those who [had] been *jinshi* in the former dynasty [were] not allowed to take the imperial examination. Officials who [had] been dismissed, artists who

[37] Eight-legged style, *bagu* in Chinese, is a literary form stipulated in imperial examination prevailing mainly during Ming and Qing period. The content of the eight-legged essay must be in the tone of the ancients, and the candidates were not allowed to play freely. The length of the sentence, the complexity of the words, and the tone of the voice were also confined under some specific requirements, while the number of words is also limited. Eight-legged essay has always been widely criticized, although not abolished till the termination of imperial examination in 1905.

[38] Yu (2016, p. 21).

[39] Hua and Wang (2014, p. 71).

> [were] engaged in singing and dancing and prostitutes [were] also not allowed to participate. All others, including those who [had] no fixed place to live, could participate in the exam.[40]

The merchants, naturally, belonged to the group of 'all others'. Although they had to undergo long-distance treks due to business needs, they were not excluded from the imperial examinations. In addition to the exam, the Confucian school regulations in Ming China stated that, 'regarding all military and civil issues, retired officials, people with lofty ideals, unadorned peasants, merchants, and craftsmen were all allowed to put forward suggestions, and no one could obstruct that'.[41] Here, merchants were also juxtaposed with other occupations, who were allowed to play their roles.

As far as the actual situation was concerned, the merchants made a long trek to engage in commerce, and the difficulties of their own and their offspring returning to their origins for the exam were outstanding. The Ming government also realized this dilemma faced by the merchants. Therefore, during the era of Emperor Jiajing,[42] there were already some examples of those who obtained *fuji* (transient registration in their place of residence). And in the thirteenth year of Emperor Wanli (1585), the court began to systematically solve this dilemma by adding a separate *shangji* ('merchants' registration') and then increasing the admission quota in this group. 'The shangji was invented during the era of Emperor Wanli. According to the proposal of Censor Cai, the offspring of the merchants in Yangzhou were allowed to take the imperial examinations locally, and their enrolment adhered to the same standards as the indigenous candidates' (Wen, 1962 [1630], 164: p. 2984). The merchants, thereafter, can more easily participated in the imperial exams.

Traditional views often overemphasize the role of imperial power. While the importance of imperial power still holds true in Ming China, the imperial examination became another core of the whole power struggle. All the things involved in the imperial examination system were essentially national affairs. The imperial examination in Ming China was more mature than any former dynasty, and thus became an essential basic

[40] Gu (1977 [1690], Vol. 4, p. 1525).

[41] Shen (1989 [1587], Vol. 78, p. 452).

[42] Emperor Jiajing reigned from 1522 to 1566.

system of the country, which affected the development of commerce and the status of merchants.

2.1.3 Fiscal Policy Design: State Monopoly

Among all the issues dealt by the ancient Chinese rulers, the grasp of state power over the national economy and the citizens' livelihood was particularly prominent. They must believe that 'political pressure acted as a pumping mechanism to create a circulation of goods of which economic demand by itself was incapable'.[43] Thus, the ruler often monopolised their state by prohibiting or restricting private entities from engaging in any industry considered to be pertinent to the national economy and people's livelihood, particularly those profitable industries or those vital natural resources related. The Chinese term *jinque* specifically referred to any government monopoly system that banned private management of extremely important commodities.[44]

The feeling of individuals was, unfortunately, seldom within the prior consideration of the rulers in ancient China. As Prof. Schefold pointed out, 'individual well-being is not so much regarded as a primary and independent goal but as the likely result of the realisation of this order'.[45] Meanwhile, commerce was often under the control of political powers where it could be manipulated by officials, who also had the convenience to do so since they were usually 'housed in cities that also served as capitals at lower levels'.[46] We may also find some clue in Montesquieu's record,[47] 'our men of commerce,..., can rather be consulted about the banditry of the mandarins [in China]'.[48] The daily activities of merchants were often closely monitored. At times, the wealth of merchants was plundered in a partially or completely public manner, and the development of private commerce was vigorously controlled.

[43] Elvin (1973, p. 165).

[44] Wu (2004, Vol. 2, pp. 283–284).

[45] Schefold (2019, p. 154).

[46] Skinner and Baker (1977, p. 93).

[47] The records of Montesquieu, however, may not be a firm evidence, since his description might only apply to officials in Qing China instead of Ming China, considering the publish date of his work.

[48] Montesquieu (1989 [1748], p. 127).

As Sombart put it,

> State enterprises were always on a large scale; there was something big about them. In an age when the accumulation of capital was not extensive, the state was able to devote considerable sums of money to its undertakings, and often enough the state was the only agency with sufficient means to commence an undertaking.[49]

During the Spring and Autumn period, Guan Zhong served as prime minister in the Duke Huan of Qi period. He conducted a theoretical exploration and preliminary trial of a state monopoly system named *guan shanhai* (control of mountains and oceans).[50] It is understandable, since natural resources like salt and iron were always hidden deep in mountainous terrain or in other inaccessible places like remote coastal areas. During that period, the Qi state had still not enforced a monopolistic system over resources such as salt and iron. It was not until Western Han when Emperor Han Wudi's government monopolised salt, iron, and wine, thereby representing the first formal establishment of a state monopoly in ancient China due to political issues at the time (such as wars with barbarians and famine). Emperor Han Wudi appointed Sang Hongyang[51] to preside over the salt, iron, and wine monopolies throughout the country, under which the government controlled the production and distribution while strictly forbidding individuals from any unauthorised involvement in the operation of these industries.

Sang Hongyang pointed out that 'if areas harbouring the wealth of the country and the assets of the monarch were governed by himself and his appointees, the country would stay strong; otherwise, the empire would collapse'.[52] If areas like these that could generate considerable wealth were allowed to fall into the hands of local princes or civil tyrants, it

[49] Sombart (1913, p. 83).

[50] Hu (1998 [1965], Vol. 1, pp. 358–359).

[51] Sang Hongyang (152–80 BC) was a Chinese politician. He was a prominent official of the Han Dynasty, who served Emperor Wu of Han and his successor Emperor Zhao. He is famous for his economic policies during the reign of Emperor Wu, the best known of which include the state monopolies over iron and salt.

[52] Huan (1992 [c.66–49 BC], p. 120).

would be very easy, in Sang's view, to 'become a treacherous and hypocritical industry that would give rise to local power'.[53] Also, the demise of centralised governing would pose a serious threat to the unification of royal power. And one obvious way to maintain such royal power may be supported by 'the additional revenue that could be raised and used to supplement the funds available for defence',[54] which should be ensured by state monopoly. Since Emperor Han Wudi, the major industries of salt, iron, and wine became the core monopolised products for most later dynasties,[55] including Ming China.

During the reign of Emperor Han Wudi, the legalists argued that 'it is difficult to see, in these conditions, how we could prevent the soldiers who defend the Great Wall from dying of cold and hunger. Suppress the state monopolies and you deliver a fatal blow to the nation'.[56] Thus, in order to allow the court to control and regulate all national markets and provide maximum pressure on the profit streams of private merchants, Sang Hongyang devised a system with far-reaching consequences called 'equitable delivery' (*junshu*) in which he 'sought to improve the efficiency of military logistics by redistributing tax revenues collected in affluent regions to the deficit-ridden frontier territories'.[57] As part of another policy known as the 'balanced standard' (*pingzhun*), government agents throughout the empire used public funds—including revenue from monopolistic practices—to smooth out price fluctuations by 'buying goods when prices were low and selling when prices were high'.[58]

The equitable delivery programme managed the entire wholesale market infrastructure and controlled travelling merchants by negating opportunities in extra-regional trade. The balanced standard programme managed all retail markets and effectively restricted merchants to owning local stalls. The two policies complimented each other: Equitable delivery relied on a constant supply of goods guaranteed by the balanced standard, while the products supplied by the balanced standard needed to be sold

[53] Huan (1992 [c.66–49 BC], pp. 78–79).

[54] Loewe (1974, p. 100).

[55] Since Tang China, tea also became a state-controlled commodity, mainly for the purpose of border trade with ethnic minority.

[56] Mark (2002, p. 33).

[57] Von Glahn (2016, p. 116).

[58] Hu (1998 [1965], Vol. 3, p. 357).

quickly and in large volumes by equitable delivery. These programmes constituted a unified system of state-run commerce that largely excluded private merchants.

The reforms of renowned economist and politician Wang Anshi[59] during the Northern Song Dynasty included extreme monopolistic policies that ratcheted up the enmity of a 'state competing with its own people' to the extreme. It was not so surprising, since the thought of Wang 'was closer to the Legalist theories than that of most Confucianists'.[60] Under his administration, the entire court became a quasi-government company with an unprecedented expansion of power. First, the government deployed special agents such as *shiyi si* (the Department of Market Trade) to enforce market regulations.[61] Next, special funds were allocated from the state treasury as capital to bankroll the equitable delivery system and monopolise the city's retail commodity industry.[62] The civilians' daily use and consumption were monitored, and even the most trivial items like fruits and vegetables were controlled by the state monopoly. Finally, the government uniformly fixed all pricing and sold at inflated prices to civilians.[63] It is fair to conclude that Wang Anshi's policies reached the limits of the *Qingzhong* theory initiated by *Guanzi*. The government interfered with all economic activity and dictated the commercial markets, thereby becoming the largest if not the only relevant merchant. They manipulated the currency, balanced prices to thwart merchants, adjusted supply and demand, and consolidated the power of distribution to ensure their ultimate utopian goal was achieved, namely, 'a country free from loitering merchants where wealth was evenly distributed among all people'.[64]

[59] Wang Anshi (1021–1086) was a Chinese economist, poet, and politician during the Song dynasty. He served as chancellor who attempted major and controversial socioeconomic reforms known as the New Policies.

[60] Liu (1959, p. 45).

[61] Wu (2004, Vol. 2, p. 827).

[62] Wu (2004, Vol. 2, p. 828).

[63] Wu (2004, Vol. 2, p. 828).

[64] Wu (2004, Vol. 2, p. 829).

2.1.4 Public Goods: Roads and Posthouse

In Ming China, the policies such as equitable delivery and balanced standards continuously provided some significant benefits by stabilising prices and eradicating problems related to poverty through state intervention. And in order to facilitate these two systems, the Ming court invested a lot in the construction of infrastructure, to be more specific, roads, canals, and posthouses. This may be regarded as another important advantage of state force. After all, no matter in the West or in the East, 'merchants' market-oriented calculations required more frequent and more exact information about distant events'.[65] And infrastructure like roads and posthouses were undoubtedly quite essential, especially for merchants.

As public goods, these are unlikely to be built by individuals. With the state's effort, during Mongolian's rule, some posthouses near the capital city can already 'provide fresh fruits like pears and papaya'.[66] And when it comes to Ming China, roads and posthouses were 'densely covered, including the border areas',[67] and 'some gorgeous hotels along the main communication artery look high-ranking and tasteful'.[68] And a very similar system like the 'kind of guild-based system of correspondence' organized by the merchants appearing in Europe 'from the fourteenth century on'[69] also appears in Ming China.[70] And the state force was behind these.

Thus, the state monopoly may not be all that 'evil' as many scholars claimed. Sombart's words seem to be appropriated here, 'the state had at its disposal the necessary organization for these undertakings. The advantage in this respect which the state possessed over the private undertaker goes without saying. The state had the administrative machine ready;

65 Habermas (1989, p. 16).

66 Zang (2009, p. 122).

67 Zang (2009, p. 134).

68 Zang (2009, p. 139).

69 Habermas (1989, p. 16).

70 Before Ming China, delivering information and letters is the privilege of the royal, aristocrat, and high-level officials. Specifically, before Song China, delivering private letters by using the postal system was illegal. And it is not until Mongolian's rule and Ming period that individuals (including low-level officials and merchants) can also benefit from the postal system and spending the night in hotels along the main roads.

the private undertaker had first to provide it'.[71] However, when viewed from the perspective of overall commercial development and the relationship between the state and merchants, major institutional disadvantages of state intervention remained. The fundamental purpose of these policies was to increase the fiscal revenue of 'the central government and the royal family'.[72] Similar to Hayek's famous assertion that 'a danger with any attempt to move toward a centrally planned economic system is that the concentration of economic power is likely to lead to a concentration of political power',[73] the ancient Chinese version of a 'planned economy' increased the state's fiscal revenue in a short period of time. However, when political power completely usurped the regulatory role normally played by market mechanisms, rejection of the free market's role in commerce negated opportunities for private merchants, as we will see in Chapter 3.

2.1.5 *Market Control: Intention and Real Effect*

Investigating its essence, the 'suppression of merchants' in ancient China has always been based on none other than some 'stability requirements'. In the West, according to Weber, 'the emphasis on the ascetic importance of a fixed calling provided an ethical justification of the modern specialized division of labour. In a similar way the providential interpretation of profit-making justified the activities of the business man'.[74] Under Confucianism, however, no such views existed. Thus, while using the development of the commerce to bring various benefits to the country, the rulers were particularly wary of the excessive expansion of merchants' forces to threaten their own rule. Although the development of commerce was indispensable for monarchy, it can under no circumstances be allowed to grow too strongly. Thus its status was quite embarrassing. Fu Xuan[75] of

[71] Sombart (1967 [1915], p. 86).

[72] Zhang (1999, p. 192).

[73] Hayek (1988, p. 202).

[74] Weber (2001 [1904], p. 109).

[75] Fu Xuan (217–278) was a Chinese historian, poet, and politician who lived in the state of Cao Wei during the Three Kingdoms period and later under the Jin dynasty.

the Jin Dynasty summarized in a very simple and straightforward manner: 'Merchants can be despised, while commerce cannot be abolished'.[76]

Ancient Chinese rulers used the power of their regimes to strengthen their control of markets as early as the Western Zhou dynasty. Excerpts from ancient literature, such as *Zhouli* and *Liji* (the *Book of Rites*), reveal that Zhou China[77] deployed systematic supervision and restrictions on commodities and merchants, and they organised and managed all transaction markets.[78] The measures recorded in *Zhouli* include the following: restricting the trade of market commodities outside the official market; prohibiting nobles from directly participating in market transactions; government regulation of different types of markets, determination of the types and prices of commodities, as well as setting time limits for transactions; and implementation of full-time management controls and the maintenance of market order.[79] In sum, the state's market control during the Zhou dynasty included strict government regulations on private commodity trading behaviour at all times with the ultimate goal of maximising the corresponding system of *gongshang shiguan*[80] (i.e. craftsmen and merchants were essentially slaves under government control). Clearly, commerce at the time 'can be influenced by non-economic considerations',[81] and these practices were consistent with the strict ritual order of the society at that time.

By the start of the Sui (581–618) and Tang eras, the old system of *gongshang shiguan* had disappeared; nevertheless, the *Fangshi* system[82] that replaced it still restrained merchants.[83] In essence, the court established the markets, sent specific officials to manage them, determined the authorised market locations, limited transaction times, and controlled all transaction behaviour and pricing, etc.[84]

[76] Fu (2010 [278], p. 22).

[77] Zhou China existed from 1046 BC to 256 BC.

[78] Hu (1998 [1965], Vol. 1, p. 37).

[79] Hu (1998 [1965], Vol. 1, p. 37).

[80] Zhou (2004 [c.400–100 BC], p. 167).

[81] Horvath (2020, p. 120).

[82] In the *Fangshi* system, the residential and market areas were separated.

[83] Wu (2004, Vol. 2, p. 64).

[84] Wu (2004, Vol. 2, p. 65).

The *Fangshi* system was abolished prior to the Song Dynasty, as was the traditional government-owned market practice of 'forbidding the establishment of markets lower than county level'.[85] However, merchants remained under the control of ubiquitous imperial power. Government officials were sent to supervise markets and levy taxes, and many important grassroot-level markets were upgraded to county, thereby 'ensuring more comprehensive control'.[86]

This kind of control over markets and merchants, however, really suffered a dilution in Ming China, although it was clearly against the will of the Ming rulers.

The merchants' itinerant and unmanageable nature forced the state to work harder in order to control them by all conceivable means, maybe due to the fear that 'as commercialized economy reached a certain limit, commerce would contribute to the disintegration of the traditional social structure'.[87] In Ming China, if merchants wanted to obtain legal residency and authorisation to conduct commerce in a particular city, they had to 'visit government offices to register and declare their intentions'.[88] Anyone who passed the investigation could obtain a permit called *shiji* (market registration). This *shiji* was initiated by Emperor Hongwu, and 'continued after the death of the founding emperor in 1398'.[89]

However, the policy itself and its real practice can be totally different. The statistics shows that for Ming government, it is the 'weak control' rather than the widely acknowledged 'strong control' reflects the real situation of markets and inner merchants,

> The Ming civil service was very small. In 1371 provincial and local officials totalled only 5,488... Even in the early sixteenth century when the offices had been significantly enlarged, there were still only 20,400 civil officials throughout the empire. The lesser functionaries totalled about 51,000 persons but they served both the civil government and the army.[90]

[85] Wu (2004, Vol. 2, p. 71).

[86] Wu (2004, Vol. 2, pp. 82–83).

[87] Tang (2017, p. 7).

[88] Xu (2011, p. 228).

[89] Ho (1959, p. 4).

[90] Huang (1974, p. 48).

With so few government officials, it is very difficult to achieve effective control of society, so many functions that should be undertaken by the government were often forced to handed over to grassroots units, where kinship played its essential role again.

Geographically speaking, the intended control seems to be confronted with a bigger drawback in the southern region, especially Jiangnan region, as 'the upper basin of the Yangtse-Kiang[91]...was a zone of scattered settlements isolated from each other, whereas in China proper, the population was concentrated in centres'.[92]

In Ming China, despite some aggressive policies and regulations, on many occasions merchants actually had considerable autonomy. In particular, the circulation of commodities in grassroots societies and the economic exchanges between villages and towns often resembled a laissez-faire state in actual practice, depending on 'autonomous political power'.[93] Merchants, like other civilians, were often free to purchase real estate, relocate to new premises, hire employees, and participate in other related economic activities. At the same time, most rulers and various levels of government (especially local governments) understood the important role played by commerce and merchants in social development when 'correcting surpluses and balancing regional wealth disparities'.[94] Some local officials even realized, at least subconsciously, that 'competitive markets work for the best, allocating resources among alternative uses, among different households and agents'.[95] It resulted in the fact that the centralization of power and market control even did not work within the bureaucracy in Ming China: the local governments often disobey the orders from the court mainly due to different interest, as we will see in this book, especially Chapter 5.

[91] Yangtze river is the longest river in Asia, the third-longest in the world and the longest in the world to flow entirely within one country.

[92] Braudel (1979, p. 61).

[93] McDermott (2013, p. 213).

[94] Ban (1962 [92], Vol. 84, p. 1691).

[95] Haliassos (1990, p. 907).

2.2 Economic Thought Origin: Pro-Agriculture and Egalitarianism

2.2.1 Why Was Agriculture Emphasised in Ancient China?

Ancient China was an agricultural society dependent on the natural economy. This essence did not change substantially in Ming China despite the rapid development of commerce in the middle and late periods, and 'most of the population remained little affected by commerce'.[96] The small peasant economy based on simple production on rural lands satisfied most of the continuous daily needs of the population. It was the sector with the least amount of change in the entire society, due to ancient China's 'long-stationary condition of the civilization' and 'its fixity and conservatism' nature.[97] 'The wealth of the empire was based on agricultural production, from the single-minded pursuit of which the manufacture of anything other than essential tools of production or necessities for survival was seen as a potentially unsettling distraction'.[98] Therefore, farmers had always been the principle creators of social wealth and the cornerstone to ensure the maintenance of social order. Throughout history, this was not unique to Eastern civilisations, 'until the late modern era, more than ninety percent of humans were peasants who rose each morning to till the land by the sweat of their brows. The extra they produced fed the tiny minority of elites—kings, government officials, soldiers, priests, artists and thinkers'.[99] And a good example from the perspective of economic thought is that 'the influence of the Chinese upon the French physiocrats was probably more extensive and more significant than it has generally been appreciated'.[100]

All rulers of ancient China understood a simple truth: Only by firmly binding the peasants to the land and strictly controlling them could the

[96] Elvin (1973, p. 165).

[97] Haney (1911, p. 48).

[98] Clunas (1991, p. 141).

[99] Harari (2014, p. 97).

[100] Klump (2004, p. 179).

collection of taxes and search of labour be facilitated. As *Hanshu*[101] stated, 'The principle of people management was based on land'. The economic impact of the above illustrated bureaucracy was 'very positive for agriculture', since 'it was the key sector from which they could squeeze a surplus in the form of taxes and compulsory levies'.[102] Similar approval of ancient China's emphasis on agriculture can be found in the words of Pierre Poivre,[103] who was sent to 'Vietnam as a representative of the Compagnie des Indes which wanted to expand trade relations with Indochina'.[104] He 'praised the Chinese economic and political system in which he saw the reason for the great economic success of the country'.[105] He believed that in ancient China, 'the many agricultural innovations and the high agricultural productivity were entirely due to a wise government which obeyed the natural order',[106] which also had a great influence on Vietnamese economic policies, represented by 'the case of Ponthiamas under the Ming Chinese rulers'.[107]

However, although agriculture was most directly responsible for the country's prosperity, countless historical facts showed that the peasants—who were the foundation of the state—lived in perpetual poverty, bore the heaviest burden of taxes, were always the first to face conscription, and endured frequent oppression from the ruling class. In contrast, merchants

[101] *Hanshu*, or the Book of Han, is a history of China finished in 111, covering the Western, or Former Han dynasty from the first emperor in 206 BCE to the fall of Wang Mang in 23 CE. The work was composed by Ban Gu (AD 32–92), a court official, with the help of his sister Ban Zhao, continuing the work of their father, Ban Biao. They modeled their work on the Records of the Grand Historian.

[102] Maddison (2007, p. 16).

[103] Pierre Poivrc (1719–1786) was a typical representative of the French bourgeoisie during the era of the Enlightenment. He was born in Lyon, and in 1740, he was sent to Macau, Canton and Tongking (the northern part of Vietnam). His special interest was the differences in agricultural productivity among the different states. He always tried to relate the state of agriculture in a country which he was able to consider with the professional eyes of an educated agronomist to the existing laws and institutions. Poivre's treatise on the travellings of a philosopher ends with a long description of China. For details, please refer to Klump (2004).

[104] Klump (2004, pp. 174–175).

[105] Klump (2004, p. 175).

[106] Klump (2004, pp. 175–176).

[107] Klump (2004, p. 181).

who appeared to be idle most days had a better chance of enjoying luxurious lifestyles with seemingly little or no effort.

This social reality with its inherent moral implications that were contrary to social practice had long been valued by some economic thinkers. Sima Qian said, 'In terms of wealth accumulation, farmers were not as good as craftsmen, and craftsmen were not as good as merchants. It was more profitable to sit in the market rather than do embroidery work'.[108] Gu Yanwu was a well-known Confucian in the late Ming period. He said, 'The profit from farming was the lowest while labour costs were the highest. The profits of merchants were several times that of peasants, but the labour invested was minimal'.[109]

When we look at the West thinkers, Xenophon's emphasis on 'profound respect for the practice of farming'[110] was an attempt to maintain slavery in ancient Greece,

> The farmer must often exhort his workers no less than the general his soldiers; and good hopes are no less necessary to slaves than to the free, but rather more so, that they may be willing to remain. Whoever said that farming is the mother and nurse of all the other arts spoke finely indeed. For when farming goes well, all the other arts also flourish, but when the earth is compelled to lie barren, the other arts almost cease to exist.[111]

The rise and fall of the ancient Greek and Roman slavery systems was based on the successes and failures of foreign conquests. Looking back to ancient China, the theory of four occupational groups put forth by *Guanzi* placed the most importance on agriculture and best served the political aspirations of the Qi state. The unified order was a traditional political reality based on ideals established and strengthened since the Shang and Zhou dynasties.[112]

[108] Sima (1959 [86 BC], p. 241).

[109] Gu (1985 [1682], p. 165).

[110] Strauss (1998, p. 119).

[111] Strauss (1998, p. 25).

[112] The Shang dynasty was a Chinese dynasty that ruled in the Lower Yellow River Valley in the second millennium BC, succeeding the semi-mythical Xia dynasty and followed by the Zhou dynasty. The Shang ruled from 1766 to 1122 BC. And as for Zhou, the military control of China by the royal house, surnamed Ji, lasted initially from 1046 until 771 BC for a period known as the Western Zhou and the political sphere of influence it created continued well into Eastern Zhou for another 500 years.

Many economic thinkers in ancient China (including Ming) believed that agriculture was 'the only source of wealth',[113] the only foundation of the national economy and the citizens' livelihood. Industry and commerce hindered agricultural production, especially the unequal exchanges in commerce and merchant hoarding that would divide the income of farmers and accelerate their poverty. In a deeper sense, the manic obsession with social stability in ancient China suggests that the state was keenly wary of all social groups with potential resistance characteristics. Merchants did not produce in any specific place and were highly mobile, thus making it easier for them to circumvent centralised governmental control. Those operating successful businesses often accumulated significantly more wealth. Merchants comprised the social group that was most problematic for rulers. In short, elevating the importance of peasants while restraining merchants were two sides of the same issue.

Therefore, it can be said that the emphasis on agriculture and peasants rather than commerce and merchants was a form of 'natural selection'. The rationale for this emphasis was directly associated with the feasibility of suppressing commerce and merchants. However, the rationale behind the suppression of commerce and merchants has already been revealed as a major dissimilarity between China and the early days of Western development. Early Western economic thought remained reasonable by despising commerce and merchants that eventually led to tolerance followed by acceptance. In China, thoughts about commerce evolved into extreme suppression of merchants that dominated ancient economic theories since the Qin Dynasty till at least Song China.

2.2.2 A Firm Stance on Commerce

Theories valuing agriculture more than commerce clarified the primary and secondary relationships between agriculture and commerce; however, they did not suggest that the two formed a single substitution relationship (or, a zero sum relationship). Therefore, the idea of valuing agriculture over commerce should not have ruled out the possibility of a complementary relationship between the two. Unfortunately, throughout the history of ancient China, this seemingly 'unreasonable' hostility toward merchants actually happened. In particular, the characteristics of

[113] Klump (2004, p. 179).

ancient Chinese economic thought regarding commerce and merchants are summarised as follows.

First, the economic thinkers in ancient China were more contentious and divergent regarding their thoughts and despisal of commerce and merchants. Mencius, Sima Qian, Su Shi,[114] Ye Shi,[115] and several other important thinkers affirmed the value of commerce to levels that might have been even more resolute than early Western thought. They were most likely to promote or at least accept a solution where peasants and merchants could be equally emphasised. Conversely, ancient legalist thinkers like Shang Yang and Han Fei, as well as Wang Fuzhi during the Ming Dynasty, held contemptuous attitudes toward commerce and merchants that were obviously more radical and extreme than any of the early Western theories about commerce. They were advocates for the suppression of merchants and 'simply believed in maximal power to the state'.[116] Han Fei even listed craftsmen and merchants among the 'Five Vermin of the State'.[117]

The second characteristic is that the divergence of thoughts despising merchants generally revealed opposite trends in China and the West. In the West, the despisal of merchants during the ancient Greek and Roman periods was more distinctive and popular than in the middle ages. However, the despisal of merchants in China before the middle Warring States period was far less serious and widespread than after. In other words, the despisal of merchants in the ancient West gradually dissipated as civilisations evolved, while the despisal of merchants gradually strengthened over time in ancient China.

The prevailing economic thought that emphasised agriculture and peasants elevated the importance of agriculture as the *benye* (the roots) in ancient China,[118] while the widespread despisal of commerce and

[114] Su Shi (1037–1101) was a Chinese calligrapher, gastronome, painter, pharmacologist, poet, politician, and writer of the Song dynasty. A major personality of the Song era, Su was an important figure in Song Dynasty politics, aligning himself with Sima Guang and others, against the New Policy party led by Wang Anshi.

[115] Ye Shi (1150–1223) was a Chinese neo-Confucian of the Song dynasty. He was the most famous figure of the Yongjia School, a neo-Confucianism School composed mostly of philosophers from Wenzhou Prefecture in Zhejiang province.

[116] Rothbard (2006, p. 23).

[117] Clunas (1991, p. 141).

[118] Clunas (1991, p. 141).

merchants relegated commerce to the status of *moye* (the branch industry). As long as agriculture was considered the primary economic provider, those involved with commerce had really no choice but to remain marginalised in a subordinate field, or even worse, trail behind all other occupations.

In fact, the theory of four occupational groups presented by the author of *Guanzi* can be considered a turning point in ancient Chinese economic thought. Before then, thoughts valuing agriculture were emphasised, such as King Wen of Zhou[119] who considered agriculture as 'the monarch's top task' and 'cultivated the fields in order to stabilise the people and reclaim the land'.[120] Such thoughts conveyed the message that agriculture remained the state's top priority. However, at that time there were no indications of major criticism of commerce or merchants. Thoughts of suppressing merchants gradually became dominant in the state's orthodox policies after Guan Zhong, the widely acknowledged author of *Guanzi*, who aimed to 'strengthen the state power of Qi'.[121] Others sharing similar goals were Shang Yang and Han Fei for Qin, as well as Sang Hongyang who aimed to strengthen the country's power under Emperor Han Wudi. For instance, after *Hanshu*, the official history books no longer wrote biographies about merchants.

The third characteristic is that Chinese and Western economic thoughts on commerce had diverse theoretical focuses. It is true that both Chinese and Western economists included ethical considerations by condemning fraud and exploitation in commercial activities, and neither denied the positive economic function of commerce. However, as mentioned previously, Chinese economic thoughts were divided into two groups based on their moderate or aggressive despisal of merchants. Both groups focused on debates related to the state's control of commercial activities. For instance, the *qingzhong* theory ('light and heavy')[122] raised

[119] King Wen of Zhou (1112–1050 BC, the Civilizing King) was count of Zhou during the late Shang dynasty in ancient China. Although it was his son Wu who conquered the Shang following the Battle of Muye, Count Wen was posthumously honored as the founder of the Zhou dynasty and titled King. Some consider him the first epic hero of Chinese history.

[120] Hu (1998 [1965], Vol. 1, p. 30).

[121] Hu (1998 [1965], Vol. 1, p. 291).

[122] Hu (1998 [1965], Vol. 1, p. 318).

by *Guanzi* and the theory of *shanyin*[123] (similar to Laissez-faire policy) put forth by Sima Qian were representative of the prevailing thoughts of the time. Conversely, the Greek and Roman despisal of commerce and merchants was based primarily on their desire to maintain their slavery systems. Since the middle ages, however, Western debate on commercial theories focused primarily on just pricing for commercial transactions.

As Prof. Schefold pointed out, in ancient China, 'early on it was at least ideologically an aim to displace large private traders through bureaucratic redistribution'.[124] Thus, the above characteristics clearly shows a tendency of suppressing merchants rather than assuming more reasonable policies became the orthodox economic thought in ancient China before Ming. Whether it continued or changed in Ming China will be elaborated in this whole book.

2.2.3 *Thoughts on Egalitarianism*

As previously mentioned, the natural economic structure of ancient China was historically dominated by a combination of the production of small-scale farming peasants and household handicrafts. This simple production relationship created a stable state and a fixed social hierarchy, thereby maintaining the stability of imperial power. Meanwhile, due to the extremely fragile nature of the natural economy, the key to the ruler's distribution of social wealth was to ensure basic production and livelihood guarantees for citizens at the bottom tier of society. The most ideal situation was to adhere to the social hierarchy and account for the interests of all strata to achieve economic and social equality. This equalisation in ancient China was among many a thing that is crucial to understand economic thoughts related to Ming China, including the propaganda of levying commercial and agricultural taxes.

As Smith pointed out, 'the poverty of the lower ranks of people in China far surpasses that of the most beggarly nations in Europe'.[125] Thus, if the high profitability of commerce (compared to agriculture) were allowed, the free development of commerce would inevitably exacerbate the social disparity between the rich and the poor. Eventually it exceeded

[123] Hu (1998 [1965], Vol. 1, p. 54).

[124] Schefold (2016, p. 340).

[125] Smith (1979 [1776], p. 89).

the limits of social development and led to the intensification of social contradictions. Therefore, in a certain sense, the idea of egalitarianism became intrinsically related to the culture of merchant restraint, as stated in Sect. 2.1. By suppressing the commercial activity of merchants, rulers could achieve better equalisation of personal wealth and thus balance the economy. This in turn benefitted the stability and prosperity of all social classes.

As early as ancient China, Yu (the third of the three Sage Kings in ancient times) took measures to regulate the supply of goods in different regions to solve food shortages and 'equalise the princes' wealth'. Xunzi praised Yao (the first of the three Sage Kings in ancient times) forfor his magnanimity and for sharing profits 'evenly among the people'.[126] The ideal of 'the average' was no longer a purely economic adjustment method during the Zhou dynasty, and it became a political mandate that the ruler incorporated as part of his plan to govern the country. A very important duty of the prime minister as recorded in *Zhouli* was 'to balance the different states, to ensure fairness among officials, and to equalise the wealth of all citizens'.[127] In short, 'average' was always an ideal principle for the distribution of social wealth in ancient China. Its purpose was to guarantee the most basic living conditions for all people to enable the entire society to achieve balanced and stable development.

In fact, pre-Qin thinkers almost unanimously proposed wealth distribution or 'economic averaging', and they criticised the social phenomenon of wide income disparity between the rich and the poor. *Laozi* was famous for his dialectical point of view, believing that 'a dichotomy always existed in all kinds of things, and each would transform into its antithesis'.[128] He started from the idea of '*wuwei*' (taking no action)[129] and denounced both the distribution of wealth by levels and the inequality between the rich and the poor that were becoming all too common in Chinese society. He famously asserted that 'The *Tao* of heaven reduced surpluses to manufacture scarcity, while the *Tao* of man reduced scarcity and paid tribute to surpluses'.[130] *Laozi* also believed that this 'reduction of scarcity and

[126] Hu (1998 [1965], Vol. 1, p. 426).

[127] Zhou (2004 [c.400–100 BC], p. 252).

[128] Shen (1996, Vol. 1, p. 30).

[129] Hu (1998 [1965], Vol. 1, p. 207).

[130] Hu (1998 [1965], Vol. 1, p. 208).

paying tribute to surpluses' was irrational and had caused extreme poverty among the people.[131] The author of *Guanzi* believed that 'everything should be evenly distributed to ensure a sense of fairness among the people'.[132] He equated the idea of balancing the rich and the poor to governing the country and fighting for hegemony:

> A monarch must be able to redistribute hoarded goods, adjust surpluses, diversify the financial benefits of mergers or partnerships, and regulate the people's consumption of goods. Even if this strengthened agriculture, stimulated production, and minted endless currency, in essence it only caused people to enslave each other. How could this be regarded as a good rule for the country?[133] (my transl.)

Mozi[134] and Han Fei belonged to different schools; however, they both believed that the equal distribution of wealth was the key to governing the country. For instance, Mozi pointed out that 'the ancient Sage Kings did not dare divide the wealth unequally'.[135] Han Fei believed that 'the Sage King who governed the country should obtain property in accordance with current affairs and determine the balance of taxation to regulate the relative percentages [allotted] for the rich and the poor. This was a calculated political measure that greatly benefitted the emperor'.[136]

Confucian thinkers had unique and incisive interpretations of the concept of equality. Confucius advocated equality based on the rules of etiquette and believed that 'what tortured people was inequality rather than the scarcity of labour forces, and what gnawed their souls was chaos rather than poverty'.[137] Therefore, the state should provide 'averages free of poverty and promote harmony without disagreement'. By using Hu's word, 'it [has] been generally understood by Confucians that what was being talked about was the relationship between the distribution of wealth

[131] Hu (1998 [1965], Vol. 1, pp. 208–209).

[132] Guan (1965 [c.400–100 BC], p. 318).

[133] Guan (1965 [c.400–100 BC], p. 318).

[134] Mozi (470–391 BC), original name Mo Di, was a Chinese philosopher who founded the school of Mohism.

[135] Hu (1998 [1965], Vol. 1, p. 127).

[136] Hu (1998 [1965], Vol. 1, p. 470).

[137] Hu (1998 [1965], Vol. 1, p. 92).

and the problem of equality',[138] thus casting Confucius in the role of an egalitarian.[139]

Mencius proposed his famous ideal of benevolence:

> How can something like the entrapment of people occur under the rule of a benevolent man? An intelligent ruler would regulate the livelihood of the people to ensure that, for those above them, they would have sufficient wherewithal to serve their parents. For those below them, they would have sufficient resources to support their wives and children. In good years they would always be abundantly satisfied, and in bad years they would escape the danger of perishing.[140] (my transl.)

Mencius believed that as long as each farmer could be offered 'a house occupying five acres and one hundred acres of fields',[141] they could live and work in peace and contentment, and 'there would no longer be hunger or discomfort'.[142] The Confucians believed that wealth distribution and equality was best reflected in a social ideal called '*Datong*' (great harmony) that essentially referred to an egalitarian society featuring 'equality and comradery'.[143] It also represented the limits of the imagination of Confucian thinkers regarding the equal distribution of social wealth.

The familiar egalitarian argument stated that,

> If the utility functions of the rich and the poor are comparable, the redistribution of wealth from the rich to the poor makes sense, as long as it may be assumed that the marginal utility of the former, because of their greater level of consumption, is lower than that of the latter.[144]

This tallies with the common ideology of thinkers from various schools during the pre-Qin dynasties, and their successors generally adhered to this concept of equal distribution of wealth and adjustments between the

[138] Hu (1988, p. 49).

[139] Cheng et al. (2014, p. 10).

[140] Hu (1998 [1965], Vol. 1, p. 231).

[141] Hu (1998 [1965], Vol. 1, p. 236).

[142] Hu (1998 [1965], Vol. 1, p. 239).

[143] Hu (1998 [1965], Vol. 1, p. 111).

[144] Schefold (2017, p. 187).

rich and the poor. Meanwhile, egalitarianism became the basic guiding policy for authorities when adjusting the distribution of social property. It featured social balance and an orderly political ideal for governing the country while retaining national significance. In a well-balanced society, the people 'respectively lived and worked in peace, enjoyed delicious food, and wore attractive clothes. Even when they saw luxurious [items] or others wearing beautiful clothing, they were not envious. Wealth was sufficient for everyone and nobody wanted to compete with others'.[145] These social characteristics undoubtedly fell short of reaching the goals of the *Datong* society that Confucians had envisioned. Nevertheless, this 'low level version' of *Datong* was a relatively easy goal to achieve by normal state governance in order to maintain the livelihood and well-being of the people. This was precisely the type of realistic pursuit sought by promising rulers of all dynasties, and Ming China was no exception.

However, the core component of economic egalitarianism was to achieve balanced distribution of social wealth, at least in accordance with the Confucian etiquette hierarchy. This would inevitably impair the rich to a great extent in order to support the poor. Some would even call this robbing the rich to help the poor. In particular, several Taoist and Moist ideas of absolute equal distribution of wealth provided the theoretical basis for 'robbing behaviour'.[146] In ancient China, the lives of the common people who comprised the majority of the population had always been difficult. The trending social disparity between the rich and the poor was increasingly magnified, and wealth equalisation became their most urgent and important need. Expressions of hatred by merchants for the wealthy class were actually in line with the spiritual consciousness of the vast majority of people in ancient China.

However, Egalitarian must come simultaneously with certain inefficiency. In this regard, among Western economic thinkers, Wagner, for instance, proposed 'seeking a 'middle point' consisting of the reform of economic law and an efficient combination of private and communal enterprise'.[147] In ancient China, however, this kind of egalitarian often

[145] Hu (1998 [1965], Vol. 1, p. 113).

[146] Hu (1998 [1965], Vol. 1, pp. 125, 206).

[147] Schefold (2016, p. 315).

became simply 'robbing the rich to help the poor'[148] during the long periods before Ming. This may at least contribute partly to the simplistic mentalities of individual farmers and their limited literacy levels. Their highest ideals were ominously forecasted to be 'starving together when food was in short supply, sharing meat when food was abundant, and trying their best to avoid poverty'.[149] Therefore, the most common slogan during the peasant uprisings of ancient China regardless of the dynasty was the basic request for income equality, 'balance the wealth between the rich and the poor, stop unfair distribution, and divide the fields evenly'.[150]

Under these 'revolutionary declarations', merchants were seen as spokespersons of wealth, and their 'unearned' dirty money often became the primary targets of plunder and division during the uprisings. For long periods, the idea of 'robbing the rich to help the poor' was considered righteous and fair among commoners. Merchants not only faced oppression and extortion from imperial powers and their bureaucratic agents; they also faced pressure from the lower classes. This was one of the most important reasons why members of the merchant class struggled to expand their wealth and raise their status in ancient China.

Restraining merchants was the extreme version of despising merchants because it resulted in detrimental actions in practice rather than involve only social feelings. As long as the prevalent orthodox thought centring on certain egalitarianism in ancient Chinese ideology was perpetuated, the thought of restraining merchants remained a potential outcome, thereby creating choices and options for rulers to 'stamp out diversity among individuals and groups'.[151] Egalitarian concepts and theories supporting peasants at the expense of merchants remained the predominant thoughts determining the status of merchants that were passed between generations after being inherited by dynasties from their predecessors.

However, questions remain. In Ming China, did these 'original thoughts' continue to dominate, and did the despisal of merchants continue as the orthodox position? Also, did the relative status of

148 In Chinese, we actually have an idiomatic expression (which is usually made up of four characters) for 'robbing the rich to help the poor', called *jiefu jipin*.

149 Hu (1998 [1965], Vol. 1, p. 93).

150 Hu (1998 [1965], Vol. 1, p. 93).

151 Rothbard (2000, p. xvii).

merchants change among the four occupations? The remaining sections of this book will analyse the status of merchants within the state-merchant relationship and their relative status compared with scholars, peasants, and craftsmen by examining economic thoughts and relevant historical facts that help answer the aforementioned questions.

References

Reference in German

Sombart, W. (1913). *Der Bourgeois*. Duncker & Humblot.

Reference in English

Braudel, F. (1979). *Civilization and capitalism, 15th-18th century, volume II, the wheels of commerce. Translation from the French by Sian Reynolds*. Book Club Associates.

Cheng, L., Peach, T., & Wang, F. (2014). *The history of ancient Chinese economic thought*. Routledge.

Clunas, C. (1991). *Superfluous things: Material culture and social status in early modern China*. Polity Press.

Elvin, M. (1973). *The pattern of the Chinese past*. Stanford University Press.

Guan, Z., et al. (1965 [c.400–100 BC]). *Guanzi*. Taiwan Commercial Press.

Habermas, J. (1989). *The structural transformation of the public sphere* (T. Burger, Trans.). MIT Press.

Haliassos, M., & Tobin, J. (1990). The macroeconomics of government finance. *Handbook of Monetary Economics, 2*, 889–959.

Haney, L. H. (1911). *History of economic thought: A critical account of the origin and development of the economic theories of the leading thinkers in the leading nations*. Macmillan.

Harari, Y. N. (2014). *Sapiens: A brief history of humankind*. Penguin Random House.

Hayek, F. A. (1988). *The fatal conceit: The errors of socialism, Collected works of F. A. Hayek* (Vol. I). Routledge.

Ho, P. (1959). *Studies on the population of China, 1368–1953*. Harvard University Press.

Horvath, J. (2020). *An Introduction to the History of Economic Thought in Central Europe*. Palgrave Macmillan.

Hu, J. (1988). *A concise history of Chinese economic thought*. Foreign Languages Press.

Huang, R. (1974). *Taxation and governmental finance in sixteenth-century Ming China*. Cambridge University Press.

Hucker, C. (1958). Governmental organization of the Ming dynasty. *Harvard Journal of Asiatic Studies, 21*, 1–66.
Klump, R. (2004). The kingdom of Ponthiamas—A physiocratic model state in Indochina: A note on the international exchange of economic thought and of concepts for economic reforms in the 18th century. In I. Barens, V. Caspari, & B. Schefold (Eds.), *Political events and economic ideas* (pp. 173–183). Elgar.
Li, Z. (2019). *A history of classical Chinese thought. Translated, with a philosophical introduction, by Andrew Lambert*. Routledge.
Liu, Z. (1959). *Reform in Sung China: Wang An-shih (1021–1086) and his new policies*. Harvard University Press.
Loewe, M. (1974). *Crisis and conflict in Han China*. George Allen & Unwin.
Maddison, A. (2007). *Chinese economic performance in the long run: 960–2030 AD*. OECD Development Centre Studies.
Mark, K. (2002). *Salt: A world history*. Walker and Co.
McCloskey, D. N., & DeMartino, G. F. (2016). *The Oxford handbook of professional economic ethics*. Oxford University Press.
McDermott, J. (2013). *The making of a new rural order in South China*. Hong Kong University Press.
Montesquieu, C. (1989 [1748]). *The spirit of the laws* (A. M. Cohler, B. C. Miller, and H. S. Stone, Trans.). Cambridge University Press.
Mosca, M. (2018). *Power in economic thought*. Palgrave Macmillan.
Rickett, W. A. (1998). *Guanzi: Political, economic, and philosophical essays from Early China* (Vol. 1). Princeton University Press.
Rothbard, M. N. (2000). *Egalitarianism as a revolt against nature and other essays*. Ludwig von Mises Institute.
Rothbard, M. N. (2006). *Economic thought before Adam Smith*. Edward Elgar.
Russell, B. (1922). *The problem of China*. George Allen and Unwin Ltd.
Schefold, B. (2016). *Great economic thinkers from antiquity to the historical school: Historical school, old and young*. Routledge.
Schefold, B. (2017). *Great economic thinkers from the classicals to the moderns: Translations from the series Klassiker der Nationalökonomie*. Routledge.
Schefold, B. (2019). A western perspective on the Yantie lun. In L. Cheng, T. Peach, & F. Wang (Eds.), *The political economy of the Han dynasty and its legacy* (pp. 153–174). Routledge.
Skinner, G. W., & Baker, H. D. (1977). *The city in late imperial China*. Stanford University Press.
Smith, A. (1979 [1776]). *The wealth of nations: An inquiry into the nature and causes of the wealth of nations*. Clarendon Press.
Sombart, W. (1967 [1915]). *The quintessence of capitalism: A study of the history and psychology of the modern business man* (M. Epstein, Trans. and Ed.). Howard Fertig.

Strauss, L. (1998). *Xenophon's socratic discourse: An interpretation of the Oeconomicus*. St. Augustine's Press.
Tang, L. (2017). *Merchants and society in modern China: Rise of merchant groups*. Routledge.
Von Glahn, R. (2016). *An economic history of China: From antiquity to the nineteenth century*. Cambridge University Press.
Weber, M. (2001 [1904]). *The protestant ethic and the 'spirit' of capitalism*. Penguin.
Weber, M., Runciman, W. G., & Matthews, E. (1978). *Max Weber: Selections in translation*. Cambridge University Press.
Weber, M., & Whimster, S. (2004). *The essential Weber: A reader*. Routledge.
Wittfogel, K. (1949). *History of Chinese society: Liao (907–1125)*. Lancaster Press.
Yu, Y. (2016). *Chinese history and culture* (Vol. 2). Columbia University Press.

Reference in Chinese

Ban, G. (1962 [92]). *Book of Han*. Zhonghua Publishing House.
Fu, X. (2010 [278]). *Commentary of Fuzi (Fuzi pinzhu)*. Tianjin Ancient Books Publishing House.
Gu, Y. (1985 [1682]). *Tianxia Junguo Libing Shu*. The Commercial Press.
Gu, Y. (1977 [1690]). *Chronicle of the Ming dynasty (Mingshi Jishi Benmo)*. Zhonghua Publishing House.
Guan, W. (1995). *A study of the political system of the Ming dynasty*. China Social Science Press.
Hu, J. (1998 [1965]). *History of Chinese economic thoughts* (Vol. 1–3). Shanghai University of Finance and Economics Press.
Hua, T., & Wang, R. (2014). *The years of studying abroad*. China Tourism Press.
Huan, K. (1992 [c.66–49BC]). *Discourses on salt and iron (Yantie Lun)*. Zhonghua Publishing House.
Li, D. (2004). *A study of imperial power in Ming Dynasty*. China Social Science Press.
Shen, M. (1996). *History (Lishi)*, Vol. 1 and 3. Shanghai: Shanghai Education Press.
Shen, S. (1989 [1587]). *Ming Huidian*. Zhonghua Publishing House.
Sima, Q. (1959 [86BC]). *Records of the grand historian*. Zhonghua Publishing House.
Sun, W., & Sun, Z. (2002). *Introduction to international finance*. Tongji University Press.
Wang, D. (2015). *Advanced lecture notes on the history of economic thought*. Shanghai Renmin Press.
Wen, T. (1962 [1630]). *Ming Shilu, record of Emperor Wanli*. Institute of History and Language.

Wu, H. (2004). *Chinese commerce history*. The Finance and Economics Press.

Wu, X. (2012). *Mighty for two thousand years (Haodang Liangqian Nian)*. Zhongxin Press.

Xu, H. (2011). *Study of Ming history in China in the 20th century*. Taiwan University Press.

Zang, R. (2009). *Posthouses and postal service in ancient China*. China International Broadcasting Press.

Zhang, Z. (1999). *Political system of the Ming dynasty*. Wunan Book Press.

Zhou, G. (2004 [c.400–100 BC]). *Zhouli*. Shanghai Ancient Books Publishing House.

CHAPTER 3

Monopoly: Merchants and Monarchy

In Ming China, whether the state should control commerce and what kind of role the merchants can play in it continued to be a popular topic of debate among philosophers and economic thinkers. Generally, economic thinkers stood in two opposing camps, respectively, opposing and supporting state-operated commerce. Let's start with the faction that opposed state-operated commerce during this period, which was represented by Qiu Jun. He might possess the closest thoughts with Adam Smith in Ming China, or perhaps, even the whole traditional China period.

3.1 Against State-Run Commerce

3.1.1 Supply and Demand: Qiu Jun and His Complex Attitudes Towards Monopoly

Qiu Jun was a well-known Ming politician and economist who served as the Grand Secretary and Minister of the Board of Revenue. His economic philosophy was concentrated in his masterpiece, *Daxue Yanyi Bu*.[1] This

[1] *Daxue Yanyi Bu* is an influential Confucian classic annotation written by Qiu Jun in Ming Dynasty, which mainly studies the economic system and legal system. It was first

T. Hua, *Merchants, Market and Monarchy*,
Palgrave Studies in the History of Economic Thought,
https://doi.org/10.1007/978-3-030-77189-8_3

book aimed to provide the rulers of the Ming Dynasty with the principles of 'ruling a country', and the section that contained his views on economic issues was an important part of it. Just as Sima Qian had during the Western Han Dynasty and Sima Guang[2] and Ouyang Xiu[3] had during the Northern Song Dynasty, Qiu Jun opposed excessive economic intervention by the state, due to the Confucianism's dogma that 'government should maintain a policy of non-interference'.[4] This coincides with Smith's most well-known 'invisible hand' assertion, 'by directing that industry in such a manner as its produce may be of the greatest value, he intends only his own gain, and he is in this, as in many other cases, led by an invisible hand to promote an end which was no part of his intention'.[5]

His logic, quite similar to the law of demand and supply, was as follows: individuals cannot produce all the things needed for daily life, thus their needs must be satisfied through exchanges, which confirms the essential role of merchants. As a result, the market thrives, and the number of goods on the market is bound to increase, so 'the price [is] naturally not very high'.[6] When prices stay stable or even decrease, 'people can have whatever they want' (the intersection of demand and supply), and the country can become rich as well.

Just as Smith's saying that 'it is not from the benevolence of the butcher, the brewer, or the baker, that we expect our dinner, but from their regard to their own interest',[7] Qiu Jun also agreed that seeking profits was the natural instinct of man and the need for social survival.[8]

published in the early years of Emperor Hongzhi and reprinted at Emperor Wanli time. Emperor Wanli himself wrote a preface in person for the republish of this book.

[2] Sima Guang (1019–1086) was a Chinese historian, writer, and politician. He was a high-ranking Song dynasty scholar-official and historian who authored the monumental history book *Zizhi Tongjian*. Sima was a political conservative who opposed Wang Anshi's reforms.

[3] Ouyang Xiu (1007–1072) was a Chinese essayist, historian, poet, calligrapher, politician, and epigrapher of the Song dynasty. A much celebrated writer, both among his contemporaries and in subsequent centuries, Ouyang Xiu is considered the central figure of the Eight Masters of the Tang and Song.

[4] Chang (1987, p. 487).

[5] Smith (1979 [1776], p. 456).

[6] Qiu (1986 [1487], Vol. 25, p. 385).

[7] Smith (1979 [1776], p. 27).

[8] Qiu (1986 [1487], p. 522).

Thus, he advocated that the state should '*min ziwei shi*'[9] ('let the commoners deal with each other by themselves'), and he believed that encouraging private commerce was an important part of the emperor's administrative duties:

> Detailed plans should be made to enable the people to participate in commercial activities. People who can sell goods should be responsible for selling, while those who cannot should assist merchants and buyers, and those who have spare money should buy goods so that the people can get what they want. This [is] definitely part of the emperor's administrative duties.[10]

However, Qiu Jun made it clear that making 'detailed plans' did not mean that the state should bring commerce under its control.[11] He held a negative attitude towards Sang Hongyang's practice of 'equitable delivery' *(junshu)* and a 'balanced standard'[12] *(pingzhun)* and Wang Anshi's practice of *shiyi*, and he supported the state's monopoly on commodities even less. According to him,

> since the reform by Sang Hongyang, the disadvantages of the state-owned monopoly system ha[ve] existed, and, if the talents of future generations cannot be compared to those of Sang Hongyang, how can the implementation be effective? When people [were] allowed to engage in free trade, the quality and price of goods could generally be guaranteed through fair and transparent trading. However, when the government ma[de] deals with commoners, the commoners [were] compelled to provide the best products while the price [was] fixed. In addition, it [was] too difficult for the agents to be fair, since they often seem[ed] to be greedy and selfish. Thus, it [was] better for rulers not to be involved in these things.[13] (my transl.)

[9] Qiu (1986 [1487], Vol. 25, p. 370).

[10] Qiu (1986 [1487], Vol. 25, p. 372).

[11] Qiu (1986 [1487], Vol. 25, p. 375).

[12] By using the description from Von Glahn (2016), 'Under the balanced standard policy, government agents throughout the empire used public funds, including monopoly revenues, to smooth out price fluctuations by buying up goods when prices were low and selling them when prices were high'.

[13] Qiu (1986 [1487], Vol. 25, p. 375).

Furthermore, Qiu Jun clearly opposed the government 'competing with merchants for profits' in business.[14] According to him,

> The imperial court [was] engaged in the trade traditionally done by merchants, so private merchants ha[d] no way to earn profits. Even things like robbing the rich and helping the poor could not be done, not to mention that the imperial court was competing with private merchants and stealing their profits. This kind of behaviour [was] very disgraceful![15]

Similarly, Adam Smith pointed out that 'the oppression of the poor must establish the monopoly of the rich, who, by engrossing the whole trade to themselves, will be able to make very large profits'.[16]

Qiu Jun not only opposed the direct management of various commodities used by commoners by the imperial government but also the establishment of *fang wu*[17] to force the purchase of commodities for the court by the government.[18] Instead, he advocated that the government should send people to buy commodities from the private market according to the principle of public sale and demanded that the buyers sent by the government and court abide by the official commerce management policy.[19] In fact, Qiu Jun's idea was to apply the principle of equality of commodities to the imperial government and turn it, and even the 'sacred' court, into equals of the commoners when trading commodities, asking it and private merchants to recognize each other as private entities.

Qiu initially recognized the difference between state management of the economy and direct state intrusion in commerce activities. Because of this awareness, his theory of 'letting commoners deal with each other themselves' can be considered an offshoot of the theories of Sima Qian, who pointed out that 'minimal government made for an abundance of food and clothing, as did the abstinence of the government from competing with private merchants'.[20]

[14] Qiu (1986 [1487], Vol. 25, p. 377).

[15] Qiu (1986 [1487], Vol. 25, p. 377).

[16] Smith (1979 [1776], p. 113).

[17] *Fang wu* refers to a market monopolised by the imperial state.

[18] Qiu (1986 [1487], Vol. 25, p. 378).

[19] Qiu (1986 [1487], Vol. 25, p. 378).

[20] Rothbard (2006, p. 26).

China's classical Confucians always considered 'restraining commerce and merchants' the foundation of governing the country. They particularly insisted on firmly suppressing rich merchants. Qiu Jun, however, believed that the livelihood of the common people depended on the rich, who were also a symbol of the country's wealth.[21] Therefore, he put forward the idea of 'placating the rich' and the view that a 'policy of taking money from the rich and giving it to the poor is unjustified'.[22] Some views at the time held that state-run business could create a situation in which 'merchants had nothing to gain' and the benefits that they received would be attributed to the state. Qiu Jun also strongly opposed this view. He retorted, 'how can the supreme emperor take the profits instead of merchants? It is a great shame for the government, which surely occupies an elevated position, to do business'.[23]

From the remarks above, we can see that Qiu Jun held a resolute attitude against the government intervening in the market. Compared with Sima Guang and Su Shi, Qiu Jun held a position that was closer to that of the merchant class. Although the former philosophers saw the disadvantages of Wang Anshi's reform, their thoughts were still trapped in the moral dichotomy of good and evil found in classical Confucianism, eschewing systematic consideration of the economic regime. Qiu Jun, however, clearly distinguished the government's functions from the laws of commerce.

However, Qiu's attitude against state monopolies was still reserved, just as Hu Jichuang pointed out, 'the traditional dogmas made him vacillate between old and new ideas'.[24] Qiu clearly opposed the inherent notion that originated during the Western Zhou Dynasty that 'mountains, forests, and rivers [were] state-owned resources'.[25] He used this as the basis of his arguments against state monopolies, pointing out that the elements of heaven and earth [were] 'public' and should be shared and used for the purpose of 'feeding people'.[26] According to him, 'The task of a monarch [was] to prohibit the privatization of public

[21] Qiu (1986 [1487], Vol. 25, p. 385).

[22] Qiu (1986 [1487], Vol. 25, p. 385).

[23] Qiu (1986 [1487], Vol. 25, p. 385).

[24] Hu (1988, p. 448).

[25] Qiu (1986 [1487], Vol. 25, p. 407).

[26] Qiu (1986 [1487], Vol. 25, p. 407).

resources'.[27] However, regarding monopolies on various commodities (salt, tea, wine, grain, etc.), Qiu's economic philosophy and his general position of opposing state monopolies became inconsistent.

First, regarding salt, based on his own interests in the salt industry, he clearly opposed the 'salt monopoly' that was being implemented at the time, which is totally the opposite of Sang Hongyang's thought. In his view, salt was a natural resource and an element of 'heaven and earth' that should be 'shared by the public'.[28] The government monopolized the salt business and 'sen[t] officials to manage it', which contravened the 'meaning of it being an element of heaven and earth'.[29] He called for the abolition of the salt monopoly and changes in the system of private production and distribution.[30] The court allowed the people to cook salt by themselves. Households that intended to produce salt only needed to apply to the government in advance and obtain the required certificate and salt-cooking tools from the government to produce it.

However, regarding tea and wine, Qiu expressed only half as much support in opposing the state monopolies. During the Ming Dynasty, the tea monopoly was mainly divided into the export and domestic markets, with the former accounting for most of the sales. That is, tea was mainly exchanged for horses in border areas, while the volume of the domestic tea trade was very small. In addition, the tea tax was very light, thus it had no appreciable impact on the national fiscal revenue. Therefore, Qiu stated that 'since salt [is] a necessity, a state monopoly can increase the fiscal revenue of the central government'.[31] However, tea was not a necessity. Thus, according to Qiu's reasoning, if it was monopolized by the state when the price was high or the quality was poor, the people

[27] Qiu (1986 [1487], Vol. 25, p. 407).

[28] Qiu (1986 [1487], Vol. 25, p. 408).

[29] Qiu (1986 [1487], Vol. 25, p. 408).

[30] Qiu (1986 [1487], Vol. 25, p. 408).

[31] Qiu (1986 [1487], Vol. 25, p. 410).

could buy less of it or even none[32] (demand decreases), making it difficult for the state to 'grab the profits'.[33]

However, regarding the export market for tea, Qiu clearly admitted that 'if the state transfer[red] the profits from exported tea to private merchants, it [would] not be conducive to the accumulation of central fiscal revenue'.[34] Thus, it was evident that he supported the state's control of the tea trade at borders. However, tea was a necessity for all ethnic groups in the northwest, while the commoners within the state's borders needed horses. This practical need, therefore, could not be erased by a government decree, so the monopoly had to end despite Qiu's rationale for supporting a state monopoly on tea exports.

Qiu's thought on wine[35] trade can be seen from both the supply and demand side. On the supply side, although he did not support the complete state monopoly on wine, he saw many downsides in private merchants taking control of the wine industry: wine production would consume a lot of grain, which will raise the grain price (not good for the grain security and state stability). On the demand side, Qiu proposed an idea: although the wine industry was unsuitable for a state monopoly, the consumption of wine should be 'limited' to only the rich, who 'could be allowed the luxury of drinking a little wine'.[36] Moreover, drinking too much alcohol was 'harmful to people's health',[37] and the commoners should thus be abstinent from alcohol. Although Qiu was opposed to the state monopoly on wine, he strongly disapproved of the liberalization of wine production and sales.

Qiu has always been regarded as a rare Ming Dynasty opponent of state-owned commerce. However, as can be seen from the economic arguments outlined above, contrary to this stereotype, Qiu did not deny

[32] A higher quality substitute often decreases the demand of the product. The salt does not really have substitutes in ancient China. However, people can choose to consume fewer salt in daily diet. According to the historical record, when in hard times (war, dry spell, famine, limited supply of salt, etc.), ordinary people often choose to experience '*danshi* season'' (the period when very little or no salt put in the food when cooking).

[33] Qiu (1986 [1487], Vol. 25, p. 410).

[34] Qiu (1986 [1487], Vol. 25, p. 410).

[35] The wine here mainly refers to yellow rice wine, which is the most popular wine in ancient China.

[36] Qiu (1986 [1487], Vol. 25, p. 433).

[37] Qiu (1986 [1487], Vol. 25, p. 430).

the role of the state in governing commerce. In addition to the 'semi-support' he showed for the state monopolies on tea and wine, his support for the state-run grain trade is an even better example of his philosophy. His thoughts on grain circulation and prices were clearly influenced by the ideas in *Guanzi*. He advocated a complete separation of the free market and the grain trade. According to him, 'the state's control over the sale of grain could still be allowed because it [was] a daily necessity for the people. Although it [was] managed by the state, the aim [was] still to benefit the people'.[38] He affirmed the philosophy of *Guanzi* on stabilizing food prices and advocated cyclical control of grain prices.[39]

It can be concluded that, although Qiu did not generally emphasize the impact of state monopolies on the country's fiscal revenue, his opinions against monopolies were contradictory. In addition to expressing clear objections to the state's control of the salt industry, he expressed either clear or implicit support for state monopolies on tea, wine, grain, and other important daily commodities. His so-called 'opposition' to state monopolies was essentially the same as the support of Sang Hongyang and some other philosophers for them. Although Qiu explicitly criticized *Guanzi*'s theory of *qing zhong* and Sang Hongyang's *junshu* concept, he did not hesitate to absorb the parts of their views on monopolies that furthered national interests. Considering that he was in the Grand Secretariat during the Emperor Hongzhi era, these views, from the perspective of the interests of the country, may not be so difficult to understand.

3.1.2 Jiangyou School: Zhang Juzheng and His Economic Views

Wang Yangming, the founder of the Yangming School, was a great Confucian scholar of the Ming Dynasty. He himself did not hold much comment on the issues surrounding state-operated commerce. After his death, the Yangming school was divided into two branches. The Jiangyou School, which is regarded as the right-wing of the Yangming School, was represented by Zhang Juzheng, the Grand Secretary during the first decade of the Emperor Wanli era. As I mentioned in Chapter 1, the Jiangyou School's thought was relatively 'orthodox' because its disciples entered the court as officials. Therefore, most of their thoughts on

[38] Qiu (1986 [1487], Vol. 25, p. 415).

[39] Qiu (1986 [1487], Vol. 25, p. 415).

merchants came from the perspective of the interests of the court rather than the welfare of merchants.

Thus, it is not difficult to understand why Zhang clearly opposed state monopolies. He criticized the policy enacted by Sang Hongyang, saying,

> I once read *Yantie Lun*[40] (Debate on Salt and Iron) and saw that during the Emperor Yuandi period[41] Sang's policies [were] continuously followed, while the masses live[d] in dire poverty. The rulers at the time argued that Sang's policy was correct and that a monopoly should be pursued. This kind of remark [was] like pedantry. Before that, Emperor Zhaodi[42] briefly abandoned Sang's policy, and the people's standard of living noticeably improved. In ancient times, fiscal management was too frivolous and spendthrift, and there was no long-term plan for the country's development.[43]

The context of Zhang Juzheng's remarks was that, during the late Jiajing period, the Grand Secretary, Yan Song,[44] had a lot of power and was regarded as using it to reap substantial profits for his family. The central intent of Zhang's remarks was indeed to oppose state monopolies, but what he really wanted to express was his dissatisfaction with the court politicians who were imitating private merchants to reap profits. He implicitly mocked Yan Song, saying that 'now the highest position at court [was] occupied by the merchant, and money [was] continuously

[40] *Yantie Lun* is a celebrated historical book compiled according to the records of the famous 'salt and iron conference'. Its literary genre is dialogue. The author is Huan Kuan (the year of his birth and death remains unknown) of the Western Han Dynasty. The book records a great debate on politics, economy, military affairs, and diplomacy during the period of Emperor Zhao of Han. The core of the argument about the theory of salt and iron is the argument between state monopoly and free economy advocated by sang Hongyang. For further details and analysis in English, please refer to Hu (1988), Von Glahn (2016) and Schefold (2019).

[41] Emperor Yuandi of Western Han reigned from 49 to 33 B.C.

[42] Emperor Zhaodi of Western Han reigned from 86 to 74 B.C.

[43] Zhang (1937 [1582], p. 213).

[44] Yan Song (1480–1567) was a Chinese politician in Ming China. He usually had a bad reputation for being corrupt during his control over the Ming court for over two decades during the reign of the Jiajing Emperor. At the time, Emperor Jiajing (reigns from 1522 to 1567) was busy eating elixir and seeking immortality. This gave Yan Song great power space. Yan Song was finally defeated by Xu Jie (1503–1583). He was dismissed from office and his property was confiscated in 1564. He died of poverty two years after.

flowing to the upper class as well'.[45] Therefore, rather than casting Zhang's objection as one to the state's intervention in commerce, it is more accurate to say that he was instead opposed to high-level court officials seeking power for personal gain and pocketing the state's income. In other words, if the profits had not wound up in the pockets of corrupt officials, but had instead gone into the state treasury, then Zhang would not have put forward any opposition to state monopolies.

However, it is worth noting that, although Zhang still put the interests of the state first, compared to prior thinkers, he was focused more on the idea of 'treating merchants generously' as the basis of opposing state monopolies.[46] Zhang's attitude towards private merchants was much milder than that of Sang Hongyang and Wang Anshi. He not only proposed supporting small- and medium-sized merchants (e.g. in state–merchant cooperation in the salt business) like Liu Yan had during the Tang period but also advocated funding them and treating them favourably. According to him,

> The best way to keep the country's material capacity high [was] to reduce the imposition of agricultural taxes. Since the farmers [were] treated well, they ha[d] adequate funds to buy goods, which was thought to benefit the merchants eventually. In order to keep the commoners' level of consumption high, it was necessary to reduce commercial taxes. Since the merchants [were] treated well, they [were] able to circulate more goods, which was thought to benefit the farmers eventually.[47] (my transl.)

However, it is ironic that Zhang Juzheng himself was a deeply corrupt official as well. Although he was more affectionate to the people than his predecessors, he was no less inclined to use his power for personal gain than they had been. Zhang Juzheng was also a first-rate master of wealth accumulation, and he was not particularly different from Yan Song, whom he mocked, or Xu Jie, the man who had been the Grand Secretary shortly before he assumed the position. He enjoyed an extravagant lifestyle. After Zhang's death, Emperor Wanli searched the Zhang family home and collected more than ten thousand taels of gold and more than

[45] Zhang (1937 [1582], p. 211).

[46] Zhang (1937 [1582], p. 211).

[47] Zhang (1937 [1582], p. 212).

one hundred thousand taels of silver.[48] Zhang was among the richest people in the empire, and, while he used his power as the Grand Secretary to seek economic benefits for his family, he directly and indirectly acted against the interests of small- and medium-sized merchants. He was indeed opposed to state monopolies, but he had no intention of allowing ordinary merchants to profit from private business.

It is thus easy to see that, although Zhang's economic views seemed to favour small- and medium-sized merchants, the policies he implemented were often beneficial to the country and wealthy merchants in practice. The best illustration of this was his well-known *yitiao bianfa* ('Single Whip Law').[49] He believed that a newly designed measure could simplify the complex fiscal code of Ming law by converting most obligations towards the central government (for instance, land and poll taxes and the labour obligations of the peasantry) into a single silver payment. At first glance, the Single Whip Law was indeed beneficial to farmers and the people at the bottom of the economic hierarchy. However, since, according to the new law, *huze* (the original division of the people into several levels according to the amount of property they owned, with varying tax rates for each) had been nullified, all households were taxed at the same rate according to the size of the fields they owned. Thus 'the land owned by the poor [was] taxed the same as the land owned by the rich', and 'barren land [was] taxed the same as fertile land'.[50] Some wealthy merchants did not own land at all, or had a way to hide their ownership of land, so, in the end, unlucky small merchants and farmers who owned land had to bear an increased tax burden. Moreover, from the perspective of national interests, the intent of the Single Whip Law was not only to reduce the costs of tax collection but also to take advantage of an opportunity to increase the tax base. This resulted in a substantial increase in national income. From the point of view of implementation, it 'inconvenienced the ordinary small farmers and small merchants'.[51] Therefore, farmers and small business owners became increasingly enslaved to wealthy merchants to comply with the requirements of the Single Whip Law.

48 Hua (2002, p. 332).

49 Hua (2002, p. 330).

50 Hua (2002, p. 331).

51 Hua (2002, p. 331).

3.1.3 *Thoughts of Traditional Confucians: Yu Shenxing and Gu Yanwu*

A less well-known example of an official who espoused this view is Yu Shenxing[52] who served as the Minister of Ritual during the Emperor Wanli period. In his book, he also expressed opposition to the direct participation of monarchs and the court in industrial and commercial activities, seeking profits, and competing with merchants. He criticized the idea of 'increasing the country's income through the sale of public property and salt and iron monopolies'[53] in *Guanzi*, which he believed would make 'the people's equipment, clothes, and food totally depend[ent] on the country's supply so that the right to manage *qingzhong* would remain above (the country) instead of below (the people and the market), which would [leave] wealthy merchants without profits'.[54] He believed that the philosophy of *Guanzi* was indeed an 'overbearing' one that could be applied to a vassal state but not the entire world. Yu Shenxing pointed out that, to rule the country, it was indispensable to manage state finances, but 'the answer [was] in the ten chapters of *Daxue*, which [was] designed for a 'benevolent government'.[55] When discussing the issue of national finances, the ten chapters of *Daxue* illustrated its conclusion on the relationship between ethical norms and material wealth that 'maintenance of moral matters [was] fundamental, and the accumulation of wealth [was] minor'.[56] It can be seen here that Yu Shenxing's economic views were deeply influenced by traditional Confucian thought, and they represented part of the argument of senior- and mid-ranking officials during the Ming Dynasty against the state competing with commoners in commerce. However, his starting point was to make 'rich merchants' profitable, and he failed to discuss the role of ordinary merchants once the country had ceased to engage in private commerce. Similarly, Gu Yanwu opposed monopolies on salt and iron and warned the state not to impose excessive taxes upon salt

[52] Yu Shenxing (1545–1608), high-level official in Ming China, who served as Minister of Rite.

[53] Guan et al. (1965 [c. 400–200 BC], p. 143).

[54] Yu (1980 [1608], p. 78).

[55] Yu (1980 [1608], p. 38).

[56] Yu (1980 [1608], p. 128).

merchants. To Gu, 'the private activities of merchants were directly related to the welfare of the people and the state'.[57]

3.2 Supporting State Monopoly

3.2.1 Lin Xiyuan: Dredging the Source from Merchants

From the analysis above, it appears that the few thinkers who supported private commerce during the Ming Dynasty, such as Qiu Jun and Zhang Juzheng, were not completely opposed to state-run businesses, and the vast majority of Ming philosophers followed the views of the former dynasty and clearly supported state-run commerce.

Lin Xiyuan[58] is an example of this type of thought. In the tenth year of the Emperor Jiajing period, Lin Xiyuan wrote his missive 'Opinions on the Rule of the Monarch' (*Wang Zheng Fu Yan Shu*), which was over 29,000 words long. It contained 21 sections in total, and nine of them were related to economic issues.

First, Lin expressed his firm support for state monopolies. According to him, 'only wealth [was] the lifeblood of a country, just as people must eat food. People [would] have to endure hunger if they [had] no food to eat. Similarly, if the country [did] not have wealth, it [would] perish'.[59] From his point of view, 'wealth' referred to the government's fiscal revenues and expenditures. He pointed out that good financial management must rely on 'dredging the source' and 'plugging loopholes', and, to 'dredge the source', he particularly emphasized the need to extract more revenue from merchants.[60] He stated that 'The wealthy merchants amass[ed] huge profits, but they [did] not give even a slight portion to the government. If it [was] possible to impose high taxes on these merchants to ease the pressure on the commoners, [was] it not good?'[61] He also pointed out that,

[57] Lufrano (1997, p. 46).

[58] Lin Xiyuan (1481–1565), a high-ranking official in Nanjing during the Emperor Jiajing period.

[59] Lin (2015 [1565], Vol. 2, p. 458).

[60] Lin (2015 [1565], Vol. 2, p. 459).

[61] Lin (2015 [1565], Vol. 2, p. 460).

> Although the state monopoly [is] regarded as a misstep by the Tang Dynasty, today's rich evade taxation and corvée labour and [do] not produce anything, profiting everywhere in the market and throughout the country. Implementing state monopolies, however, can alleviate the pressure on peasants and simultaneously suppress the "branch" (commerce).[62] (my transl.)

3.2.2 *Li Zhi: Following Sang Hongyang*

The left-wing of the Yangming School, known as the Taizhou School, was represented by Li Zhi.[63] He also expressed support for state-run commerce. However, his views were somewhat contradictory. He was supportive of private merchants making profits. Although he believed that the lord will show the private merchants in his good time when they can amass fortunes and become rich, he also defended their efforts, saying that 'becoming rich [was] something that relied on manpower and was not determined by destiny'.[64] Regardless of whether it was 'God's will' or 'personal diligence' that made them rich, it was essentially reasonable for private merchants to amass fortunes. However, he still could not completely disabuse himself of the idea of 'suppressing the merchants', subscribing to the belief that a merchant was not 'an important person to the country',[65] Sir Thomas More had a similar thought, believing that it is not 'justice' that a merchant, 'a goldsmith, a moneylender, or someone else who makes his living by doing something not especially necessary for the commonwealth, gets to live a life of luxury and grandeur'.[66]

Based on this framework, he believed that state control of commerce was very reasonable. He regarded Sang Hongyang's state-run commerce policy as one that 'combated wealthy merchants'[67] and reallocate the wealth. He never raised the word 'utopian' that Sir Thomas More put forward, although the essence seems to be similar. In More's words

[62] Lin (2015 [1565], Vol. 2, p. 462).

[63] Li Zhi (1527–1602) was a Chinese philosopher, historian and writer of the late Ming Dynasty. A critic of the Neo-Confucianist views espoused by Zhu Xi, which was then the orthodoxy of the Ming government, he was persecuted and committed suicide in prison.

[64] Li (2001 [1602], p. 241).

[65] Li (2001 [1602], p. 242).

[66] More (2002 [1516], p. 104).

[67] Li (2001 [1602], p. 244).

explaining 'the kind of thing that Plato imagines in his republic',[68] he believes 'however superior those institutions might be', 'private property is the rule here', while 'there all things are held in common'.[69] From his perspective, 'the one and only path to the public welfare lies through equal allocation of goods', and he doubts 'whether such equality can ever be achieved where property belongs to individuals'.[70]

Li not only supported the state's intervention in commerce but also believed that 'national officials should actively participate in it'.[71] This coincides with More's faith in the officials in the 'senate' will 'consider the common interest', and they 'have enough foresight at the beginning to speak with consideration',[72] compared with some individuals who 'would rather jeopardise the general welfare than their own reputation'.[73]

Li believed that the government should use its 'power' (*shi*) to suppress the merchants' practice of 'buying low and selling high'.[74] More, similarly, asserted that some trade, 'though can't be called a monopoly because it isn't in the hands of a single person, is concentrated in so few hands'[75] (in current terminology, oligopoly), and the rich merchants and owners 'are never pressed to sell until they have a mind to, and that is only when they can get their price'.[76]

Li Zhi emphasized the importance of making the country rich. He believed that 'those who [do] not speak of money can never rule the country',[77] and, in his work, he included a section titled 'Famous Ministers Dealing with Financial Issues' that included accounts of figures such as Sang Hongyang and Liu Yan, who were usually accused of 'gathering wealth for the country'.[78]

Although he agreed that it was reasonable for merchants to amass a fortune, allowing them to become very rich would lead to 'merchants

[68] More (2002 [1516], p. 35).

[69] More (2002 [1516], p. 36).

[70] More (2002 [1516], pp. 37–38).

[71] Li (2001 [1602], p. 244).

[72] More (2002 [1516], p. 48).

[73] More (2002 [1516], p. 48).

[74] Li (2001 [1602], p. 244).

[75] More (2002 [1516], p. 19).

[76] More (2002 [1516], p. 19).

[77] Li (2001 [1602], p. 245).

[78] Li (2001 [1602], p. 245).

not listening to the state',[79] which would thus constitute a threat to the rule of the country. This threat is that, in More's words, 'where money is the measure of everything, many vain and completely superfluous trades are bound to be carried on simply to satisfy luxury and licentiousness',[80] which surely runs counter to the design of More's Utopia. Under this circumstance, the state needed to monopolize related businesses and suppress wealthy merchants. From the perspective of the state, of course, rich merchants who 'could not support the country's urgent needs' should be restrained through means such as 'heavy taxation'; on the other hand, if they could, the state would not have any issues with them. In any case, it was required that wealthy merchants, in addition to paying normal commercial taxes, should 'support the state' through additional contributions. Li's thought shows a clear continuation of the views of the Western Han thinkers on state monopolies, and all effort should be made to 'support the state', or support the 'common wealth' by using More's words.

3.2.3 Wang Fuzhi: The Role of Wealthy Merchants

Wang Fuzhi was another famous late Ming philosopher who thought that the government should directly control the trade in salt and tea. According to him,

> The wealthy merchants manipulated the interest rate and suppressed the income of the farmers who ploughed the fields, while the incomes of the army and the state were highly inadequate. The people pursuing commerce [were] getting richer, whereas the hard-working peasants [were] getting poorer. The uneven distribution of wealth [would] become the biggest hidden danger in suppressing the development of the national economy and people's livelihoods.[81] (my transl.)

He criticized the attitude of 'the Confucians trying to return salt profits to commoners' in *Yantie Lun*, pointing out that their suggestion would only benefit the rich and the big merchants.[82] He was supportive of Liu Yan's

[79] Li (2001 [1602], p. 245).

[80] More (2002 [1516], p. 51).

[81] Wang (1975 [1692], Vol. 9, p. 48).

[82] Wang (1975 [1692], Vol. 9, p. 48).

belief that 'if the country [gave] up the profits from salt, they [would] only flow into the pockets of profiteers and crafty merchants, not the ordinary people who consume[d] it'.[83] Therefore, he believed that the state needed to insert itself in the trade and implement Liu Yan's views and policies.

Wang also affirmed the role of 'wealthy merchants'. In the conflict between 'seeking wealth' and 'seeking moderation', contrary to the values of traditional Confucianism, he valued the former more.[84] He considered the wealthy merchants and the rich 'the lifeblood of the country'.[85] This rhetoric was not inconsistent with his usual idea of restraining merchants. He believed that the country should focus on the rich merchants, not the ordinary ones. Other similar views were expressed in his work, such as the view that 'If there [were] no rich people in the country, ordinary people might have an economic crisis and no way to carry out effective production'.[86]

Wang believed that wealthy merchants and the rich could play the role of 'circulating money and corn and supporting vulnerable populations'.[87] When droughts and floods occurred, government relief was often delayed. In this situation, poor people who were short of food only needed to 'hold a hundred cents and inconvertible coupons issued by the government and knock on the doors of the rich, then they [would] get enough food to survive'.[88] Wang believed that 'wealthy merchants and the rich' could serve as 'the lifeblood of the country' in this way. He criticized the corrupt officials who satisfied their personal needs in the name of 'eradicating the mighty', asserting that this resulted in 'stifling the circulation of money and corn' and a situation in which 'the poor and the weak wandering the streets could not receive help'.[89] Therefore, he advocated 'severe punishment for corrupt officials and preservation of the strength of the rich'.[90]

[83] Wang (1975 [1692], Vol. 9, p. 49).
[84] Wang (1975 [1692], Vol. 24, p. 115).
[85] Wang (1975 [1692], Vol. 24, p. 115).
[86] Wang (1975 [1692], Vol. 24, p. 118).
[87] Wang (1975 [1692], Vol. 2, p. 14).
[88] Wang (1975 [1692], Vol. 2, p. 15).
[89] Wang (1975 [1692], Vol. 2, p. 15).
[90] Wang (1975 [1692], Vol. 2, p. 15).

3.2.4 Li Wen: Comments on Previous Financial Governors

Similarly, Li Wen[91] attached great importance to the social role of wealthy merchants and regarded the people who became rich (mainly landowners and wealthy merchants) as the backbone of society. He believed that the rich made a great contribution to raising the standard of living of ordinary people. Taking aim at the traditional concept of restraining merchants and landowners that had prevailed in China for thousands of years, Li Wen exclaimed, 'What [was] the crime of these rich people?'[92] In his view, the rich were not only not guilty of anything but they also contributed to society in two ways. One was 'feeding the general public'.[93] He believed that the rich bought land from the poor, rented it to them to cultivate, paid taxes on their behalf, and provided them with clothes and food. Therefore, Li Wen concluded that rich merchants were 'the mother of the poor'. The second was 'feeding the monarch'.[94] Li Wen believed that the poor and nomads were unable to contribute to the economy, and the emperor 'could rely on only the rich' as the source of income for the country.[95]

From the standpoint of protecting the rich, Li Wen advised the emperor to reduce the burden on them. First, he asked the emperor to treat the rich and well-connected, powerful figures differently and to adopt different conscription and tax policies for them.[96] Li Wen analysed the differences between the rich and the powerful and pointed out that, by virtue of their political rights, the latter engaged in more predatory behaviour towards the poor.[97] The rich, however, furthered their interests through their own hard work (e.g. wealthy businessmen who became rich through business ventures). This was different from the powerful plundering the resources of the ordinary folk. Moreover, the powerful used their positions to evade their financial and military duties to the country and passed on the burden to the rich and poor alike.

[91] Li Wen (1608–1647) was a low-ranking official during the late Ming dynasty.

[92] Li (2000 [1647], p. 34).

[93] Li (2000 [1647], p. 34).

[94] Li (2000 [1647], p. 35).

[95] Li (2000 [1647], p. 35).

[96] Li (2000 [1647], p. 37).

[97] Li (2000 [1647], p. 37).

However, although, like Yu Shenxing, Li Wen emphasized the positive role of wealthy merchants in society, he then came to the opposite conclusion on whether the country should control principal resources and commodities. That is, Li believed the court should still control them.[98] He discussed his economic views in his missive to Emperor Chongzhen titled *Financial Expenditure* (*Caiyong*).

In view of the financial difficulties of the central government and the famine that was plaguing many regions at the time, he believed that salt and the mountains containing copper, iron, and wood should be controlled by the government. In turn, the court would give all those who actively cultivated the fields and brought the grain to it (in Li Wen's thought, wealthy merchants undoubtedly accounted for most of the 'people' who contributed to the court) copper, iron, wood, or salt of equivalent value and an exemption from taxes.[99] In this way, those who needed these things would 'actively grow grains', and there would be no shortage of cereal. Li Wen believed that the role of state monopolies lie in providing incentives to wealthy merchants who were encouraged to participate in increasing the national fiscal revenue and providing disaster relief.[100] Moreover, Li Wen's view that 'agriculture came first' can also be seen clearly here. The thoughts stated above may be another evidence of the state's emphasis on grain and stability, thus long-lasting famine is intolerable. Even with Emperor Wanli who was 'typically viewed as a weak and ineffectual ruler', the state ruling in his name 'was able to mount a famine relief campaign' that 'prepared local reports and released grain from the local granaries'.[101] This kind of achievement should at least be attributed to thinkers (who are often officials as well) at the time, such as Li Wen.

In another article titled *Salt Policy* (*Yan Ce*), he summarized the gains and losses of the salt policies of previous dynasties and advanced his opinions on the salt policy of the Ming Dynasty. Li Wen regarded the production and sale of salt as a purely commercial activity and opposed government intervention in it. However, he also made it clear that his

[98] Li (2000 [1647], p. 38).

[99] Li (2000 [1647], p. 39).

[100] Li (2000 [1647], p. 39).

[101] Tanimoto and Wong (2019, p. 138).

views were only applicable to the salt trade in the south-eastern region.[102] The salt industry in the north-western region, however, should still be run by the government because trade was being conducted close to the capital and the frontier fortress. Moreover, Li also affirmed that salt was the most important source of state revenue: 'Salt [was] in the biggest demand in the world, and there [was] no other product more lucrative'.[103] He quoted the discussion about the salt policy in *Guanzi*, explaining that, during Duke Huan of Qi's era, 'the profit from boiling the sea ma[de] the whole world rich'.[104] Li praised Sang Hongyang's salt and iron monopoly: 'Without these policies, Emperor Han Wudi would have had to increase the taxes on the peasants and may have triggered grievances or even rebellion by the people'.[105] Therefore, although he was, to some extent, an advocate of free trade economics, he also said that 'the words of the literati cannot all have been correct, while the words of Sang Hongyang cannot all have been wrong'.[106] He said, 'The Confucian scholars of later generations thought that the state would have enough money to spend without imposing additional taxes or finding other sources of income. They believed that Sang Hongyang's state monopoly was deceptive to Emperor Han Wudi. What these Confucian scholars did not understand [was] that Sang Hongyang's policy [was] actually the best strategy to make the country rich and strong!'.[107]

He also criticized Wang Anshi, saying that, regarding the implementation of state monopolies, 'The Confucian Wang Anshi's policies resulted in malpractice and abuses (due to inexperience), while Sang Hongyang, born to a merchant family, turn[ed] out to be more successful'.[108]

However, he did not explain why Confucianism's promotion of state monopolies encouraged abuses. As for Liu Yan, Li regarded him highly. He believed that the reason Liu Yan had successfully provided over half of the country's fiscal revenue through the salt industry was that Liu took the advantage of the merchants who enjoyed certain freedoms in

[102] Li (2000 [1647], p. 87).
[103] Li (2000 [1647], p. 88).
[104] Li (2000 [1647], p. 88).
[105] Li (2000 [1647], p. 89).
[106] Li (2000 [1647], p. 89).
[107] Li (2000 [1647], pp. 89–90).
[108] Li (2000 [1647], p. 91).

the production and sales of salt and that 'there [were] no other novel technologies'.[109] As mentioned earlier, Liu Yan's conversion of the country's complete control over important industries to the use of merchants to conduct trade was a turning point in the history of Chinese economic thought regarding state monopolies. Obviously, the recognition of this fact was reflected in Li Wen's views.

Against this backdrop, it is apparent that most philosophers during the Ming Dynasty were still supportive of state monopolies and that some of them defended merchants, mainly the wealthy ones, since they could be very useful to the country, regardless of whether their cooperation was needed in business matters or in aiding the victims of natural calamities. In the opinions of these philosophers, consideration of the welfare of merchants should come completely from the perspective of national interests. If they proved to be useless to the country or harmful to the interests of state monopolies, then they should be ruthlessly discarded.

3.3 State–Merchant Cooperation in the Salt Business

3.3.1 The Kaizhong *Method and the Role of Merchants*

The status of merchants in the state monopoly in Ming China was best reflected in the state-owned salt industry activities. 'The Ming state's principal intervention in the commercial economy took the form of monopolies controlling aspects of the production and distribution of major commodities',[110] such as salt. Although 'only the state could authorize the making of salt, and only state salt was permitted to circulate',[111] yet it was not a state enterprise. The actual circulation and sale of salt was contracted from private merchants, who therefore played an important role in the operation. Within a few years of the dynasty's founding, the famous *Kaizhong* policy (the institution of border delivery) was established,

> In the salt administration, no method was better than the *Kaizhong*. The merchants were called to transport grain and animal fodder up to the

[109] Li (2000 [1647], p. 91).

[110] Twitchett and Mote (1998, Vol. 8, p. 678).

[111] Twitchett and Mote (1998, Vol. 8, p. 678).

> border, and then the corresponding lucrative *yan yin* (salt licenses) to sell government salt was distributed according to the amount of grain delivered. This is called *Kaizhong*. Since then, almost all the border provinces followed this mode. Most of them recruited merchants to transport grain, which was kept as a reserve for the troops.[112] (my transl.)

To be more specific, the *Kaizhong* method could be roughly divided into three steps: transferring the grain and getting the salt license, collecting the salt in designated salt fields by using the salt license, and selling salt in the designated areas. However, the court 'starved the salt monopoly by failing to provide adequate financial support to producers while disbursing excessive quantities of salt certificates'.[113] The immoderate issue of salt licenses had begun since the years of Emperor Yongle, which led to the stagnation of step two, that is, merchants had to wait according to the order of precedence for salt, sometimes even for years at a time. 'Some merchants [had] been waiting for salt since the middle of Emperor Yongle, and the waiting sometimes cost three generations' time'.[114] In the fifteenth century, 'over thirty years' delay of honouring the licenses were common'.[115] In order to alleviate the hardships of merchants, the limitation of collecting salt in designated fields had been relaxed. 'In the tenth year of Emperor Yongle (1413), the emperor ordered that if a merchant [had] waited for salt for many years, he [could] go to the neighbouring fields to collect salt if he [was] willing to do so. If not, he [had] to continue to wait in line'.[116]

The continuous delay resulted in the finance deficit of state monopoly of salt. To solve this issue, the court first put off the current delivery obligations, then sold the currently available stock at a much higher price. Thus, the new purchasers who could pay in cash immediately were given priority over previous buyers.

Thus, in the fifth year of Emperor Zhengtong (1440), a second way showed up, which was to divide salt into two categories, respectively *Changgu* salt and *Cunji* salt. 'Eighty percent of the salt produced in

[112] Zhang (1974 [1739], Vol. 80, p. 1935).

[113] Von Glahn (2016, p. 288).

[114] Zhang (1974 [1739], Vol. 80, p. 1937).

[115] Liu (1962 [1491], pp. 4103–4104).

[116] Shen (1989 [1587], Vol. 34, p. 238).

Lianghuai, Liangzhe and Changlu [was] reserved for the merchants who wait[ed] in the line in the field, called the *Changgu* salt. And the other twenty percent [was] stored in the official warehouse, known as *Cunji* salt'.[117] Although 'the price of *Changgu* salt [was] much lower',[118] 'the salt [was] paid for on the spot when the merchant and his grain arrive[d], while *Cunji* salt [was to] be distributed according to the order of precedence and the quality and quantity of the grain the merchant delivered'.[119] Therefore, 'the merchants who [had] suffered from long-time waiting [were] scrambling for the *Cunji* salt'.[120]

In the thirteenth year of Emperor Zhengtong (1449), the government 'increased the *Cunji* salt (reserve stock) to sixty percent while the *Changgu* salt (regular stock) dropped to only forty percent'.[121] The merchants who held granary receipts for *Changgu* salt were told at the salt field that only reserve stock was available. And the situation could sometimes be the opposite. Some salt yards preferred to sell their salt as *Changgu* salt first, thus 'the merchants who held granary receipts for *Cunji* salt had to wait', although they actually had the priority according to the classification.[122]

The phenomenon was exacerbated in the years of Emperor Hongzhi[123] which was followed by the transformation of the salt laws. 'In the fifth year of Emperor Hongzhi, due to the merchants being trapped in the waiting for salts, Ye Qi, the Minister of Revenue, proposed commuting merchant transport to payment in silver'.[124] Although the price of one *yin*[125] of salt had therefore increased, the merchants were scrambling for it.

Why was the increasing price actually beneficial to some merchants? The answer pointed to the benefits of the different merchant groups. From the late fifteenth century, two types of merchants appeared in the

[117] Zhang (1974 [1739], Vol. 80, p. 1937).

[118] Zhang (1974 [1739], Vol. 80, p. 1937).

[119] Shen (1989 [1587], Vol. 34, p. 238).

[120] Zhang (1974 [1739], Vol. 80, pp. 1937–1938).

[121] Zhu (2002 [1529], Vol. 4, p. 8).

[122] Gu (1985 [1682], Vol. 21, p. 36).

[123] Emperor Hongzhi reigned from 1488 to 1505.

[124] Zhang (1974 [1739], Vol. 80, p. 1939).

[125] One *yin* stands for one piece of salt license.

salt business. The so-called *bian shang* ('border merchants') delivered grain to the border garrisons and then sold the granary receipts to the so-called *nei shang* ('internal merchants'). The benefits of *Kaizhong* mainly belonged to the border merchants, of which the northern locals like Shanxi and Shaanxi merchants were the main force, and the merchants who bought the salt licenses and collected the salt were often the internal merchants, of which the merchants near the state salt yards were the mainstay. This was a necessary division according to the fact that the waiting period for the salt was at least three years and often reached around ten years, despite the improvement of efficiency in the sixteenth century.

When the border merchants sold the salt license to the internal merchants, they certainly charged an extortionate price. If the salt licenses were hoarded and monopolized by the merchants who had relations with powerful officials, the price was even higher. Thus, it is quite understandable that these merchants, who had a sufficient amount of resources to collect the salt on the spot, lobbied the Ministry of Revenue, making known their position that they wanted to monopolize the sales of salt in the cost of increasing price:

> The Huizhou merchants discussed with Ye Qi that previously if they want[ed] to get the permission of selling salt, they had to transport the grain to the border themselves, or buy the salt licenses from the border merchants. However, if silver [were to be] accepted as payment instead of grain, the benefit [would have] become much bigger and the operation [would have] become more efficient (no need for long-time waiting anymore).'[126] (my transl.)

Ye Qi originally came from Huai'an[127] in the Lianghuai area, and the salt merchants (who were mainly Huizhou merchants) were the mainstay in the Lianghuai area, though they did not originally come from the same region. Under the new policies, the border merchants would be crowded out. Moreover, although after the reform the merchants had to pay more money for one *yin* of salt, the costs could have been offset by the premium they were forced to pay to the border merchants, which led to no loss for the Huizhou merchants.[128]

[126] Chen (1985 [1521], Vol. 2, p. 83).

[127] Huai'an was a prefecture-level city, located in the current central Jiangsu province.

[128] Wu (2004, Vol. 3, pp. 795–796).

The new policy formulated by Ye 'enabled the Huizhou merchants to wrest control of the salt trade from their Shanxi rivals'.[129] Thus, Ye Qi was accused of 'promoting the interest of the merchants due to his selfishness' by the opposition faction in the court.[130] After Ye retired, the *Kaizhong* system was revived. However, almost a century later, Pang also realized that compared with the incompetent *Kaizhong* system, 'Ye's reform supporting cash payments was much more efficient'.[131] Therefore, in fact, the discussion of the salt policy by different forces in the court also reflected the infighting between the merchant groups in different regions they represented.

Sometimes, the internal merchants generally settled in Yangzhou did not participate directly in the salt sales as well. Instead, they 'sold the stock issued by the checking stations to the small-sized distributing merchants'.[132] The internal merchants sat idle and enjoyed the fruits of other merchants' work due to their fiscal strength. As the only buyers, they could manipulate the border merchants into accepting their quote for granary receipts. And as the only salt suppliers of the distributing merchants, they also had the decisive power over the price. In the fourth year of Emperor Longqing (1570), a granary receipt for one *yin* of salt cost the merchants half taels of silver at the salt field, while the price sold to the internal merchants is only 0.04 more taels. When the delivery cost was included, the border merchants were actually doing loss-making business. Thus, the governors had to make some concession and lower the official salt price since 'otherwise the border merchants would be unwilling to participate in the system'.[133]

Thus, it is obvious that like most dynasties after Qin, the status of merchants in the state–merchant cooperation was still not high. Behind the seemingly essential appearance, the merchants of the Ming Dynasty could only serve the national interest. Moreover, the fate of merchants was firmly in the hands of the officials who were in charge of the country's economy at the time. For example, when Ye Qi took power, the

[129] Von Glahn (2016, p. 305).

[130] Sun and DeFrancis (1966, pp. 299–308).

[131] Chen (1962 [1638], Vol. 360, p. 27).

[132] Zhang (1974 [1739], Vol. 80, p. 840).

[133] Chen (1962 [1638], Vol. 357, pp. 24–26).

merchants reside in the Lianghuai area obtained great economic benefits. But the situation quickly changed after Ye Qi retired. The merchants absolutely had no ability to determine their own fate. What's worse, when officials relied on state power to participate in salt sales, the merchants stayed in a real predicament. This will be analysed in the next section.

3.3.2 Rent-Seeking: The Participation of Officials and the Private Salt Sale

One of the reasons for the immoderate issuance of salt licenses mentioned above was the participation of officials or well-connected merchant families. The state's control and participation in the salt trade inevitably bred officials who used their control of the country's policies and power to seek private gain, becoming corrupt. This problem also existed in Western Han, when 'government policies had legitimised profit-seeking behaviour, created a class of newly rich, wealth flaunting government officials'.[134] In modern economics' word, there existed certain 'rent-seeking' in Ming salt business. Like Sombart said,

> The power of the state was the almighty influence that was to be looked to for one's interests, whether for the disposal of men or commodities; or an indirect influence which aided in a sale or a bargain- say, the granting of a concession, privilege, or monopoly. This gave birth to an important sub-species of undertaking. Influential members of the nobility associated themselves with the moneyed sections of the middle classes, or with impoverished inventors, for the purpose of common gain.[135]

The fact that officials started to exploit the loopholes in the *kaizhong* system was the essence of this problem and directly opposed the interests of the merchant class.

'In the twenty-seventh year of Emperor Hongwu[136] (1395), the emperor ordered that the dukes, the counts, and the officials higher than the fourth rank were forbidden from allowing their attendants to

[134] Cheng et al. (2019, p. 8).

[135] Sombart (1967 [1915], p. 77).

[136] Emperor Hongwu, the founder of the Ming dynasty, named Zhu Yuanzhang, reigned from 1368 to 1398.

participate in the salt business'.[137] However, despite the court's repeated warnings and orders, neither the smuggling nor the officials' participation had been eliminated in reality. First of all, officials seemed to have no intention of reining themselves in the salt business. During the years of Emperor Jingtai,[138] there were already high-ranking officials who designated their retainers to engage in the salt business. They 'occup[ied] quite a few salt licenses, and [sold] them to others with a high price, which undermine[d] the country's laws and seized the interests of merchants'.[139] During the Emperor Chenghua years,[140]

> A rich man Lu Ming and some others entrusted some senior officials with asking for some salt licenses of Lianghuai salt (the salt with the highest quality), and their request was approved. Ma Ang, the Minister of Revenue could not be fair in his administration, thus the salt law began to erode. Many eminent figures participated in this business.[141] (my transl.)

How to solve a problem like private salt? It was even more knotty because the government introduced a new policy that actually condoned private salt trading. In theory, all the salt produced must be acquired by the government. However, in order to support the salt price, the official quota was often far lower than the actual salt production, resulting in a great deal of excess salt. This salt could not be sold due to the ban on private salt trading, which was called *yuyan* ('residual salt'). In order to dredge the clogged uncashed salt licenses, in addition to the above-mentioned method of fetching salt from nearby saltyards, in the second year of Emperor Hongzhi (1489), the court began to allow producers to sell these salt to the merchants after paying a proportional amount of *yuyan yin* ('residual salt silver'), that is, the tax on the 'residual salt'.[142]

As a result of this proclamation, many salt merchants stopped caring whether their granary receipts could be redeemed. The salt license became the only thing they were eager to acquire because it enabled them to

[137] Shen (1989 [1587], Vol. 34, p. 240).

[138] Emperor Jingtai reigned from 1450 to 1456.

[139] Zhang (1974 [1739], Vol. 164, p. 4450).

[140] Emperor Chenghua reigned from 1465 to 1487.

[141] Zhang (1974 [1739], Vol. 80, p. 1938).

[142] Fei (1962 [1525], p. 2878).

purchase salt directly from producers and thus 'broke through the restrictions on the salt purchase limit, allowing smuggling of excess salt'.[143] This regulation ostensibly helped to resolve the excessive salt license issue without damaging the salt monopoly system. However, in practice, this meant that merchants had to pay twice as much for the same amount of salt, first to the salt producers and then to the government (since the cost of residual salt taxes was passed on to the merchants). Even so, salt merchants were willing to do so, since 'this extra expenditure was still smaller than the interest paid over a long waiting period'.[144]

Moreover, to increase their own profits, merchants often purchased more salt than the prescribed amount of 'residual salt'. The excess amount was essentially private salt, which was illegal, but they could legitimize themselves by acquiring a salt license, after which the official salt and residual salt could be mixed. The grassroots salt officials at the salt field 'welcomed merchants who bought directly from salt producers',[145] since this would thus result in a higher proportion of trade on the official records (which represented higher political achievement). Therefore, grassroots officials gave free reign to the de facto smuggling activities.

Therefore, it can be assumed that a lot of salt was diverted as residual salt and that it competed with 'official' salt. As mentioned above, powerful officials were also actively engaged in these activities, and they even 'adopted some tactics to induce the emperor to authorise them to participate'.[146] Once dignitaries got salt licenses, they 'might reuse the licenses, sometimes for many years',[147] and no action was taken against them, since local officials were fearful of their powerful connections. Other merchants 'obtained trading privileges by paying an intermediary agent', usually a friend or relative of a government official.[148]

In this context, the court had tried several times since the late fifteenth century to attract legitimate salt merchants by lowering the price of official salt.[149] In the twelfth year of Emperor Chenghua (1476), 'one *yin* (of

[143] Chen (1962 [1638], Vol. 474, pp. 26–27).

[144] Zhu (2002 [1529], Vol. 7, pp. 5–6).

[145] Zhu (2002 [1529], Vol. 4, p. 29).

[146] Li (1962 [1509], p. 3593).

[147] Fei (1962 [1525], p. 506).

[148] Zhu (2002 [1529], Vol. 7, p. 53).

[149] Fei (1962 [1525], p. 1019).

salt) in the northern border town was worth only 0.15 taels'.[150] In the tenth year of Emperor Chenghua (1474), 'one hundred kilograms of salt in Hedong[151] were only worth 0.05, evidently lower than the production cost'.[152] However, this practice further hindered the issuance of salt licenses. By the twenty-ninth year of Emperor Jiajing (1550), the Ministry of Revenue estimated that 'the court actually collected only forty percent of the total salt produced by the Lianghuai area, and the remaining sixty percent was under the control of smugglers'.[153] These smugglers were predominantly members of powerful families and the treacherous merchants who served them.

Therefore, the salt revenue collected by the Ming court was very small. Although the salt administrations during the middle and late Ming Dynasty periods collected a total income of 2 million taels per year, under the Tang Dynasty merely 'the Lianghuai area was capable of producing an annual income of 6 million taels from salt per year'.[154] The salt management departments at all levels were under great pressure, and each increase in pressure was transmitted from top to bottom to the most vulnerable part of the monopoly system, that is, the poor and powerless salt producers. The salt merchants who bought residual salt directly from producers 'were also involved in persecuting the producers'.[155] Meanwhile, since the official price of salt was not competitive, legitimate producers could not compete with the illegal salt market. By the end of the sixteenth century, 'salt management agencies were unable to force merchants to sell salt in designated areas anymore'.[156]

Timothy Brook, in his *The Confusions of Pleasure*, asserted that 'the state's relationship to commodity markets in the mid-Ming was only moderately extractive'.[157] In most cases this was true. However, in the context of the salt monopoly, this expression might not have painted a completely accurate picture, at least from the perspective of salt

[150] Liu (1962 [1491], p. 2891).

[151] Hedong was located in currently Linyi, Shandong Province.

[152] Liu (1962 [1491], p. 2434).

[153] Zhang (1962 [1577], p. 6420).

[154] Chen (1962 [1638], Vol. 476, p. 1).

[155] Gu (1985 [1682], Vol. 12, p. 41).

[156] Chen (1962 [1638], Vol. 357, p. 31).

[157] Brook (1999, p. 108).

merchants' funding. First, before the official checkpoints issued the salt, the merchants had to pay the residual salt tax. Except for the wealthy salt merchants who could immediately raise the required funds, most merchants could not recover the funds for the next round of trade until the previous one had been completed. This meant that the volume of small merchants was highly limited and that 'these official checkpoints demanded huge amount of merchants' funds'.[158]

Second, the repeated collection of excessive tariffs and fines was relatively common. Although, as mentioned above, the grassroots salt officials present at the salt fields often tolerated merchants smuggling salt privately, the scrutiny of the officials responsible for regulating salt sales at ports and land checkpoints was very intense. The punishment for exceeding the weight limit was very severe. 'Even if the excess portion weighed under five pounds, one would be fined according to the total weight instead of the excess portion'.[159] In addition, although, in theory, 'official' salt produced by those with licenses should be tax-free when passing through checkpoints, there was no guarantee that no additional taxes would be assessed on it. The officials in charge of the checkpoints often imposed additional tariffs on the goods. In fact, many local officials also 'imposed a tax of 0.1 tael for every one hundred *yin* of salt in transit and 1 tael for every one hundred *yin* of salt sold locally'.[160] Although the tax imposed on salt in transit did not seem high, the total amount was disproportionate, since almost all the counties it passed through collected taxes on it.

> 'The treatment that the merchants received depended on the sense of fair play of the officials ... It is true that, when merchants were ill-treated, the censorial officials were obliged to protest, but they did so more out of a feeling that harsh treatment of imperial subjects conflicted with the ideal of governmental benevolence rather than out of concern for individual justice'.[161] Reforms only occurred when officials who genuinely cared about the interests of small merchants were in power. For example, when Pang Shangpeng[162] was in charge of the salt administration in the

[158] Chen (1962 [1638], Vol. 357, p. 29).

[159] Gu (1985 [1682], Vol. 12, p. 44).

[160] Hai (1962 [1587], p. 50).

[161] Huang (1974, p. 201).

[162] Pang Shangpeng (1524–1580) was governor of Fujian.

> Lianghuai area in the late sixteenth century, 'the amount of residual salt tax was reduced so that merchants who had to pay taxes at the official checkpoints in the first place could pay the residual salt tax more easily'.[163] However, most officials were more interested in increasing their personal incomes. In the early seventeenth century, 'a superintendent-level salt officer spent three thousand taels' for an initial appointment, while his personal income 'during a one-year term reached thirty thousand taels'.[164] In fact, the imperfections of the system itself seemed to breed dishonesty. In the sixteenth century, 'if a person was appointed as a salt officer, his reputation would immediately be tarnished'.[165] In the late sixteenth century, 'when a grassroots official was promoted to vice-director of the Changlu[166] branch of the salt administration, one of his friends wrote to him, expressing deep regret'.[167]

In addition, since the court never provided sufficient capital investment or service facilities to the salt administration, the management department did not possess its own vessels, and 'the funds for dredging the canals were very scarce',[168] resulting in some salt fields in the Lianghuai area, through which the canal passed, being unprofitable. Merchants found that the cost of transporting salt from these salt fields 'actually exceeded the purchase price'.[169] In addition, 'the clearance documents issued by the checkpoint' were expensive.[170] These costs were passed on to consumers, that is, the ordinary people, by 'raising the price of salt'.[171] 'A labourer's annual allotment of salt cost him four days' wages. When the price soared three or four times higher than this, as happened in Huguang[172] in the

[163] Chen (1962 [1638], Vol. 357, p. 15).

[164] Zhou (1985 [1586], p. 48).

[165] Chen (1962 [1638], Vol. 475, p. 24).

[166] Changlu was located near the current Tianjin, along the Bohai Gulf.

[167] Chen (1962 [1638], Vol. 383, p. 21).

[168] Chen (1962 [1638], Vol. 474, p. 26).

[169] Chen (1962 [1638], Vol. 474, p. 29).

[170] Chen (1962 [1638], Vol. 474, p. 26).

[171] Chen (1962 [1638], Vol. 474, p. 23).

[172] Huguang was a province of China during the Yuan and Ming dynasties. During the Yuan dynasty it included the areas of modern Hubei south of the Yangtze river, Hunan, Guizhou, and Guangxi. During the Ming dynasty it came to include just the modern provinces of Hubei and Hunan, in the process adding areas north of the Yangtze.

1610s, it became clear that salt was no longer within reach of the common people'.[173]

Since the fifteenth century, quite a few officials had noticed that the salt trade was increasingly being carried out by relatively few powerful, well-connected families that took advantage of the state monopoly. Members of powerful families increasingly dominated the salt market and took a disproportionate share of the salt licenses issued.

3.3.3 *Ye Qi: Salt Merchants' Representative*

Ye Qi[174] believed that the problems of the state-owned salt industry were essentially contradictions caused by the intermingling of two distinct systems of logic. He believed that, on the one hand, the salt-regulation system was the lifeblood of the national economy. Although the government had incorporated it into the state monopoly, its actual operation still had to follow the market's own economic logic. On the other hand, border defence was ensured by various systems implemented by the state, which were largely limited by the country's external environment. These systems relied on the government's control through administrative, foreign, and ethnic policies. Thus, since the government's leading position in the salt law system had been overemphasized, border politics had completely overtaken it, which had led to the indiscriminate issuance of salt licenses and caused issues with supply and demand. The cascading reaction resulted in the weakening of enthusiasm among merchants. Therefore, the real issue with the implementation of the salt law was that the merchants could not obtain the status they desired and were unwilling to participate in the *kaizhong* system because it did not suit their own interests. Therefore, to restore the fundamental role of the market in the allocation of resources, Ye believed that the salt market and the Ming Dynasty's national economy could be reinvigorated by accepting silver as payment.

However, the root of Ye's economic views regarding merchants' interests was his status as a representative of the interests of salt merchants in the Lianghuai region. From the late fifteenth century onwards, two

173 Huang (1974, p. 219).

174 Ye Qi (1426–1501) was Minister of Revenue. During his term of office, he conducted the reform of salt laws.

types of merchants appeared in the salt business. The so-called *bian shang* ('border merchants') delivered grain to the border garrisons and then sold the granary receipts to the so-called *nei shang* ('internal merchants'). The benefits of the *kaizhong* system mainly accrued to the border merchants, of which the northern locals, including the Shanxi and Shaanxi merchants, were the main faction. The merchants who bought salt licenses and collected salt were often internal ones, a group that included the merchants who were a mainstay near the state's salt flats. This was a necessary distinction because the production period for salt was at least three years, often reaching around ten, despite improvements in efficiency during the sixteenth century.

Moreover, it can be concluded from Ye Qi's views that the formation and evolution of the *kaizhong* system during the early and middle periods of the Ming Dynasty was a competition between 'despotism' and the 'rational market'. From the perspective of authoritarian rule, we can see the self-adjusting process of the Ming Dynasty's government control 'remained strong'. During the early period of the Ming Dynasty, external military threats to border areas had not yet been eradicated, and the domestic economy was in urgent need of recovery. If organizational and administrative efficiency were to be maximized, authoritarian power would need to penetrate the political, economic, national defence-related, and other sectors of the country and project the authority of the central government through various systems. This authoritarian power was rigid in Ming Dynasty China. Even when the *kaizhong* system was on the verge of collapse, the premise of Ye's views on state monopolies and the salt system reform was still to ensure the functioning of the original institutional framework with the aim of leaving space for the market's autonomous operation by accepting silver as payment. He attempted to reverse the situation and implemented a new mode of government intervention; however, the role of merchants was still very limited.

3.3.4 *Han Wen: Maintaining the State-Run System*

Under the circumstances that hindered the effectiveness of the salt law, some senior court officials still hoped to maintain the *kaizhong* system. A representative of this type of philosophy is Han Wen[175] who stated,

[175] Han Wen (1441–1526) was a mid-level official during the Emperor Hongzhi and Zhengde periods.

'The rulers of the Ming Dynasty originally hoped to help small merchants. Unfortunately, however, they are now being squeezed out of the market by powerful families',[176] Han first claimed that in the actual implementation of the *kaizhong* system, powerful families could easily obtain more salt licenses than ordinary merchants through their relationships with members of the court.[177] Second, not only did they acquire more salt licenses, but each one was often reused, which meant that they secretly sold more salt than ordinary merchants.[178] Although this obviously violated the provisions of the *kaizhong* system, no official dared to point out or put a stop to this situation. After all, they could not afford to offend the powerful families.

His colleagues, including Liu Jian, the Minister of Rites and, later, the Grand Secretary during the Emperor Hongzhi era, believed that 'too many people asking for salt licenses leads to the destruction of existing regulations'.[179] Similarly, Li Dongyang[180] thought that this also led to 'several times more people [...] selling illegal salt privately'.[181] Diverging from the views of his colleagues, who only focused superficially on the fact that there were 'too many people asking for salt licenses', Han Wen considered the imperial court the most fundamental reason for the ineffectiveness of the *kaizhong* system.[182] However, despite understanding the deeper facts of the court's non-compliance with the system, Han still did not think deeply enough regarding its most fundamental disadvantage. His goal remained to maintain the state-run *kaizhong* system, and he strived to restore its original method of implementation. Therefore, although he offered sympathy to small merchants, it was impossible for him to provide constructive insights into their situation.

[176] Chen (1962 [1638], Vol. 85, p. 752).

[177] Chen (1962 [1638], Vol. 85, p. 753).

[178] Chen (1962 [1638], Vol. 85, p. 753).

[179] Chen (1962 [1638], Vol. 85, p. 757).

[180] Li Dongyang (1447–1516) was the Vice Minister of Rites and, later, the Grand Secretary during the Emperor Hongzhi and Zhengde periods.

[181] Li (1962 [1509], p. 235).

[182] Chen (1962 [1638], Vol. 85, p. 754).

3.3.5 Li Wen: Design of Salt System Reform

Regarding the Ming Dynasty's salt strategy, Li Wen affirmed its initial success but pointed out that it later began to entail increasing disadvantages, stating that 'each new bill adds a disadvantage to the merchant, and, for each additional disadvantage to the merchant, corrupt officials can obtain additional benefits'.[183]

So, how could salt profits flow 'into the hands of merchants' in response to this situation? Li Wen designed a set of blueprints for the rulers of the Ming Dynasty to allow merchants to operate freely, but his aim was to reform the salt system by 'seizing (grabbing) the illegal gains of wealthy merchants and returning them to the court'.[184] Li Wen believed that the government should give merchants portions of the salt flats and merchants should subsequently purchase the production materials by themselves, hire salt boilers independently, and operate freely.[185] The state could only exercise taxation rights in return for providing various services for them, and taxes could only be levied once in the salt-producing area, after which merchants would be allowed to sell their salt anywhere they wanted without paying additional taxes. In order to avoid opposition from powerful families (people with vested interests) and reduce resistance to the implementation of his plan, Li Wen advocated that powerful families and general merchants be allocated equal portions of the salt flats, requiring powerful families to engage in commerce just like ordinary merchants.[186]

Li Wen explained the advantages of doing so. One was that there would be no black-market salt anymore. All salt would be considered 'official' salt. He thought this approach could thus 'release the salt merchants from being accused of selling black-market salt and augment the enthusiasm of the salt merchants for production and operation',[187] which would increase the country's tax revenue. The second advantage was that this approach would no longer allow the powerful and nobles to rely on their political power to reap excessive profits; instead, they would only

[183] Li (2000 [1647], p. 121).

[184] Li (2000 [1647], p. 123).

[185] Li (2000 [1647], p. 123).

[186] Li (2000 [1647], pp. 123–124).

[187] Li (2000 [1647], p. 124).

be able to profit from their own commercial capabilities like ordinary merchants, ensuring social stability.[188]

In this way, this approach could not only make ordinary merchants rich but also increase the country's fiscal revenue. Obviously, Li Wen's views went a step further than Liu Yan's had during the Tang Dynasty. In the salt policy designed by Li, the government was no longer a participant, or even a manager, but a 'service provider' that provided necessary services to salt merchants. Although Li Wen's ideas were not incorporated into the actual policy of the imperial court, the appearance of such ground-breaking views proves how much the state's control over state-run commerce had weakened during the Ming Dynasty, especially the late Ming period (whether due to reduced capabilities or willingness).

3.3.6 Pang Shangpeng and Yuan Shizhen: States' Interest First

The views of the officials in charge of the salt administration are also worth exploring. In the second year of Emperor Longqing (1568), Pang Shangpeng was ordered to lead the salt administration in Lianghuai area, Changlu, Shandong, and other essential places of salt production and sales as well as the border area, in effect serving as the head of the national salt administration. He believed that the state and merchants should cooperate with each other and reap profits together. Pang understood that border merchants (*bian shang*) and internal merchants (*nei shang*) worked hard, and he mediated the conflicts of interest between the two parties.[189] He believed that 'the price of salt should be controlled by the state so that the price [would] not become low enough to cause the country to lose money or high enough to make it difficult for merchants difficult to sell salt'.[190] He believed that both the border merchants and domestic merchants could benefit from making concessions to each other. He believed that this would not only ensure that salt was taxed by the government but also guarantee the livelihoods of all merchants.[191] Effective cooperation between the state and merchants would lead to a closer relationship between the two.

[188] Li (2000 [1647], p. 126).

[189] Chen (1962 [1638], Vol. 357, p. 3848).

[190] Chen (1962 [1638], Vol. 357, p. 3848).

[191] Chen (1962 [1638], Vol. 357, p. 3859).

In the forty-fifth year of Emperor Chenghua (1617), Yuan Shizhen[192] a relatively upright official who, like Pang, took charge of the national salt administration, made some reforms. At the time, many merchants who had already obtained granary receipts abandoned them since they were unable to pay the residual salt tax in advance as required by the salt administration. Yuan was aware that this would lead to serious consequences if the income from the residual salt tax failed to reach the amount that had to be paid to Beijing.[193] Therefore, Yuan stipulated that merchants who paid the residual salt tax would receive the promised amount of salt immediately regardless of their positions on the waiting list to encourage more of them to pay the residual salt tax.[194] However, like many other policies in China, the sound ideas of high-level officials were greatly undermined by the actual operation of the grassroots framework. Despite the new regulation, 'some merchants still did not receive salt after paying the residual salt tax in advance three times'.[195] Thus, some merchants could only afford to pay some extra fees, such as the bribes paid to officials to obtain priority in collecting salt.

In Yuan Shizhen's view, ensuring the smooth operation of the salt business, which was fundamental to the national economy, was a top priority. Like that of Pang Shangpeng, Yuan Shizhen's reform of the Salt Law still comprehensively considered the relationship between the state and salt merchants. He believed that, 'while border merchants and domestic merchants [were] considered distinct types of merchants, they [were] actually mutually dependent'.[196] People who hoarded salt for speculation (called *tun hu*) and manipulated both the border merchants and domestic merchants would 'make merchants miserable' and thus 'make the state miserable', with the result that 'the border defence of the country [would] be in danger'.[197] Yuan accused the crafty merchants and hoarders who deceived the government of 'stealing tax money from the state', treating them as 'treacherous people'.[198] However, he also said

[192] Yuan Shizhen served as the Vice Minister of Revenue in late Ming.

[193] Chen (1962 [1638], Vol. 474, pp. 5204–5205).

[194] Chen (1962 [1638], Vol. 474, p. 5207).

[195] Chen (1962 [1638], Vol. 476, p. 5244).

[196] Chen (1962 [1638], Vol. 475, p. 5224).

[197] Chen (1962 [1638], Vol. 475, p. 5224).

[198] Chen (1962 [1638], Vol. 475, p. 5227).

that 'hoarders also belong[ed] to the class of merchants' and that they were 'a type of domestic merchant with higher capabilities'.[199] In view of the overall situation of the salt administration, the government's implementation of the new reform urgently required the assistance and support of these hoarders. Therefore, Yuan advocated that the government make appropriate compromises, 'placat[ing] the hoarders' and integrating them into the state's formal salt system to benefit the country and merchants alike.[200]

Pang Shangpeng and Yuan Shizhen, as the leaders of the national salt administration and representatives of the scholar-officials, put the state's interests first when thinking about the issue of the salt administration. They put forward the idea of criticizing its drawbacks, but they failed to view the issue from the perspective of the core drawbacks of the state monopoly, thus also failing to take the interests of merchants into consideration. Even if the hoarders were reviled as 'treacherous' by scholars like Pang and Yuan, since the government needed their assistance implementing reforms in the salt system, these officials were willing to take 'consolation' measures when dealing with hoarders. Thus, the status of ordinary merchants was compromised.

3.3.7 Other Scholars: Guiding Merchants

From the perspective of many scholars, the goal of circulating commercial goods and enriching the country relied on the government guiding merchants behave in advantageous ways by providing incentives to do so. The following are some examples of this type of thought. Zhao Bingran[201] emphasized the need for the government to take the initiative in state–merchant cooperation:

> Financial management [is] the primary task of managing the country, and the state must firmly hold the right to profit from financial management. With the right to interest in hand, market management can be flexible ... The profit [is] in its hands, and the treacherous merchants ha[ve] no

[199] Chen (1962 [1638], Vol. 475, p. 5229).

[200] Chen (1962 [1638], Vol. 476, p. 5245).

[201] Zhao Bingran (1507–1569) once served as Minister of Military.

> way to monopolise the trade, thus the prices of the (salt) market can be stabilised, and the cost of border defence can be reduced.[202]

Liu Yingqiu[203] examined the gains and losses from the salt policies and linked the long-term interests of merchants, border armies, and the country:

> The official salt industry became increasingly stagnant, thus provisions for the border armies ha[d] become scarce ... Once there [was] an emergency at the border, and merchants [were] not responding to the state's calls anymore, so the troops receive[d] insufficient military supplies, which [was] bad for the army and merchants and thus affect[ed] the country. [Was] it really a good thing?[204]

Lu Shen[205] also stated the significance of merchants to the *kaizhong* system: 'The main purpose of establishing the *kaizhong* system [was] to make business activities smoother. In general, the smoother the merchants' activities were, the richer the state [became]'.[206]

Guo Weixian,[207] a high-level censor during the Wanli period, believed that 'the purpose of guaranteeing the fairness of the salt law [was] to make the country rich, and, to make the country rich, we had to first benefit merchants ... If you could save a penny, it [was] equivalent to the merchant receiving an extra penny from the country'.[208] Similarly, Xu Guo[209] believed that,

> The nature of a merchant's business [was] to make a profit. Without the temptation of heavy profits, you cannot motivate a merchant ... If you squeeze[d] less from the merchants, then they [would] be happy to participate in the *kaizhong* system to support border defence. Once the merchants ma[de] a profit, the country's fiscal revenue would be adequate.

[202] Chen (1962 [1638], Vol. 252, p. 2648).

[203] Liu Yingqiu (1547–1620) once served as Governor of Nanjing.

[204] Chen (1962 [1638], Vol. 431, p. 4718).

[205] Lu Shen (1477–1544) was a famous scholar and calligrapher in mid Ming.

[206] Chen (1962 [1638], Vol. 155, pp. 1551–1552).

[207] Guo Weixian once served as Governnor of Huguang.

[208] Chen (1962 [1638], Vol. 406, pp. 4417–4418).

[209] Xu Guo (1527–1596) once served as Minister of Rites.

> The country [does] not seem to reap too high a profit according to this method, but, in fact (through this method), the country's income will always be stable.[210]

3.4 Short Summary

Qiu Jun's and Zhang Juzheng's opposition to state monopolies obviously did not become the mainstream position in Ming China. They were only a few high-level officials during the Ming Dynasty who opposed state monopolies (and they themselves were seeking power for personal gain). Although both men served as Grand Secretary, the two were in power for fewer than 12 years altogether. In the context of the Ming Dynasty, which lasted for 276 years, this length of time was almost negligible. More importantly, even Qiu and Zhang did not completely oppose state-run commerce, leaving room for their respective views on it. Although Qiu generally denied the positive impact of state-run commerce on the country's fiscal revenue, he was relatively supportive of the state's monopoly on the grain trade. In fact, his attitude was no different from Sang's towards the state monopolies on salt and iron, since, like grain, salt and iron were integral to the stability of the country and people's livelihoods. Regarding Zhang, the starting point of his views was that the money gained from such monopolies could not enter the pockets of corrupt officials. As long as money flowed into the national treasury smoothly, he did not oppose state monopolies. Moreover, as a high-level corrupt official who used his power for personal gain, it would have been unrealistic for Zhang to consider economic issues from the perspective of ordinary private merchants.

The country's use of merchants was best reflected in the state–merchant cooperation in the salt business. The low status of merchants was reflected in the arbitrariness and corruption of the bureaucracy, which exploited them instead of facilitating their activities. The central government's intentions and actual operations were extremely mismatched. Emperors seemed, on occasion, to have tried to protect the merchants in light of their economic function, but rulers could not control the state apparatus completely, resulting in a discrepancy between formally equitable laws and the realities of the salt trade. The design of the monopoly system in Ming China was full of loopholes. Although the ruling class

[210] Xu (2000 [1596], Vol. 4, p. 449).

showed concern for the happiness of the people when attempting to implement laws when the top-level design was implemented at the grass-roots level, its effect was often different from the original intention. In the state monopoly on salt, wealthy salt merchants who had the backing of officials turned out to be the group that profited the most. Small- and medium-sized merchants were easily squeezed out of the lucrative business by large ones because of the former group's financial constraints and lack of power, while those who could afford to be flexible still made good money by smuggling excess residual salt. Nevertheless, in the salt monopoly, although the status of merchants might have been considered unacceptable, salt producers and the final consumers of salt (i.e. the commoners) were even more oppressed. The former could only earn a meagre income and were even oppressed by merchants during some special periods, while the latter often had to bear increases in salt prices largely due to the extra costs incurred by merchants.

Although officials held varied opinions on the salt administration, the evidence in this chapter shows that state–merchant relations in Ming China served only the state's interests. That is, if merchants, salt producers, and corrupt officials were colluding to decrease state revenue, then they should be punished, or the administrative system should be changed to close the loopholes. Otherwise, they could be tolerated to some extent.

References

Reference in English

Brook, T. (1999). *The confusions of pleasure: Commerce and culture in Ming China*. University of California Press.

Chang, J. L. (1987). History of Chinese economic thought: Overview and recent works. *History of Political Economy, 19*(3), 481–502.

Cheng, L., Peach, T., & Wang, F. (2019). *The political economy of the Han Dynasty and its legacy*. Routledge.

Hu, J. (1988). *A concise history of Chinese economic thought*. Foreign Languages Press.

Huang, R. (1974). *Taxation and governmental finance in sixteenth-century Ming China*. Cambridge University Press.

Lufrano, R. J. (1997). *Honorable merchants: Commerce and self-cultivation in late imperial China*. University of Hawaii Press.

More, T. (2002 [1516]). *Utopia*. Cambridge University Press.

Rothbard, M. N. (2006). *Economic thought before Adam Smith*. Edward Elgar.
Schefold, B. (2019). A western perspective on the Yantie lun. In L. Cheng, T. Peach, & F. Wang (Eds.), *The political economy of the Han Dynasty and its legacy*, 153–174. Routledge.
Smith, A. (1979 [1776]). *The Wealth of Nations: An inquiry into the nature and causes of the Wealth of Nations*. Clarendon Press.
Sombart, W. (1967 [1915]). *The quintessence of capitalism: A study of the history and psychology of the modern business man* (M. Epstein, Trans. and Ed.). Howard Fertig.
Sun, E., & DeFrancis, J. (1966). *Chinese social history: Translations of selected studies, 7*. Octagon Books.
Tanimoto, M., & Wong, R. B. (2019). *Public goods provision in the early modern economy: Comparative perspectives from Japan, China, and Europe*. University of California Press.
Twitchett, D., & Mote, F. (1998). *The Cambridge history of China: Volume 8, the Ming dynasty, 1368–1644*. Cambridge University Press.
Von Glahn, R. (2016). *An economic history of China: From antiquity to the nineteenth century*. Cambridge University Press.

Reference in Chinese

Chen, H. (1985 [1521]). *Jishi Jiwen*. Zhonghua Publishing House.
Chen, Z. (1962 [1638]). *Compile of memorials to the emperor in the Ming Dynasty (Ming jingshi wenbian)*. Zhonghua Publishing House.
Fei, H. (1962 [1525]). *Ming Shilu, record of Emperor Zhengde*. Institute of History and Language.
Gu, Y. (1985 [1682]). *Tianxia Junguo Libing Shu*. Peking: The Commercial Press.
Guan, Z., et al. (1965 [c. 400–100 BC]). *Guanzi*. Taipei: Taiwan Commercial Press.
Hai, R. (1962 [1587]). *Collected work of Hai Rui* (Vol. 1). Zhonghua Publishing House.
Hua, Q. (2002). *General history of China*. Shanghai Ancient Books Publishing House.
Li, D. (1962 [1509]). *Ming Shilu, record of Emperor Hongzhi*. Institute of History and Language.
Li, W. (2000 [1647]). *Liaozhai Ji*. Peking Press.
Li, Z. (2001 [1602]). *Fen Shu*. Yuanfang Press.
Lin, X. (2015 [1565]). *Lin Ciya Xiansheng Wenji*. Xiamen University Press.
Liu, J. (1962 [1491]). *Ming Shilu, record of Emperor Chenghua*. Institute of History and Language.
Qiu, J. (1986 [1487]). *Daxue Yanyi Bu*. Taiwan Commercial Press.

Shen, S. (1989 [1587]). *Ming Huidian*. Zhonghua Publishing House.

Wang, F. (1975 [1692]). *Discussion on Zizhi Tongjian (Du Tongjian Lun)*. Zhonghua Publishing House.

Wu, H. (2004). *Chinese commerce history*. The Finance and Economics Press.

Xu, G. (2000 [1596]). *Xu Wenmugong Ji*. Peking Press.

Yu, S. (1980 [1608]). *Gushan Bizhu*. Jiangsu Renmin Press.

Zhang, J. (1937 [1582]). *Zhang Wenzhonggong Quanji*. The Commercial Press.

Zhang, R. (1962 [1577]). *Ming Shilu, record of Emperor Jiajing*. Institute of History and Language.

Zhang, T. (1974 [1739]). *The history of Ming*. Institute of History and Language.

Zhou, X. (1985 [1586]). *Jinglin Xuji*. Zhonghua Publishing House.

Zhu, T. (2002 [1529]). *Yanzheng Zhi*. Shanghai Ancient Books Publishing House.

CHAPTER 4

Taxation: Levy on Merchants

The commercial taxation and related thoughts also reflected the role and status of merchants. First, I would like to clarify why I divide this chapter chronologically by early, middle, and late Ming. Unlike the state monopoly in the last chapter, which lasted for the whole Ming period, commercial taxation and related thought appeared to be quite different among different periods in Ming China.

During early Ming, the first several emperors, especially Emperor Hongwu and Emperor Yongle, focused mostly on the economic development and recovery from the ruin done by Mongolians. Mongolians were famous for their comparatively uncivilized behaviour, such as massacring the inhabitants of a conquered city, thus it is not difficult to imagine the dilapidation at the beginning of Ming. Therefore, the emperors cannot tolerate the evasion of commercial tax. Meanwhile, they planned to obtain more 'commercial tax' from the wealthy merchants, especially those who seems to be too powerful to threaten their rule, such as Shen Wansan, allegedly the richest merchant in Jiangnan region at the time. Nonetheless, to the small merchants, the emperors still show great empathy and care.

During middle Ming, as the economy recovered to its normal level, some thought regarding reducing commercial taxation began to emerge, although this kind of thought was still limited to some specific categories

T. Hua, *Merchants, Market and Monarchy*,
Palgrave Studies in the History of Economic Thought,
https://doi.org/10.1007/978-3-030-77189-8_4

of taxes during this period. At the same time, 'pro-agriculture' and 'Egalitarianism' also appear in the thought on commercial taxation. For some thinkers, taxing more on the merchants may after all be regarded as an appropriate and effective way to reduce the burden of the peasants. Moreover, while severe punishment on some merchants for tax evasion turned out to be quite effective during the early years of Ming China, the officials often turn a blind eye to the tax evasion during mid-Ming period.

When it comes to late Ming, the Donglin School, the major representative of the merchant class at the court,[1] appeared to be one of the major power. The Donglin thinkers vigorously agitate for cutting down commercial taxation, although there were actually very little room for further reduction. And quite a few thinkers in other schools still strived for adding commercial taxation, which, they believe, could save the peasants. We will see in this chapter how different their opinions and perspectives were, considering where they were sitting and how much percentage of moral issue occupied their minds.

4.1 Early Ming: Crackdown on Tax Evasion

4.1.1 Emperor Hongwu: Hostility Towards Wealthy Merchants

At the beginning of almost every dynasty in ancient China, the government imposed loose restrictions, allowing some commercial freedom and restoring the vitality of the people. Despite Emperor Hongwu's views on the small-scale peasant economy, the Ming Dynasty was no exception to this rule: 'in keeping with Hongwu's intent to reduce the logistical and administrative costs of the government, the Ming fiscal system generated a low level of income compared to that of the Song Dynasty'.[2]

In line with the reduction of state fiscal expenditures, Emperor Hongwu proposed a large-scale tax reduction plan after he ascended the throne, targeting both farmers and merchants. Emperor Hongwu ordered officials at all levels not to disturb merchants. Later, since the heavy toll tax (*tongxing shui*) led to merchants' goods being abandoned, he followed the advice of the ministers and lowered the toll tax rate because he believed that, only in this way, 'could profits flow and the army's supply

[1] As I expressed already in Chapter 1, quite a few members of Donglin Party have close relations with merchant families, or even, they themselves were merchants.

[2] Von Glahn (2016, p. 287).

be sufficient'.[3] Meanwhile, Zhu ordered a reduction in general commercial taxes (*shang shui*), since 'these taxes were too high and the people were damaged'.[4] Finally, the general commercial tax rate was set at 'one out of thirty'[5] (around 3.33 percent). All taxes collected in excess of this limit were considered illegal. Compared with that of the previous dynasty, the commercial tax rate of the Ming Dynasty was relatively low.

These efforts to lower commercial taxes can be adequate evidence of Emperor Hongwu's compassion for merchants. Emperor Hongwu advocated a reduction in commercial taxes, which can indeed be traced back to Confucius's appeal to 'reduce the tax on customs'.[6] Confucius resolutely opposed the idea of setting up checkpoints and collecting heavy commercial taxes, considering this 'an unjust act'.[7] What Emperor Hongwu was facing was pieces left by the Mongolian, and it is wise for him to adopt similar policies like Emperor Gaozu and Emperor Wendi of Western Han. However, this seemingly enlightened idea was aimed at helping only small- and medium-sized merchants, a group that did not threaten his rule. Despite the traditional theory of four occupational groups, he grouped small merchants and peasants into a single category in practice.[8] This does not mean that making the common people rich was his top priority since the vast majority of farmers and small merchants were still very poor. They might have been relieved of some burdens, but they were not encouraged to become rich. The rich group, represented by wealthy merchants, was the real threat to imperial rule and was, no doubt, Emperor Hongwu's target.

Emperor Hongwu was hostile towards wealthy merchants. His plan of 'collecting commercial taxes' from large merchants was simple: crude forfeiture of their assets. Examples of his lack of sympathy for large merchants were endless. In the first year of Emperor Hongwu's rule (1368), he forced the relocation of 140,000 merchants in the Jiangnan area to his hometown of Fengyang in Anhui province, which was still

[3] Xie (1962 [1411], Vol. 106, p. 1777).

[4] Gu (1985 [1682], p. 1176).

[5] Chou, Edward (1974, p. 132).

[6] Hu (1998 [1965], Vol. 1, p. 90).

[7] Hu (1998 [1965], Vol. 1, p. 90).

[8] Xie (1962 [1411], Vol. 132, p. 2096).

underdeveloped.[9] After the capital was established in Nanjing, Emperor Hongwu relocated another 67,000 wealthy merchants to Nanjing.[10] Emperor Hongwu's slaughter of the entire family of Shen Wansan was another example. Shen Wansan was said to provide Emperor Hongwu with a considerable amount of funding and military support at the beginning of his rule, but he, unfortunately, ended up having his assets confiscated.[11]

Emperor Hongwu was not the first to employ the strategy of using the wealthy merchants first and then discarding it. Former emperors, such as Emperor Gaozu of Western Han (Liu Bang) and Emperor Guangwudi of Eastern Han (Liu Xiu), did similar things. Emperor Hongwu himself expressed his thoughts very clearly. He said that 'Previously Emperor Gaozu of Western Han moved the wealthy merchants to Guanzhong region. I felt confused at first, but now I know that it is necessary to relocate the merchants since the capital city is the foundation of the country. There is no other way to ensure the stability of the country'.[12] Emperor Hongwu was obviously still a firm supporter of 'agriculture being the root and commerce being the branch', and controlling wealthy merchants was an essential part of maintaining the country's stability. The low commercial tax rate was enacted merely for the benefit of the small merchants who constituted no threat to the ruler.

4.1.2 The Severe Punishment: Measures to Prevent Tax Evasion

In the context of having inherited a policy of 'implementing strict criminal laws', the classical position of Legalism, the use of 'severe criminal laws to deter merchants' became a major guiding ideology of the rulers during early Ming period who aimed to prevent merchants from evading taxes.

Some records seem to be a little bit too arbitrary. For example, some editor of *The History of Ming* took it for granted that 'merchants often have the motive to engage in tax evasion to reap more profits, but he did not provide any specific examples. He proposed a method of punishment:

[9] Wu (2012, p. 217).

[10] Wu (2012, p. 217).

[11] Wu (2012, p. 219).

[12] Zhang (1974 [1739], Vol. 81, p. 1980).

'all the goods should be confiscated by the government. The punishments are determined according to the law, but it [is] best to add fifty extra lashes'.[13] The Ming Code, which was followed by the government at the time, stipulated that 'for every merchant or person who [sold] wine and vinegar and [did] not pay tax, half of their stock of wine or vinegar [would] be confiscated by the government, and they [would] be lashed fifty times'.[14] Obviously, the method proposed was meant to punish merchants more severely than the Ming Code.

More reliable information can be seen from the records of some other scholars. For instance, Gao An[15] stated,

> Historically, the commercial tax has amounted to 6,000 *liang* annually. Since the founding of our dynasty, some of the shops and wine vinegar providers in our region have closed ... while some have been newly opened, but, since there has been no new round of investigation since the founding of our dynasty, there [are] bound to be a lot of shops and itinerant merchants that have not paid the slightest bit of taxes. Many people feel that it is unfair to collect taxes like this.[16] (my transl.)

He suggested a new round of investigation of, and tax collection from, merchants, preventing newly established shops and merchants from evading taxes. Another example is He Liangjun,[17] who proposed a system of 'joint punishment', that is, one inspired by a similar archaic method proposed by *Zhouli*:

> Every ten families were grouped into one *jia*, with one of the families chosen as the head. The ten households had to check with each other whether any fault or omission in the taxes they had paid existed. If any hidden assets or tax evasion [were] found by the government, the other nine families [would] be punished along with the criminal family.[18] (my transl.)

[13] Zhang (1974 [1739], Vol. 83, p. 2009).

[14] Zhang (1974 [1739], Vol. 45, p. 1078).

[15] Gao An once served as the prefecture of Hangzhou, Zhejiang Province.

[16] Zhang (1974 [1739], Vol. 86, p. 2046).

[17] He Liangjun (1506–1573) was a famous scholar and traditional opera theoretician.

[18] Zhang (1974 [1739], Vol. 86, p. 2047).

Obviously, from statements by the rulers and philosophers of the early Ming period, it may be inferred that they considered merchants as untrustworthy from the beginning. They may to some extent care for the grassroots whereas inclined to believe in the preconceived notion that merchants had an incentive to evade taxes.

4.2 Mid-Ming: The Objections to Fixed-Quota Commercial Taxes

4.2.1 Taxing Merchants: Reducing the Burden of Peasants

Around the middle of the Ming Dynasty, commerce began to boom, especially in traditionally wealthy regions, such as Jiangnan and Guanzhong.[19] However, the development of commerce brought even more anxiety to the ruling class and the scholars who served them. Some scholars were clearly inclined to justify the imposition of commercial taxes on merchants. For instance, Liu Ying said in his missive that 'the ancient emperors restrain[ed] merchants not for their own personal gain. If commercial taxes had not been levied, there would have been no source of funds for the country. By levying taxes, emperors can relieve the burden on farmers'.[20] He said that, although the imposition of commercial taxes seemed to curb the profits of merchants, its real purpose was still to control border defence.

This view can also be confirmed by examining the memorials[21] of Ma Qing[22] and Xu Lingdian.[23] Ma Qing explained that the levying of commercial taxes was conducted in accordance with the ancient sage king law and because the state treasury was almost empty at the time, he said,

[19] Guanzhong region in Ming China includes approximately five cities currently in Shaanxi province, respectively Xi'an, Baoji, Xianyang, Weinan and Tongchuan.

[20] Zhang (1974 [1739], Vol. 95, p. 2254).

[21] A memorial to the throne, *zouzhe* in Chinese, was an official communication to the Emperor in Ming China. They were generally careful essays in classical Chinese and their presentation was a formal affair directed by government officials.

[22] Ma Qing (1480–1536) once served as the highest governor in charge of domestic grain transportation, and the Governor of Fengyang.

[23] Xu Lingdian once served as a senior official in Ministry of Military.

> The purpose of our country establishing customs [was] not to increase the country's fiscal revenue but to prevent too many people from becoming merchants and to encourage them to return to agriculture. Ancient sages and wise kings attached great importance to agriculture, the top priority for survival. Thus, they value[d] grain and humbled jade, which [was] a very sound idea. Therefore, levying commercial taxes on merchants can maintain the ancient law of the wise kings while enrich[ing] the state treasury. Collecting commercial taxes on merchants should be considered a means of reaping a profit by following the correct path, while levying agricultural taxes on farmers should be considered a means of amassing great wealth by fleecing the people. The differences between the two should be readily apparent.[24] (my transl.)

Here, he seemed to provide an explanation for the moral rationale behind levying commercial taxes. Next, he said that 'Merchants who trade[d] between the North and South [were] taxed when they pass[ed] through Linqing[25] and other customs checkpoints, but merchants who travel[led] west along the Huai River were not taxed when they pass[ed] through Zhengyang.[26] It [was] very unreasonable'.[27] Therefore, from the perspective of ensuring consistency in commercial taxes across the country, he suggested opening new a customs checkpoint in Zhengyang.

Xu Lingdian expressed similar thoughts: 'The demands imposed by official salaries, rituals, sacrifices, post offices, military expenses, and palace repair expenditures could not be met. The king had a benevolent heart. The funds needed for these huge expenses could not be taken from ordinary people, so it [was] natural to tax merchants'.[28]

Wang Shizhen[29] explained the rationale behind levying taxes on merchants and analysed the relationship between merchants and the country. He suggested a milder method of collecting commercial taxes. He stated,

[24] Chen (1962 [1638], Vol. 169, p. 1726).

[25] Linqing was the then most important commercial city in Shandong province.

[26] Zhengyang is a county in current Henan Province.

[27] Chen (1962 [1638], Vol. 169, p. 1727).

[28] Chen (1962 [1638], Vol. 179, p. 1867).

[29] Wang Shizhen (1526–1590) was a famous scholar and historian in Ming China.

> The practice of levying taxes on merchants at customs began during the troubled times of the Warring States period. At the time, due to the demands of war, countries had to strengthen inspections and obtain commercial contributions and levy fines to subsidise military expenses. During the Han Dynasty, the monarchs' tastes were extravagant, and the peasants were quite poor, so the rulers could only collect taxes from merchants. However, our founding emperor (Emperor Hongwu) respected frugality. He believed that the collection of commercial taxes should be appropriate. Otherwise, if officials violate[d] the rules of collection due to selfishness, it [would] eventually lead to problems for both the state and merchants.[30] (my transl.)

Therefore, it can be inferred that the state's fiscal revenue was considered something that must be obtained from either merchants or farmers. To ensure the stability of the peasant economy, Ming rulers chose to collect taxes from merchants, of course. By emphasizing the importance of agriculture, scholars repeatedly made a case for 'expanding fiscal revenue by taxing merchants', often in a fierce manner.

4.2.2 The Objections to Fixed-Quota Commercial Taxes

The opposition to fixed-quota commercial taxes, which became popular around mid-Ming, may also be viewed as evidence of some merchants making more money while cutting the state out of the profits. For many years in ancient China, fixed taxes were considered fair and believed to be an effective method of wealth redistribution. However, with the rapid development of commerce and merchants' increased ability to earn money, some officials began to blame the undifferentiated fixed-quota commercial tax for 'causing a lack of socio-economic efficiency', and their targets were merchants who had the ability to earn a lot of money. In short, in ancient China, once merchants found ways to earn money, some officials had incentives to find ways to make them moneyless, inflicting 'average poverty' on the whole of society because it was conducive to ruling the people effectively.

The views of scholars were in line with (or reflected) the view of the ruling class: when the total amount of commercial taxes was small, the problem was not obvious. However, as the total amount of commerce

[30] Wang (1986 [1590], p. 855).

and trade began to increase during the mid-Ming period, officials believed that 'levying a fixed amount of commercial taxes [amounted to] increasing the relative burden of the poor (mostly farmers)', which led to the improper allocation of social resources. Many officials raised objections to fixed-quota taxes and supported differential ones. As early as the latter period of the Emperor Yongle era, Xie Jin[31] pointed out that 'fixed-quota taxes were implemented regardless of the profits or losses of business operators', which caused the 'commoners to suffer'.[32] He believed that fixed-quota commercial taxes gave merchants the opportunity to evade taxes, so he argued that commercial taxes should be 'collected according to actual sales'.[33] This was a clear contradiction to the commercial tax quota system that had prevailed since the early years of the Northern Song Dynasty and had been inherited by Ming China, but Xie did not propose a detailed method of levying taxes 'according to actual sales'. Thus, it can be inferred that Xie simply wanted to levy a differential tax proportional to the amount of profits earned by merchants.

In the early years of Emperor Wanli's reign, Shen Jiwen[34] wrote that 'the regulation of taxation should lean toward taxing rich people, while poor people should be exempt'.[35] Shen used a metaphor to illustrate his rationale: 'Taxing rich merchants [was] only harvesting their excess, while levying commercial taxes on small merchants [was] like cutting the fat from their abdomens'.[36] He proposed that industries like pawning and usury should be taxed at the highest rate. Regarding the small merchants who '[sold] flatbread and soy milk all day long but could only earn a few silver pieces',[37] Shen believed that the government should collect only a small amount of tax or even that such merchants should be exempt from taxes. Shen Jiwen thus wanted to levy a differential tax according to the amount of profits yielded by various industries.

Chen Yan similarly believed that differential taxes should be levied according to the type of goods that merchants sold. For example, he

[31] Xie Jin (1369–1415), was a famous scholar and once served as the Grand Secretary.

[32] Chen (1962 [1638], p. 76).

[33] Chen (1962 [1638], Vol. 11, p. 76).

[34] Shen Jiwen once served as the Governor of Henan Province.

[35] Wen (1962 [1630], p. 569).

[36] Wen (1962 [1630], p. 569).

[37] Wen (1962 [1630], p. 569).

thought that taxes on alcohol should not be equal to taxes on food. He believed there were three benefits to restricting wine production and levying higher taxes on it: first, 'farmers can harvest more grains if they do not plant sorghum (the raw material for making wine)', encouraging food production.[38] Second, the number of people who abused alcohol would be reduced, and 'commoners in the four occupations can be saved from neglecting their jobs'.[39] Third, even if an increase in taxes raised the price of alcohol, it would not 'damage the commoners'.[40] He also pointed out that, since those who consumed alcohol and tea were mostly members of wealthy families, although raising taxes and fees would increase prices, the demand would not change much and would not affect the collection of taxes (since these families would still be able to afford such commodities), thus the profits of the wine merchants would be unaffected. On the contrary, if the tax rate were increased for commodities, such as food, that the poor had to consume every day, the price increases would 'embroil innocent people'[41] in conflict, which was unfair. In Chen's views, we can see vague hints at the concept of price elasticity of demand in modern economics.

The negative attitude towards fixed-quota commercial taxes and the increasing support for differential taxes at the time reflected the unfair distribution of wealth during the Ming Dynasty and the wide disparity between the rich and the poor to some extent. It more clearly reflected the fear of the ruling class and scholar-officers of merchants' ability to earn money. They hoped that, by changing the tax collection system and reallocating social resources, these merchants would not be allowed to accumulate too much wealth.

4.2.3 Increasingly Rampant Tax Evasion

During middle and late Ming, commercial tax itself remains very low despite its booming economy, compared with previous dynasties. The major reason, if not the only reason, maybe that the income the commercial tax provided was 'too small and too scattered for it to be regarded

[38] Xie (1980, p. 281).

[39] Xie (1980, p. 281).

[40] Xie (1980, p. 282).

[41] Xie (1980, p. 282).

as a major source of revenue'.[42] For instance, 'some Ming officials were surprised to read in the histories that under the Tang the Lianghuai region alone produced an annual income from salt of over 6 million strings of copper cash'.[43] And tax evasion began to be quite common. This can be seen from the records of Alvaro Semedo, a Portuguese missionary staying in China at that time,

> In the Custom-house (for there is a very famous one here) there is not so much honour done the Merchant, but more favour. There is no house where the Merchandise is deposited, weighed or visited; neither is it taken out of the barke; but only a moderate rate is paid for it by the eye, and according to the Merchants book of accounts. If the passenger be no merchant, although he go alone in a Barke with his servants, and carry five or six chests, and several other things, which are usually transported from one country to another, they are not searched nor opened, neither do they pay any custom. A good example for the Custom and Gabell-houses of Europe, where a poor traveler is so beastly and barbarously, robbed and spoiled; when all he carries with him is not worth so much as they ask him for custom.[44]

Judging from this record, the so-called inspection of merchants' goods is just some kind of formalism. Generally, the merchants may pay as much commercial tax as they like. Even, if you pretend not to be a merchant, no matter how many goods you brought, you would not be taxed.

Under this pretentious inspection, a lot of tax evasion may happen in the vast majority of all commercial transactions. And many tax evasion behaviours were even the result of government officials' indulgence and encouragement. They seem to think that as long as the tax they have collected can be paid, the others are ignored. Ray Huang described the following weird things.

> This was the case when Ho Tsun was in charge of the Sha-shih station in the decade after 1510. Once the quota was met he offered the timber merchants a general reduction on the scheduled rates. Shao Chingpang, who was in charge of the same station in the 1520s, adopted an even more striking solution. After making up the annual quota in three months he

[42] Huang (1974, p. 232).

[43] Huang (1974, p. 216).

[44] Semedo (1655 [1636], p. 12).

> apparently closed down the office and for the rest of the year allowed the timber merchants to pass through the station tax-free. In the 1560s Yang Shih-ch'iao established an honour system at the Hang-chou station, and based his tax assessments on the merchants' own declarations. Significantly, these three officials all won high praise from the traditional historians.[45]

It is precisely because of such absurd things that we can understand why the following situations happen,

> In the early years of the dynasty there were more than 400 stations collecting local business taxes but by the early seventeenth century only 112 remained in operation. The rest had become unprofitable and had been closed. 27 In 1568 the ministry of revenue reported that at one particular station labour costs amounted to about 400 taels a year while it netted only 110 taels in taxes.[46]

The commercial taxes collected were not even enough to pay the salaries of tax collectors, and indeed the stations can only be closed. And this kind of situation actually worsened during the late Ming.

4.3 Late Ming: Further Reduction of Commercial Tax

4.3.1 Critiques of Additional Commercial Taxes: State Interest

The views regarding commercial taxation during the late Ming Dynasty essentially revolved around Emperor Wanli dispatching additional tax collectors, which caused serious disruptions to the country's normal taxation system. For instance, Zhao Shiqing[47] wrote to the emperor and analysed the reasons for the tariff reduction:

> The purpose of the state in establishing customs [was] to levy a reasonable amount of taxes on merchants while the income of the country [was] sufficient. There [was] only a limited amount of wealth in the world. If it was collect[ed] in one place, there [would] inevitably be less to collect in

[45] Huang (1974, pp. 238–239).

[46] Huang (1974, p. 232).

[47] Zhao Shiqing (1540–1618) once served as the Vice Minister of Revenue, and was once in charge of the salt business nationwide.

> other places. Do you (the emperor) expect to increase the capital of the court through repeated heavy taxation on merchants over successive years? You do not know what the consequences will be, and this is the reason that commercial taxes can no longer be adequately levied.[48] (my transl.)

Obviously, the state's fiscal interests were still Zhao's major concern. He believed that the biggest disadvantage of heavy taxation on commerce was that the country 'was making a thorough but unwise exploitation' and thus could not obtain enough fiscal revenue in the long run. He indeed felt sympathy for the unfortunate circumstances of merchants, but his priority was to highlight the role of collecting commercial taxes in providing sufficient fiscal revenue and stabilizing the state.

Huang Kezuan[49] expressed similar thoughts in the middle of the Wanli period. He was distressed that both farmers and merchants suffered due to the collection of additional taxes. He pointed out that 'in Linqing, after merchants [were] taxed once at customs, they [were] taxed again by additional tax collectors, which [was] harm for the state'.[50]

Although those additional tax collectors were called back by the emperor who knuckled under the public opinion, the new taxation officials sent by the court continued to collect additional taxes from sources other than customs. They behaved no differently from the previous tax collectors. How could the stability of the country be ensured and trouble and chaos avoided? Gu Yanwu provided one solution in his work: after commercial taxes had been levied on goods at the site of production, they 'should no longer be subject to any other form of taxation, giving merchants more freedom in business operations and generate more revenue for the state'.[51]

Additional taxation not only caused great hardships for merchants in relatively backward areas but even influenced merchants and businesses in wealthy areas, such as the Jiangnan region. In the ninth year of Emperor Chongzhen (1636), Zhang Guowei[52] talked about commercial taxes in Jiangnan region, saying,

[48] Chen (1962 [1638], Vol. 411, p. 4458).

[49] Huang Kezuan (1550–1634) once served as the governor of Shandong Province.

[50] Huang (2000 [1634], Vol. 4, p. 53).

[51] Gu (1985 [1682], p. 135).

[52] Zhang Guowei (1595–1646) once served as the Minister of Military.

> Jiangnan was originally a place where boats and carriages met. There were a lot of commercial activities and many merchants coming and going. However, recently merchants there had bec[o]me poorer and they did not have much ability to pay commercial taxes ... The harm of increasing commercial taxes [was] even greater than the harm of increasing farmers' land taxation rate ... Moreover, only about one-tenth of the additional commercial taxes were used by the court, while the other nine-tenths [were] all appropriated for private use by someone else.[53,54] (my transl.)

According to the scholars' view, this kind of nationwide chaos that even harmed the rich and populous regions cannot be put up with. This certainly, in the long run, would affect the stability of the country, not only financially.

4.3.2 Donglin School: Personal Interest in Commercial Tax Reduction

In addition to the above-stated ideas of levying lower commercial taxes to benefit the state's interests, some other thinkers supported the same argument with a different purpose: the interest of the merchant class. They often belong to the Donglin School, the school that represented the interests of the merchant class and demanded the reform of commercial taxes became more powerful. The Donglin members regarded any kind of increase in commercial taxation as beyond endurance. For example, Gao Panlong believed that the court should be sympathetic to merchants and opposed the government's aggressive purchasing tactics. He suggested that the government should 'compensate merchants at the market's seasonal rates, just as in ordinary deal[ings] between merchants and commoners'.[55] The members of the Donglin School criticized the plundering of those who collected additional taxes and advocated for the reduction of commercial taxes, views that were supported by urban residents (most of whom were merchants and officials involved in commerce).[56]

[53] Here, 'someone else' refers to the additional tax collectors sent by the emperor.

[54] Zhang (2000 [1646], Vol. 2, p. 645).

[55] Gao (1986 [1626], p. 233).

[56] Du (2017, p. 407).

The Donglin Party members, headed by Gu Xiancheng, were very active in opposing Emperor Wanli's policy of levying heavy commercial taxes. In 1600, just two years after Emperor Wanli began to dispatch additional tax collectors, Li Sancai[57] wrote a missive to the emperor, titled 'Petition for Stopping Additional Taxation', and he directly petitioned the emperor to stop the practice:

> Your Majesty love[d] pearls and jade, but the people still ha[d] to eat and drink. Your Majesty [considered] gold even more important than heavenly principles. The emperor want[ed] to pass his kingdom on to subsequent generations. In order to achieve this, does Your Majesty not believe that the people must be allowed to live in peace?[58] (my transl.)

Gao Panlong also pointed out that 'depriving people of their property [was] not the way for the state to earn money. There [were] only two correct ways. One [was] to promote production, and the other [was] to save money'.[59] YeXianggao, who then served[60] as Grand Secretary and was one of the core members in the Donglin School during the Emperor Chongzhen era, repeatedly asked the emperor to withdraw the additional tax collectors.[61] He also took advantage of the situation, giving lectures to the crown prince and talking about the eunuchs (the additional tax collectors were all eunuchs dispatched directly by the emperor) of the Eastern Han Dynasty, using the past to satirize the present.

Compared to traditional Confucian philosophy and Legalism, the views of the Donglin School regarding commercial taxes reflected an attitude of 'taking on the problems of the world as their own'. Instead of focusing on the welfare of peasants and entangling in metaphysics issues, in Prof. McDermott's words, they 'preferred a far more eclectic and inclusive body of thought that blended Confucianism and Buddhism. While

[57] Li Sancai (1552–1623) once served as the Minister of Revenue.

[58] Chen (1962 [1638], Vol. 417, p. 4245).

[59] Gao (1986 [1626], p. 236).

[60] Ye Xianggao (1559–1627) served in the Grand Secretariat under the Emperor Wanli from 1607 to 1614 and served as the Grand Secretary under the Emperor Tianqi from 1621 to 1624. As a member of the Donglin School, he played an essential role in staving off the court's (led by Wei Zhongxian, the grand eunuch) persecution of the Donglin members under Tianqi until his resignation in 1624.

[61] Ye (1994 [1627], Vol. 10, p. 234).

they recognized the validity of Zhu Xi's[62] orthodox thought, they gave at least equal preference to the more internal and activist teachings of Wang Yangming'.[63] Their petition for real change in the collection of commercial taxes signalled 'the end of bookishness',[64] which helped the scholarly circle, and society overall, to change the general attitude towards merchants, more or less.

4.3.3 Lü Kun: Blaming Imperial Shops

Although some were sympathetic towards merchants, repeated criticisms of commercial taxes seldom received proper responses from the emperor. It is quite understandable, from the emperor's perspective, because border wars, armies, infrastructure, famines, etc. everything needs huge expenditure from the national treasury. Commercial taxes do not really have any room for further reduction anymore during the late Ming.

As a result, the views of scholars regarding commercial taxes became passive. The most representative example was Lü Kun, who was the Vice Minister of Justice during the Emperor Wanli period. His view on commercial taxation was that the issue of merchant status in the collection of commercial taxes was not suitable for discussion at all (since a reply from the emperor could not be expected). He had learned a lesson from his predecessors and colleagues, who had criticized the dysfunctional governance of tax collection. He believed that it was futile to write to the emperor or engage in theoretical debates with officials and that solving the real problem was the only key issue.[65]

Lü Kun believed that the fundamental problem with commercial tax collection during the Emperor Wanli era was the corruption of the *huang-dian* (shops set up by the emperor or royal families) and the deep

[62] Zhu Xi (1130–1200) was a Chinese historian, philosopher, and writer during the Southern Song dynasty (1127–1279). Neo Confucianism initiated by Zhu Xi had a great influence on the Mongolians' ruling, Ming and Qing Dynasties. His philosophy dominated the ideological circle during these 6 centuries, and he was considered as the master in education after Confucius. His other major contribution includes his commentaries to the *Four Books*, which later formed the curriculum of the imperial exam from 1313 till the end.

[63] McDermott (2006, p. 191).

[64] McDermott (2006, p. 65).

[65] Handlin (1983, pp. 118–121).

involvement of powerful and well-connected families in business activities.[66] Ordinary merchants could not compete with them. As a sober scholar, Lü realized that the merchant class simply could not defeat the imperial system or the eunuchs who abused it.[67] Therefore, he believed that, for officials in relevant positions, it was more important to solve the problems that merchants encountered when heavy commercial taxes were levied on their goods than 'simply express opinions on the issue'.[68] It is thus worth emphasizing that his thought may be among the very few probing 'the basic causes inherent in the nature of the tax system'[69] rather than an abstract mumble.

4.3.4 *Wang Fuzhi: Duty Borne by Merchants Only*

With the development of commerce during the latter period of the Ming Dynasty, attitudes towards merchants did take a favourable turn. Unfortunately, this image neglected a bias. Wang Fuzhi, a famous late Ming Confucian, held views on commercial taxes that were, to some extent, representative of those of many scholars of the time, which were quite different from that of Donglin School. Wang believed that, regarding commercial industries that were not suitable for direct operation by the government, the government could increase fiscal revenue through taxation.[70] Wang believed that, since ancient times, 'the taxes that supported the soldiers and carriages used by the army ha[d] always been derived from merchants because they earned profits by selling the carriages and ox carts used by the army. The trade in goods such as leather, silk, linen, bamboo, and cloth [was] also operated by merchants'.[71] Therefore, he asserted that military costs should be borne by merchants, and taxes should also be levied on other goods.

Wang believed that taxes that should be borne by merchants could not be passed on to peasants or landowners. He believed that the reduction of commercial taxes was a manifestation of 'inhibiting the root industry

[66] Lü (2008 [1618], p. 165).

[67] Lü (2008 [1618], p. 165).

[68] Lü (2008 [1618], p. 166).

[69] Huang (1974, p. 264).

[70] Wang (1956 [1692], p. 11).

[71] Wang (1956 [1692], pp. 11–12).

and advocating the substance industry',[72] which did not help the country become rich or make the people strong. In short, taxation had to be borne by all merchants so that the tax burden would not fall entirely on the agricultural sector. Wang dismissed the idea that levying commercial taxes would raise prices or that 'peasants also suffer[ed] from this illness'.[73] According to him,

> People must first be free from freezing (after basic food and clothing needs had been met), and, only after that, [could] they seek to buy things on the market. Therefore, even if prices increase[d] slightly due to taxation, they [were] still within reach for the general public. If the public suffer[ed] from hunger, cold, and excessive taxation perennially, then there [would] be countless people who [could] not purchase anything on the market for many years. Rising prices would ha[ve] no effect on these people, how could they be harmful?[74] (my transl.)

It can be said that Wang's vision [was] not broad enough, since his perspective [was] only applicable to a self-supporting, self-sufficient economy. It could also be said that his views were limited by the realities of Ming Dynasty China.

He accused the senior officials who 'established regulations and policies at court' and 'enjoyed their lives without having to farm and lived close to the market, often buying food and daily necessities there'.[75] Thus, the policies they made were 'beneficial to merchants and themselves' (such as Xu Jie and Zhang Juzheng, who were large-scale merchants themselves). They 'often hear[d] merchants' complains but could not hear the complaints or see the hardships of farmers'.[76] He evidently thought that the policymakers at court failed to realize that the collection of commercial taxes could reduce the burden on farmers and benefit the state in practice.

In addition, Wang also reinterpreted Mencius's objection to levying commercial taxes. He explained that Mencius's proposal only applied

[72] Wang (1956 [1692], p. 37).

[73] Wang (1956 [1692], p. 37).

[74] Wang (1956 [1692], p. 39).

[75] Wang (1956 [1692], p. 39).

[76] Wang (1956 [1692], p. 40).

to the era of 'feudal separatist rule'.[77] At the time, various states were attempting to attract merchants by exempting them from commercial taxes. However, '[Ming] China ha[d] been unified, and ships and carriages shuttled between provinces. Why would anyone worry that no merchants [would] come?'[78] Thus, Wang believed that Mencius's views on the topic were outdated and that levying high commercial taxes would be reasonable in the context of Ming China.

Despite Wang's 'anti-merchant nature', the thought of Wang seems to correspond with the reality at the time. During late Ming, 'though the items were numerous the total revenue that they produced was comparatively small'.[79] Fewer than four million taels of silver collected 'seems unrealistically low when considered in terms of the fiscal requirements of the empire... considering the immensely broad coverage of this category of taxation, its level might in fact be considered quite inadequate'.[80]

It should be pointed out that 'the silver obtained from miscellaneous incomes' represented only around '17 copper cash per capita if apportioned equally on the entire population, reckoned to be 150 million or so by the late sixteenth century'.[81] Although many scholars criticized the Ming court for extortionate taxation, they did so mainly from moralistic perspective. Their major concern was to reveal 'the greed of the tax collectors and the hardship caused to individuals, rather than to probe the basic causes inherent in the nature of the tax system'.[82] Their thought and description have created the impression that the main issue was excessive commercial taxation. However, in fact, the fix was more likely due to insufficient commercial taxation.

[77] Wang (1956 [1692], p. 51).

[78] Wang (1956 [1692], p. 51).

[79] Huang (1974, p. 263).

[80] Huang (1974, p. 263).

[81] Huang (1974, p. 264).

[82] Huang (1974, p. 264).

References

Reference in English

Chou, C., & Edward, H. K. (1974). *An economic history of China*. Center for East Asian Studies, Western Washington University.

Handlin, J. F. (1983). *Action in late Ming thought: The reorientation of Lü Kun and other scholar-officials*. University of California Press.

Huang, R. (1974). *Taxation and governmental finance in sixteenth-century Ming China*. Cambridge University Press.

McDermott, J. (2006). *A social history of the Chinese Book*. Hong Kong University Press.

Semedo, A. (1655 [1636]). *The history of that great and renowned monarchy of China*. Translated by a person of quality. E. Tyler for John Crook.

Von Glahn, R. (2004). *The sinister way: The devine and the demonic in Chinese religious culture*. University of California Press.

Reference in Chinese

Chen, Z. (1962 [1638]). *Compile of memorials to the emperor in the Ming Dynasty (Ming jingshi wenbian)*. Zhonghua Publishing House.

Du, C. (2017). *Who terminated the Ming dynasty*. World Knowledge Press.

Gao, P. (1986 [1626]). *Gaozi Yishu*. Taiwan Commercial Press.

Gu, Y. (1985 [1682]). *Tianxia Junguo Libing Shu*. The Commercial Press.

Hu, J. (1998 [1965]). *History of Chinese economic thoughts* (Vol. 1–3). Shanghai University of Finance and Economics Press.

Huang, K. (2000 [1634]). *Shuma Ji*. Peking Press.

Lü, K. (2008 [1618]). *Lü Kun Quanji*. Zhonghua Publishing House.

Wang, F. (1956 [1692]). *Nightmare (E Meng)*. Zhonghua Publishing House.

Wang, S. (1986 [1590]). *Yanzhou Xugao*. Taiwan Commercial Press.

Wen, T. (1962 [1630]). *Ming Shilu, record of Emperor Wanli*. Institute of History and Language.

Wu, X. (2012). *Mighty for two thousand years (Haodang Liangqian Nian)*. Zhongxin Press.

Xie, G. (1980). *Selected social and economic historical materials of Ming dynasty*. Fujian Renmin Press.

Xie, J. (1962 [1411]). *Ming Shilu, record of Emperor Hongwu*. Institute of History and Language.

Ye, X. (1994 [1627]). *Cangxia Cao Quanji*. Peking Press.

Zhang, G. (2000 [1646]). *Zhang Zhongmingong Yiji*. Peking Press.

Zhang, T. (1974 [1739]). *The history of Ming*. Institute of History and Language.

CHAPTER 5

International Trade: Merchants' Predicament and Opportunities

In fifteenth to seventeenth-century China, the maritime merchants formed more formal organization, either a military-commercial group, which suppressed their competitors and scattered merchants, or trading diaspora that settled in Southeast Asia, where the Chinese merchants enjoyed a relatively higher status. Moreover, the Chinese merchants established mutually beneficial relationships (although fragile) with local governments, while the central government, most of the time, spared no effort to stop merchants from trading overseas.

There is a widespread set idea over the issue that Ming China lacks thought regarding foreign trade due to its long-lasting sea ban policy. It is, however, at most only half true. Forbidding the foreign trade at the official level does not mean there were no trade at all. On the contrary, just like the rule in physics that 'the tighter the spring is, the stronger the rebound is', the underground private trade and even smuggling was quite flourishing, as we will see in this chapter. In fact, the economic thoughts regarding foreign trade and merchants' role in it became more positive and had more supporters among scholars. Even though their main purpose was still to increase state revenues or improve people's welfare, these thoughts and the active role of merchants in reality did reinforce each other, enabling the Ming merchants to more or less show their strength and importance in the regional trade.

T. Hua, *Merchants, Market and Monarchy*,
Palgrave Studies in the History of Economic Thought,
https://doi.org/10.1007/978-3-030-77189-8_5

5.1 The Origin of Thoughts on Foreign Trade Before Ming

Forbidding the foreign trade at the official level does not mean scholars not discussing the topic. Not ignoring its ancient source tracing, the thoughts regarding opening overseas trade in Ming China was closely related to the commercial development at that time and the situation of international trade in China's surrounding areas (the reality and the shock brought by external forces [e.g. the arrival of European merchants] and the formation of the regional market), and it was therefore, at least to some extent, different from the traditional foreign trade thinking before the Mongolian's rule (such as *Guanzi*, Sang Hongyang, Han Yu, etc.).

In ancient China, 'oversea trade in relation to the land mass of the interior was of minor significance. Moreover, for centuries China had renounced seapower, the indispensable basis of export trade. Finally, for the sake of preserving tradition, China, as is well known, had confined foreign contact to a single port, namely Canton, and to a small number of licensed firms, specifically thirteen'.[1] Smith also noticed that 'neither the ancient Egyptians nor the Chinese encouraged foreign commerce'.[2] With such 'non-emphasis' on foreign trade, accordingly, thoughts on foreign trade were very scarce before Ming China. However, in these limited thoughts, we can still glimpse the origin of Ming Dynasty's foreign trade thoughts.

In the pre-Qin period, the author of Guanzi and Xunzi were the ones talking about foreign trade, and they both encouraged foreign trade. First of all, the author of Guanzi, like Confucians, advocated that the 'frontier pass only inspects and does not tax' the goods.[3] Further, the author of Guanzi saw the frontier pass as the 'gateway to foreign wealth',[4] which was beneficial for state finance. So, he generously gave special treatment to foreign merchants. For example, he put forward that once a guest house for foreign merchants is set up, 'if only one passenger comes, we will provide him meals; if two passengers come, we will also provide the horse

[1] Weber (1951 [1915], p. 16).

[2] Smith (1979 [1776], p. 35).

[3] Hu (1998 [1965], Vol. 1, pp. 349–350).

[4] Hu (1998 [1965], Vol. 1, p. 350).

food; and if three passengers come, we will even provide the servants food'.[5] But there was no such treatment for domestic merchants.

Xunzi also advocated actively developing foreign trade, and expressed the viewpoint of 'from the interests of the state' more clearly.[6] 'Turn the four seas into one family, no matter how remote the country is, we hope to trade with them in order to increase our fiscal interests. For remote countries, we keep actively trading with them. And for neighbouring countries, we will not hide our professional talents'.[7] So, what were the specific benefits for the state if foreign trade was actively expanded? He believed that actively developing foreign trade could obtain many rare goods that could not otherwise be produced domestically, which may increase the material enjoyment of each class in the country: 'the people of integrity and ability in the upper class can thus have more decorative items, while the commoners at the bottom can also live in peace'.[8] 'The prohibition on foreign trade reflected the impact of the notion of "*ren*" (humanity or humaneness), one of the core propositions in Confucian ideology'.[9]

Legalists, such as Shang Yang, adopted a negative attitude towards commerce, so their thoughts on international trade were naturally negative. Shang Yang used the relationship between gold and corn to explain his related thoughts. He believed that gold and corn were mutually exclusive. 'If the country obtains one or two taels of gold, then 12 *dan*[10] of corn will flow out of the country; and if the country exports one or two taels of gold from abroad, the country will see an increase of 12 *dan* of corn'.[11] The country's main source of wealth was corn, so if the state allowed gold to flow in and corn to flow out of the country, there would soon be a lack of corn in the country. 'Even if there is gold, there is no place to use it'.[12] Thus, 'filled with useless gold and having a shortage of corn leads to empty warehouses and empty government vaults'. On the

[5] Hu (1998 [1965], Vol. 1, p. 350).

[6] Hu (1998 [1965], Vol. 1, pp. 438–440).

[7] Hu (1998 [1965], Vol. 1, p. 440).

[8] Hu (1998 [1965], Vol. 1, p. 441).

[9] Li (2010, p. 24).

[10] *Dan* is a measure in ancient China. 1 *dan* approximately equals to 30 kg.

[11] Hu (1998 [1965], Vol. 1, p. 390).

[12] Hu (1998 [1965], Vol. 1, p. 390).

other hand, when gold flowed out and corn flowed in, 'gold and corn are both abundant, and warehouses and government treasuries will be full'.[13]

After China unified and established the imperial system, the thoughts on foreign trade were even more based on state interests. In the Western Han dynasty, the view of attaching importance to and advocating for the development of foreign trade was very prominent in Sang Hongyang's thoughts. Sang Hongyang believed that the development of foreign trade could mainly achieve two purposes.[14] The first was to try to control foreign countries through foreign trade by using *Guanzi*'s *qingzhong* theory.[15] The second was to exchange the surplus of domestic goods for the scarce domestic goods through foreign trade, to achieve the purpose of 'no profit leakage to the outside' and the 'richness of state expenditure'.[16] Of course, Sang's thinking on foreign trade did not consider equality and mutual benefits with foreign countries, but purely aimed at increasing the domestic wealth. Therefore, he believed that foreign trade was also completely a state action, and there was no mention at all of the role that private merchants could play in it.

Very rare thoughts were put forward from Western Han to Song regarding foreign trade. Han Yu,[17] who was among the very rare thinkers talking about foreign trade, only mentioned that obtaining plenty of exotic goods like 'jewellery, essence, ivory, and rhino horn' could be a very good thing.[18]

When it came to the Mongolian's rule (Yuan China), Lu Shirong put forward some thoughts regarding foreign trade. Regarding the land trade in the Northwest, he did not begin specific discussions. As for the sea trade along the southeast coastline, he advocated for the implementation of a state monopoly on foreign trade. The specific method was to establish an official department in Quanzhou and Hangzhou, China's largest ports

[13] Hu (1998 [1965], Vol. 1, p. 390).

[14] Hu (1998 [1965], Vol. 2, p. 81).

[15] Hu (1998 [1965], Vol. 2, p. 81).

[16] Hu (1998 [1965], Vol. 2, p. 81).

[17] Han Yu (768–824) was a Chinese prose writer, poet, and government official in Tang China.

[18] Hu (1998 [1965], Vol. 2, p. 458).

at that time, and the state even monopolized the building of all sea trade-related ships and tools.[19] Only merchants who obtained official ships and funds can engage in maritime trade.[20] In this way, the government can strictly prohibit private trade. Lu believed that once a private maritime merchant was found, the state 'first detains all the treasures collected by the merchant, and the government buys them; if there is anything hidden, the state can confiscate all the merchant's hidden goods, half of which is awarded to the whistle-blower'.[21] In his thought, not only was the role of merchants in foreign trade not mentioned, the private merchants were also considered to be the object of strict restrictions and inspections. These ideas were undoubtedly later inherited by the thinkers who supported the sea ban in Ming China.

5.2 Trade Barriers: Supporting the Sea Ban

5.2.1 Ancestral Law Must Not Be Violated

When it came to Ming China, the first argument of the thinkers who supported the sea embargo was that opening up overseas trade violated the 'ancestor's law' and shook the foundation of rule. The Ming dynasty's sea embargo idea, which greatly influenced Chinese merchants' participation in the world market, originated from Emperor Hongwu. Emperor Hongwu formally announced in the fourth year after his ascension (1371) that 'people living along the coastline must not go out to sea in private',[22] prohibiting people from all forms of contact with overseas countries (trade was surely included), and even restricting some official tributes from vassal states.[23] The tone of the sea ban in the Ming dynasty had since been determined. Although Emperor Yongle, the son of Emperor Hongwu, repeatedly sent Zheng He to carry out official trade and promote national

[19] Hu (1998 [1965], Vol. 3, pp. 257–259).

[20] Wu (2004, p. 550).

[21] Hu (1998 [1965], Vol. 3, p. 257).

[22] Xie (1962 [1411], p. 1364).

[23] Xie (1962 [1411], p. 1364).

authority.[24] He still banned private merchants from doing business overseas, and 'still regarded profit from trade as shameful'.[25] He reiterated the ban on seas issued by Emperor Hongwu at the beginning of his reign. Since then, several of the ensuing emperors had adhered to the ancestral system and enforced the sea ban.

This attitude of the emperors also received the support of many scholars and thinkers. In their attitudes towards foreign trade, the thought of preventing contact with foreign countries and piracy can be revealed. The scholars, such as Feng Zhang,[26] used the ancestor's 'legislation' all the time to severely condemn private merchants for 'going to sea to do business and communicate with foreign countries'.[27] They also reminded emperors who were more open-minded about overseas trade that 'The holy king of the ancients must cultivate his character and not pay attention to foreign goods'.[28] It is quite understandable, since overall, 'any politician who proposed that the state encouraged trade as a source of revenue risked attack on the grounds that he was subverting very ancient and deeply ingrained notions about the ordering of society'.[29]

Even in Ming society, the benevolence of Confucianism served as the role similar to the theoretical foundation of the constitution. Scholars across the country should first, as Confucian school taught, suppress individual desires and not emphasize individual rights. In a broader sense, once they were lucky enough to be placed in an official position or even in a prominent position, they could not emphasize the privileges of their region and department. For example, in our case here, the provinces along the southeast coast (Fujian, Guangdong, etc.) could have benefited from overseas trade. However, due to the need to take into account the overall situation of the whole state, the political balance of the country was maintained without insisting on such special economic benefits. Only under this premise of public interest was it possible for the central government to manage the country uniformly, without having to consider the special needs of each region, department, or individual, although this was a simple and crude approach.

[24] Shen (2009, p. 188).

[25] Li (2010, p. 7).

[26] Feng Zhang was a scholar serving as a local official near the coastline.

[27] Chen (1962 [1638], Vol. 280, p. 2965).

[28] Chen (1962 [1638], Vol. 280, p. 2745).

[29] Clunas (1991, p. 142).

5.2.2 *Comparative Disadvantage: Little Supplement to State Revenue*

Some thinkers believed that opening up overseas trade would not bring profits into the country's tax revenue and would not benefit people's lives as well. It counted for only a very small percentage of overall state revenue.

Feng Zhang believed that the goods exchanged in China's overseas trade were not only for the use of the country and the people, but due to the impact of smuggling trade, 'it cannot add a penny to the country's finances'[30]:

> The foreign traders come and bring only products like pepper and Biancaea sappan, which were not widely used by our people. The large number of these products to be sold will inevitably lead to low prices. Then, after two or three years, the merchants will not make a profit. Thus, it is bound to extinguish this trend by itself. Although the overseas trade seems to gain its legitimacy in the name of taxation, in fact, no tax can be levied by the state at all as expected.[31] (my transl.)

Feng also said that 'some sly merchants sold domestic raw silk, cotton silk, satin cloth, magnets and other valuable goods to foreign countries, but no goods were exchanged from abroad except gold and silver. After returning home, they burned their ships and then fled to other places. How can the state levy taxes in this way?'[32] In addition, he cited historical experience and argued for himself:

> I checked the old rules of the previous dynasty, such as the late Southern Song dynasty, which levied taxes on overseas trade as well. However, the goods that came at the time were ivory and spices, which were also entirely useless, and had no effect on the commoners then. The people of the Yuan dynasty lived extravagantly, and eventually fell victim to the scourge of Japanese pirates. But we are different from the Yuan dynasty. It has been peaceful for two hundred years in our country. We should plan a stable

[30] Chen (1962 [1638], Vol. 280, p. 2965).

[31] Yan (1993 [1574], Vol. 8, pp. 283–284).

[32] Chen (1962 [1638], Vol. 280, p. 2966).

plan that will benefit our children and grandchildren. Don't be greedy for a small profit.[33] (my transl.)

With this regard, Quesnay[34] had some similar assertion, saying that 'even the profits of the merchants in foreign trade damage the people of a country, because they increase the prices of the commodities imported'.[35] His thought can surely get support among some Ming thinkers.

5.2.3 *Overseas Trade: Culprit of Pirate Harassment*

Some thinkers believed that the openness of overseas trade led to emptiness in coastal defence, and according to them the culprit of harassment were Japanese pirates. First, trade led to the collusion of internal and external, which would have caused chaos. Gui Youguang[36] said that 'For those who do not belong to any registration, they will violate the imperial court order, disregard the prohibition of going out to sea privately, and seduce foreigners, which will cause a hundred years of disaster'.[37]

Second, the overseas trade led to the infidelity of a coastal defence force. Feng Zhang believed that the soldiers who were in charge of coastal defence were 'thinking about a hundred strategies to escape their duties'.[38] In particular, after seeing some people along the border go out to sea and have some fixed travel routes, they were even more negligent and lax, and their weapons and equipment wore down by the years without repair and were not trimmed. Once there was some real rebellions along the border, these coastal defence forces wouldn't have the ability to stop it at all. If the ancestral system was abolished, it would be difficult to restore once it was destroyed. Once the border was compromised by a foreign country because of opening the sea, it would have been impossible to block the border again. Feng also said,

[33] Chen (1962 [1638], Vol. 280, p. 2966).

[34] François Quesnay (1694–1774) was a well-known French economist of the Physiocrats. Quesnay once served as the consulting physician to King Louis XV at Versailles. In his lifetime he was also known as the 'European Confucius'.

[35] Vaggi (1987, p. 67).

[36] Gui Youguang (1507–1571) was a famous Chinese writer of Ming Dynasty, and once served as the *Sicheng* (certain official position) in Nanjing.

[37] Chen (1962 [1638], Vol. 283, p. 3108).

[38] Chen (1962 [1638], Vol. 280, p. 2965).

> Today, if the state is greedy for the small benefit of the overseas tax, once the policy is really implemented, it means that there are no restrictions on overseas trade any more. Foreigners are cunning, fierce and unpredictable. If they really disturb the border and exacerbate the situation, it will be totally contrary to the original intention of the ancestors to arrange the army at the border and to ban the sea to protect border security. Therefore, the ban on maritime affairs is very important.[39] (my transl.)

Third, the overseas trade caused gunpowder to flow into Japan for Japanese pirates. Feng said that 'If the sea embargo is lifted today, gunpowder will also be traded openly. We will get useless things from Japan, while the Japanese will get gunpowder from us that are useful to them. This is equivalent to helping Japan enhance their military strength!'

On the other hand, some thinkers thought that the opening up of overseas trade had led to the deterioration of the social atmosphere, and the coastal merchants were the culprits. Feng Zhang believed that 'a merchant who trades with foreign countries must be a robber who has drifted at sea for many years. He doesn't value life and meanwhile despises official law'.[40]

Wang Yu[41] had a very detailed description of domestic 'criminals' collusion with illegal foreign forces. This may be the 'facts' that many Ming thinkers who supported the prohibition of overseas trade agreed with:

> Recently, there have been more and more crafty people in Zhangzhou and Quanzhou relying on colluding with the powerful local clan, constructing large double-mast vessels without permission, brazenly carrying prohibited weapons, buying strange goods, and colluding with pirates. Meanwhile, Portugal and other foreign countries fiercely entered into the port. They pretended to talk about trade, and slaughtered and plundered after landing. And when they went back to sea, they continued to plunder merchants and wealth. Thus, not only was the national body harmed, but the endless troubles in the future is beyond words.[42] (my transl.)

[39] Chen (1962 [1638], Vol. 280, p. 2967).

[40] Chen (1962 [1638], Vol. 280, p. 2967).

[41] Wang Yu (1507–1560) once served as a military governor in Jiliao region.

[42] Chen (1962 [1638], Vol. 283, p. 2993).

5.2.4 *Continentalist Orientation*

The Emperor Jiajing's sea closure was 'usually attributed to a Chinese continentalist orientation based on a deep-seated aversion to foreign contact and a failure to appreciate the benefits of maritime contact in the South Seas. The Chinese, as the explanation goes, have always been culturally oriented to the continent'.[43] For well over a millennium, China had oscillated between an emphasis on continental and on maritime strategy. The early Ming dynasty, by contrast, focused heavily on the sea, before recalling its ambitious exploration and trading fleets in the mid-fifteenth century.[44] Why was that? The answer can be seen from both political and economic perspectives.

Politically speaking, first of all, the maritime embargo policy that was initiated by Emperor Hongwu maintained its legitimacy based on the Japanese pirates' invasion mainly in the South, the residual anti-Ming forces appeared at the end of the Yuan dynasty, and the collusion between pirate groups and foreign invaders, etc. Perhaps the Japanese pirates' (who were merchants as well) invasion was true, but the collusion between the pirate smuggling group and foreign invaders was most likely the Ming government's own imagination. But no matter what the facts were, Ming China always considered itself to be the core of the whole world.[45] Thus, the collusion with those subordinate foreign countries, or being harassed by boorish countries like Japan, was something unacceptable. Other threats such as resource depletion and concern over land-based threats from northern continental barbarians also damaged the image of the empire. Thus, it was always the number one goal for the Ming court to formulate policies and maintain the security of its rule. However, in the middle of the Ming dynasty, the main contradiction within the Ming dynasty was *dangzheng* (party struggles), which directly or indirectly made the court incapable of effectively solving the border issues and made it difficult for the court to implement an active outward policy.[46] This surely exacerbated the inclination towards a continentalist orientation.

For economic reasons, although Ming China's domestic commerce had further developed compared to Song and Yuan, as far as the overall level

[43] Brook (1999, p. 29).

[44] Calder (2012, pp. 24–25).

[45] Li (2010, p. 150).

[46] Li (1995, p. 145).

of economic development in the country at that time, it was still self-sufficient and the peasant economy continued to dominate Ming China. The commerce still mainly played the role of adjusting the surplus among small producers and regions. Commerce and handicrafts only developed in some regions, especially in the southeast coastal area. And the so-called 'capitalist buds'[47] (if it did exist, since it has no fixed conclusion yet in academia) were only sparse in these places.

Moreover, as a large country with complete economic sectors and a large internal market, the products that Ming China needed could basically be met domestically, and its dependence on external commodity imports was limited. Moreover, even the goods exported to foreign countries, such as raw silk, tea, porcelain, etc., had a wide domestic market as well. This meant that China could have survived without an overseas market. Thus, no matter how important the impact of overseas trade on some regions, some production sectors, and the population connected to it at that time, the impact of overseas trade on the overall national economy and the vast majority of the population was still extremely weak. In Ming China, the demand for overseas trade at that time stemmed mainly from the coastal provinces with overseas trade traditions. The whole country, however, had not yet generated a strong demand for overseas trade, which surely also contributed to the deepening of continentalist orientation.[48] A vivid example of this is that Lin Xiyuan, 'arrived to serve as magistrate of Qinzhou'[49] in 1536, 'stated explicitly that Dai Viet should be conquered and annexed as an administrative unit of the Ming',[50] and he got negative feedback from his colleagues 'who claimed that distant Dai Viet lacked any significance and that its subjugation would only burden the Ming'.[51]

Because of this, during the Ming dynasty, whenever a policy debate on whether to impose a sea embargo occurred in the court, most of the thoughts against a sea embargo came only from officials who worked in or originated from the coastal provinces. Moreover, at the time, objections to the ban on the sea were mainly focused on the livelihood of

47 Balazs (1967, p. 31).

48 Li (1995, p. 148).

49 Baldanza (2016, p. 115).

50 Baldanza (2016, p. 118).

51 Baldanza (2016, p. 118).

coastal residents, social stability, and court taxation, and rarely understood the role of overseas trade for the sake of country development like Western mercantilism. Thus, when the Ming ruler faced different choices and weighed the pros and cons in decision-making, political security and national stability were often given priority consideration, and this consideration was reflected in the thoughts against overseas trade, such as 'little supplement to state revenue' and 'overseas trade leading to pirate harassment'.

5.3 Free Trade: Against the Sea Ban

Proponents of opening overseas trade first demonstrated that overseas trade policies could not adhere to the rules set by their ancestors and needed to be tailored to the times, which would help to improve the situation of maritime merchants along the coastline. Tang Shu[52] emphasized the importance of overseas trade by speaking a bit of irony regarding Emperor Hongwu's proscribed sea embargo ancestor system: 'Now the senior court officials, such as Zhao Wenhua,[53] Nie Bao,[54] all put forward similar proposals to fight against the sea ban. However, at the beginning of our dynasty, the senior officials of the court presented memorials to the throne discussing the *wokou* (Japanese pirates), which was in line with the idea of the Emperor Hongwu, who wanted to abolish overseas trade. If he lives to this day, he may have to change the rules he himself set'.[55]

5.3.1 The State and the Commoners: Sharing the Same Interests

Some thinkers believed that opening up overseas trade is an important economic source for coastal people. Both the state and commoners could gain interests from overseas trading. It was exactly the opposite thought of the sea ban-supporting group, which asserted that the state can gain little or even no benefit from foreign trade.

[52] Tang Shu was a *Zhushi* (an official position) in Ministry of Justice.

[53] Zhao Wenhua (?–1557) was a Cixi (the coastline region in Zhejiang) local, and once served as the Minister of Works.

[54] Nie Bao (1487–1563) once served as Governor of Huating (part of current Shanghai) and Minister of Military.

[55] Chen (1962 [1638], Vol. 270, p. 2850).

Chen Zizhen[56] put forward the significance of 'taking foreign trade as a mission' to the national economy and people's livelihood. He mentioned that 'Fujian has a small amount of arable land while densely populated. Therefore, the people along the border and sea all consider boats as their homes, the sea as their fields, and selling goods as their livelihoods'.[57] In this situation, commerce and trade can have the effect of stabilizing people. Moreover, he believed that the sea embargo is completely unnecessary. He believed that, 'for commercial ships from the East and West, we should continue to pass the market as usual, while, for Japan, we still strictly restrict and carefully inspect its cargo. Once items such as nitrate are found, they must be detained immediately and punished.... And for Western merchant ships, we can first learn about their movements, which help us detect the situation for reference'.[58] Similarly, Xu Fuyuan[59] said,

> The farmland in the remote part of Fujian is eroded by seawater, so most of the farmland is barren, and only a very small number can be cultivated. Therefore, the people's livelihoods lie in shipping and trade, and local taxes are also dependent on these. In the past, the sea ban was severe, and led to chaos among people. Fortunately, Haicheng County was later established and trade was allowed. For decades, it has served the people's wellness and security. Recently, because pirates and trespassers have invaded border defences in succession, the related provinces all banned merchants from conducting foreign trade again. The merchants, more than a hundred ships and hundreds of millions of goods involved are all affected. The merchants' living is blocked, and they are to wait passively for their demise. Thus, we must not ban the overseas trade due to the harassment of the pirates, just like 'we must not completely ban shoes because someone has no feet.'[60] (my transl.)

[56] Chen Zizhen once served as the highest governor in Fujian.

[57] Wen (1962 [1630], Vol. 262, p. 4865).

[58] Wen (1962 [1630], Vol. 262, p. 4865).

[59] Xu Fuyuan (1600–1665) was a famous poet in late Ming.

[60] Chen (1962 [1638], Vol. 400, p. 4332).

Zhou Qiyuan[61] said more clearly about the important role of overseas trade taxation in state finances that,

> After Emperor Longqing abolished the ban on foreign trade, merchants from all countries came from the water. They bring many kinds of goods from foreign countries that are difficult to describe, and we do not need to worry that the money involved in trade will be annually less than several millions of taels. In this way, the country and the people can rely on this money, and more money can enter the emperor's vault as well.[62] Moreover, tariffs levied from overseas trade increased fiscal revenue, which was 'enough for the royal family' and the 'supply of soldiers' provisions' as well. The tariffs levied from overseas trade were thus 'an important part of making the country have adequate state expenditure.'[63] (my transl.)

In comparison, Xu Xueju[64] held similar thoughts while paying attention to more specific cases. Haicheng, a county that belongs to Fujian province, prospered rapidly after officially becoming the only legal foreign trade port on the southeast coast of Ming China. Xu Xueju elaborated the importance of tariffs imposed by overseas trade on the finance of Haicheng County's local government in his work *The First Report of Dutch People*:

> Although Haicheng is only a tiny place, due to its unique geographical location, checkpoints for taxing merchant ships should be established. If the merchant ships are going to dock in Penghu, then within two thousand miles away from Xiaoliuqiu in the east, all the brisk small merchant ships can proceed with their goods. Then where lies our court's deterrent force to them? The merchant ships coming from the Western Ocean and the small merchant ships off the coast of China are all desperado, carrying all prohibited things like knives, iron and nitre. And they are not afraid to sell anything. Even if allowing them to do business overseas, we still need to tax them! But if we don't set up checkpoints in Haicheng, how can they be taxed? This is a great matter concerning the fate of our country![65] (my transl.)

[61] Zhou Qiyuan (1571–1626) was a Haicheng local, and was one of the representative figures of Donglin School.

[62] Zhou (1987 [1626], p. 206).

[63] Zhou (1987 [1626], p. 206).

[64] Xu Xueju once served as the highest governor of Fujian.

[65] Chen (1962 [1638], Vol. 400, p. 4333).

Lin Fu,[66] the vice minister of war during the Jiajing period, proposed another foreign trade method of increasing national income: restoring tributary trade. In the eighth year of Jiajing (1529), Lin Fu cited 'Instructions of the Ancestor of the August Ming' and 'Collected Statutes of the Ming Dynasty' (hereinafter referred to as 'the two references'), and asked the court to expel the *folangji* (private Portuguese merchants),[67] and resumed the tributary trade with the vassal states mentioned in the two references. In this way, the Guangdong government could levy taxes to suffice, the commoners could sell the goods to profit, and thus both the country and private merchants could benefit from the tributary trade.

To be more specific, Lin Fu listed four advantages that the tributary trade would bring. First, overseas vassals going to Guangdong for tributary trade would definitely bring some 'private goods'. In addition to the tribute goods, the Ming dynasty could draw taxes from 'private goods' to increase the state's fiscal revenue. Secondly, regarding the taxes mentioned above, in addition to the part sent to Beijing, the rest of the money could be left at military garrisons in the border defence of the two southeast regions. Third, the goods from the vassal states could be used as provision for conquering the barbarians, thereby reducing the burden on the people. Fourth, the people can resell the goods of the vassal states to make a profit.[68]

5.3.2 *Qiu Jun and He Qiaoyuan: First Attempts to Abolish Sea Ban*

In order to solve the series of problems caused by the sea embargo, some scholars in Ming China first proposed strategies for restoring the management of overseas trade systems by the *shibosi* (Department of Shipping) during the Song and Yuan dynasties.[69] This was an earlier attempt to break the sea embargo at the ideological level, and demanded that the sea embargo be abolished to allow civilians to trade overseas. Qiu Jun was generally considered as the first one to hold this thought in Ming China, which marked the emergence of the ideological trend of abolishing the

[66] Lin Fu (?–1540) once served as the governor of Liangguang region.

[67] Please refer to Chou and Edward (1974, p. 133).

[68] Yan (1993 [1574], pp. 712–714).

[69] Qiu (1986 [1487], p. 345).

sea ban in the Ming dynasty. It was more than a century before Emperor Longqing officially opened the sea in 1567.

Qiu Jun not only advocated to not interfere in 'people's free trade with each other' domestically, but also paid particular attention to the development of overseas trade, and argued that the state should 'encourage persons living along the coast to apply to the local Bureau of Overseas Affairs if they were willing to take up the business'.[70] This kind of thinking was quite valuable in the mid-Ming dynasty, when the sea embargo was still severe. In his *Daxue Yanyi Bu*, Qiu Jun's overseas trade thoughts can be summarized as follows, after he 'studied the records of transportation of tribute during the Yuan Dynasty'.[71]

First, he believed that the state should make full use of the country's abundant products and export more goods for the benefit of the state. He thought that the products made from 'vast land and vast resources' were needed by foreign countries and thus could surely be profitable by exporting, while 'the government did not make any money at all from the tributary trade'.[72] With such high profits, 'the losses incurred in sea transportation were much less than those incurred in canal transportation'[73] and the 'sea ban' should not be implemented. Since severe penalties had been repeatedly ineffective, why not simply let merchants engage in overseas trade, which was good for both state and commoners.

Second, merchants could benefit from engaging in overseas trade, and the state could collect taxes from it, which could increase the country's fiscal revenue without disturbing its own people. He believed that this kind of 'foreign aid' was 'counted out of the normal tax each year',[74] and was enough to outweigh the various miscellaneous taxes seized by the government in the previous dynasties. If the state could encourage overseas trade, this was really much smarter than the 'excessive exploitation of people'.[75] Zhou Qiyuan (1571–1626) also expressed very similar thoughts in his work.[76]

[70] Hu (1988, p. 453).

[71] Hu (1984, p. 90).

[72] Li (2010, p. 7).

[73] Hu (1984, p. 90).

[74] Qiu (1986 [1487], pp. 345–346).

[75] Qiu (1986 [1487], p. 346).

[76] Zhou (1987 [1626], p. 208).

Third, Qiu Jun used history as a reference and believed that opening up overseas trade had not caused borderline disasters. He pointed out that,

> Regulations with foreign trade have been in place since the Han dynasty, and have been implemented throughout almost all of the previous dynasties. Some people are worried about causing trouble along the coast, and I have verified it in the history books of previous dynasties. For most foreign countries on the sea, there has been no record of invading our borders since ancient times, and countries like Siam and Java have even been blocked by the tempestuous sea from us, with no land connection. Only the treacherous people from Japan have repeatedly plundered our country's coasts. We should follow the ancestral teachings and not trade with Japan.[77] (my transl.)

Therefore, Qiu believed that it was necessary to treat different countries differently and not to sever overseas trade with other countries because of Japan. However, Qiu also pointed out that although the state should encourage merchants to engage in overseas trade, it must also strictly manage private foreign trade. Qiu believed that those who were engaged in overseas trade activities, although the vessels were allowed to be built by themselves, as mentioned above, they still needed to report to the Department of Shipping the number and tonnage of maritime trade vessels, the type and quantity of trade goods, and the countries they planned to visit. Also, the administration must ensure that they did not bring prohibited goods for export. Imported goods were subject to inspection and taxation by the Department of Shipping. In this way, the private overseas trade would not be out of control and wouldn't even damage the interests of the court.[78]

During the Song and Yuan dynasties, China's overseas trade had clearly developed. Not only could the court obtain certain economic benefits from overseas trade, and increase fiscal revenue; the private overseas trade had also opened a way for the people along the southeast coast to become rich. In the Ming dynasty, despite the imperial maritime ban policy of the imperial court, the people along the southeast coast still disregarded the ban to travel to Southeast Asia to seek a living and made

[77] Qiu (1986 [1487], p. 346).

[78] Qiu (1986 [1487], pp. 346–347).

an indelible contribution to the development of Southeast Asia. Some had even become local leaders with a huge impact (to be discussed in detail in the next section). This situation reached a crucial stage of overseas commerce development by the middle of the Ming dynasty. The decision of advocating or forbidding overseas trade would determine whether Ming China would progress or retrogress at sea. Qiu Jun's thoughts on overseas trade were of great significance. Although they were not adopted by the court at that time, it undoubtedly had a profound impact on thoughts on trade during the late Ming dynasty.

The financial crisis of the Ming dynasty since the middle and late period of Wanli was a very important and difficult problem facing the court of the Ming dynasty. He Qiaoyuan[79] had a deep understanding of the financial crisis in the late Ming dynasty. He shared the unanimous refusal to obtain financial revenue by 'adding taxation' and 'selling official positions' and supported cracking down on the sale of private salt, just like his colleagues at the court. However, in addition, as a Quanzhou local, for the people's livelihood along the coast and the increase in the court's fiscal revenue, in the early years of Emperor Chongzhen, he memorialized to the emperor, asking for abolishing the sea ban. Most of his economic thoughts were reflected in his memorial to the throne titled *Pleading for Opening the Sea*.[80]

The first part of the memorial focused on why opening the sea could 'make the country stable and make the people rich'.[81] The argument was similar to Tang's and Xu's thoughts, which I shall not go further into detail here. The middle part of the memorial mainly expounded on the 'benefit of opening up the sea' and dispelled the court's anxiety about *Hongmaofan*[82] (Dutch merchants). In his view, opening the sea was not only beneficial to the people's livelihood and merchant's profits, but also to the imperial court's access to commercial tax revenue from overseas trade to increase state use.

First of all, he affirmed the feasibility of conducting overseas trade. He said that although the merchant ships had to bear the risk of being robbed by sea pirates, the merchant ships could actually 'go with each

[79] He Qiaoyuan (1558–1632) once served as the Deputy Minister of Works.

[80] He (2015 [1631], p. 683).

[81] He (2015 [1631], p. 683).

[82] He (2015 [1631], p. 683).

other' and '[carry] firearms with them'[83] to prevent pirates from robbing them, and they had a certain ability to protect themselves. In addition, if the embargo policy was abolished, the armies along the coastline could protect the safety of the merchants.

Regarding the benefit of opening the sea, He Qiaoyuan believed that, first, opening the sea could enable the court to collect the profits of maritime trade. After the Dutch occupied Taiwan, coastal people and merchants came to Taiwan to trade with the Dutch, and the Portuguese also often traded in the Keelung and Danshui areas. Although the Ming dynasty banned overseas trade, it was actually difficult to ban the coastal merchants from trading privately, which led to the situation that 'the government can't get a single penny from it, while the profits all went to these treacherous people'.[84] Therefore, He Qiaoyuan believed that instead of 'benefiting these treacherous people', it was better to raise the sea ban and make 'both up (the state) and down (the commoners) gain'. It can be seen that He Qiaoyuan believed that the imperial ban on the court was mainly for the purpose of 'benefiting the state's fiscal revenue'.[85]

Next, he said that foreign trade could meet the purpose of 'letting people gain' (thus stabilizing people). If the court 'allowed maritime merchants to legally trade from east to west', it would undoubtedly provide a huge overseas market for the 'production of domestic silk, porcelain and other handicraft products' in the Ming dynasty.[86] In this way, the abrogation of the sea embargo was not only beneficial to the people in the coastal areas, such as Fujian, Zhejiang, and Southern Zhili, but even inland people could earn a living because of overseas trade. At that time, the thought had started to appear that 'both commerce and industry can be considered as roots just like agriculture'.[87] He Qiaoyuan himself also said that 'anyone who wants to make money today should engage in commerce. If the country can earn more tax revenue from overseas trade, then it can feed more people nationwide'. He Qiaoyuan

[83] He (2015 [1631], p. 683).

[84] He (2015 [1631], p. 684).

[85] He (2015 [1631], p. 684).

[86] He (2015 [1631], p. 687).

[87] He (2015 [1631], p. 675).

even believed that merchants and other commoners along the coast could 'carry their skills and go to Lüsong[88] for a living'.[89]

He Qiaoyuan maintained that keeping the sea ban would close 'the hole of inflow profits'.[90] Since the state had to spend a lot of money at the time, raising the sea ban was the state's best chance to increase its financial resources. Moreover, He Qiaoyuan said that after Zheng Zhilong,[91] a famous merchant (and pirate), accepted amnesty and pledged loyalty to the Ming ruler, he 'worked diligently for the court'[92] to maintain the safety of the coastline and the court should therefore distribute pay to him. How should money be raised? He Qiaoyuan advocated for the restoration of the tax system initiated in Emperor Longqing era to manage overseas trade, and provided Zheng Zhilong with the collected taxation.

5.3.3 *Pirates Became Merchants Once Trading Was Allowed*

Some thinkers believed that only by opening up overseas trade could a stable social order be maintained. To be more vivid, the most frequently used words were, quote, 'Pirates become merchants when trade is smooth, and merchants become pirates when trade is banned'.[93] This view may find its parallel in the West. As Sombart mentioned, 'in France the word *armateur* means a shipper as well as a pirate'.[94] It may suggest that the role of shipper and pirate can be swapped under different circumstances. In this way, only without wasting food and military supplies could the hidden dangers at sea be quelled by themselves. It was a tit-for-tat view of the sea ban supporters, who believed many coastal merchants and other commoners had 'secret communication with foreign people', and it had greatly influenced Ming China's thoughts and policies on overseas trade.

[88] Lüsong was then (and also today) the largest island in current Philippines.

[89] He (2015 [1631], p. 687).

[90] He (2015 [1631], p. 687).

[91] Zheng Zhilong (1604–1661), baptised as Nicholas Iquan Gaspard, was a merchant, pirate, and military leader.

[92] He (2015 [1631], p. 675).

[93] Chen (1962 [1638], Vol. 270, p. 2850).

[94] Sombart (1967 [1915], p. 72).

Tang Shu believed that the immediate cause of 'pirate infestation' during Emperor Jiajing's reign was the strict sea embargo policy implemented by the government:

> The legislation allows the government's tributary actions and prohibits private merchants from going to sea. However, since such a system of tributes exists, there will inevitably be foreign goods coming and the market opportunities that follow, so it is impossible to completely ban the overseas trade activities of private merchants.[95] (my transl.)

> It is commonplace that merchants along the coast see foreign trade as a relatively convenient way of earning a living. However, since the sixth year of the Jiajing period, local officials obeyed the central government's order to prohibit private merchants from going to sea. Commercial routes were closed, so merchants lost their means of livelihood and were forced to turn into pirates.[96] (my transl.)

On the basis of Tang Shu's thoughts, Xu Fuyuan put forward and clarified the theory that 'pirates become merchants when trade is smooth, and merchants become pirates when trade is banned'. He said,

> The Longxi and Haicheng counties under Fujian are coastal counties. Most of the land is barren land that cannot be cultivated. Most of the local people rely on maritime markets. In the early years, the central government worried that they would seduce hostile forces from overseas and the overseas trade was once banned. Local people go to sea to make a living. There is no means left for the people, and they can only gradually produce evil schemes. So they incited riots and caused disasters. In the Emperor Longqing years, the local governor abolished the ban and allowed merchants to trade at sea. And all kinds of goods from the East and the West were allowed to be sold, while only Japanese pirates have always been jeopardized by the Chinese government and are thus still banned to trade with. For more than two decades, the people's livelihoods have been comforted, and the court has collected more than twenty thousand taels per year. The military provisions in the Zhangnan area are rich due to the money flowing in from overseas trade. However, in recent years, the central government has again issued a ban on overseas trade, and people are quite worried about it.[97] (my transl.)

95 Chen (1962 [1638], Vol. 270, p. 2850).

96 Li (2010, p. 17).

97 Chen (1962 [1638], Vol. 400, p. 4332).

According to the state of affairs he witnessed while at his official post, Xu believed that there were four true hidden dangers in the local area. These four problems were as follows: (1) The fierce men will definitely ignore the sea bans of the court, and will inevitably communicate with foreign merchants. Then the central government will inevitably send troops to hunt them down. When these powerful men are forced to flee, they will gather the members of their gangs and flee to the sea, ultimately becoming dangerous forces that threaten the tranquility of the border; (2) The merchants who remain in Lüsong are far more than just thousands of people. Once the trade is no longer smooth and the ships are not moving, these merchants have no livelihood, and how can it be ensured that they will not seduce outside hostile forces and become pirates; (3) When the sea embargo comes out, not only merchant ships dare not go out to sea, but also other official ships, such as ships coming to convey the emperor's order or official sentries ships don't dare to go to sea either. Suppose that the barbaric states around them are really hatching unlawful plots, (if the sentry ships don't go to the sea to inquire about this news), then we will really be in great danger; (4) As soon as the sea ban comes out, it will lead to a lack of military supplies for the coastal border defence forces, and it will thus inevitably impose harsh taxes on the people instead. The people will become poor and their wealth will be exhausted, and it will be difficult to predict the situation afterwards.[98]

Therefore, Xu very subtly elaborated on the relationship between merchants and pirates: although the sea embargo banned trespassers, it also blocked the ordinary people's 'living opportunities',[99] and hidden dangers were thus born. From the perspective of maintaining the stability of the country, Xu believed that it was necessary to abolish the sea ban and allow private traders to participate in overseas trade.

Lin Fu also analysed the possibility of 'foreign invasion of China's borders and becoming a scourge',[100] and concluded that the vassal states such as Siam and Java, which had been included in the two references and which had been in the tributary trade with Ming China for many years, should not dare to become pirates. However, Foreign merchants such as Portuguese who were engaging in private commerce should be

[98] Chen (1962 [1638], Vol. 400, pp. 4332–4334).

[99] Chen (1962 [1638], Vol. 400, p. 4334).

[100] Fei (1962 [1525], Vol. 149, p. 2911).

expelled in general, and the inspections of Fujian and Guangdong's officers and soldiers should be strengthened. Meanwhile, Chinese and foreign merchants were forbidden from engaging in secret communication, and commoners were strictly forbidden from flowing out of the country. In the end, he believed that it would benefit the country and private merchants and bring the vassal states under control through conciliation as a result of the resumption of tributary trade.[101]

5.3.4 *The Thoughts of Xu Guangqi*

As a final supplement to the thoughts regarding foreign trade in Ming China, Xu Guangqi's relevant ideas are worth mentioning. As mentioned in Chapter 1, he first came into contact with advanced Western technology, became friends with Matteo Ricci,[102] and lived in Shanghai, part of the most commercialized area at that time, i.e. Jiangnan region. He served as the vice grand secretary during the early Emperor Chongzhen period and was a famous scientist as well. His friendship with Ricci is not a mere coincidence; as a member of the Yangming School, his pre-determined chequered endeavour in imperial exams (although he obtained the *jinshi* title at last) may contribute a lot to 'his striking sceptical and critical attitude'.[103]

Equally evident is his 'practical application'[104] attitude (in Chinese, *jingshi zhiyong*), which can be exemplified by his contribution to the thoughts regarding resisting pirates, especially Japanese pirates. Japan and China had constant economic and cultural exchanges before the Yuan dynasty, and exchanges between the two parties were conducted in a peaceful manner. After the Mongolians conquered Japan, however, the exchanges between China and Japan were greatly affected. After the establishment of the Ming dynasty, Japanese pirates repeatedly harassed the coastal areas of Ming China. For this reason, the Ming dynasty established a military defence system along the coast to prevent pirates, especially 'Japanese pirates'.[105] The relationship between the Ming dynasty and

[101] Fei (1962 [1525], Vol. 149, pp. 2911–2912).

[102] Shen (2009, p. 235).

[103] Sun (2009, p. 136).

[104] Sun (2009, p. 138).

[105] Xu (1984 [1633], p. 37).

Japan had been poor due to robberies in the coastal areas of the Ming dynasty. The Ming dynasty regarded Japan as an important external problem. How to resist pirates was an important part of the Ming dynasty's foreign strategy.

In the late Wanli period, Xu Guangqi, as the later cabinet (i.e. Grand Secretariat)'s second assistant, put forward a very creative idea of resisting pirates: allowing Japan and the Ming dynasty to mutually tribute trade, which was aimed at resisting pirates.[106] In Xu Guangqi's opinion, Japan had a huge dependence on Ming China's goods, which could only be obtained through the development of trade with Ming China.[107] During the Emperor Hongwu and Emperor Yongle periods, although Japan joined the Ming tribute system, the Ming dynasty set restrictions such as the tribute period, the number of ships, and the number of people for the Japanese tribute. Therefore, Japan could not obtain enough goods through the tribute trade. And the private merchants in Japan and Ming China developed a 'private market'.[108] However, after Zhu Zhi strictly enforced the maritime embargo, the 'private market' was hit by the government, and the merchants turned into pirates. Xu Guangqi believed that 'the state should eliminate pirates, not merchants, and it should prohibit the official market, not the private market'.[109]

Regarding this, Malthus once commented that 'with other laws and institutions, and if foreign commerce were had in honour, she [China] might still be much richer'.[110] Further, he pointed out that 'it is evident that if trade and foreign commerce were held in great honour in China; from the plenty of labourers, and the cheapness of labour, she might work up manufactures for foreign sale to an immense amount'.[111] Malthus believed that foreign trade is unlikely to surpass agriculture to be the supporting industry of China, 'an immense capital could not be employed in China in preparing manufactures for foreign trade, without taking off

[106] Xu (1984 [1633], p. 37).

[107] Xu (1984 [1633], pp. 39–40).

[108] Xu (1984 [1633], p. 40).

[109] Xu (1984 [1633], p. 47).

[110] Malthus (1966 [1798], p. 322).

[111] Malthus (1966 [1798], p. 322).

so many labourers from agriculture, ... and in some degree to diminish the produce of the country'.[112]

Finally, the above thought is also related with Malthus' most famous 'population theory', believing that population growth will always tend to outrun the food supply. He did some maths as well, 'throughout all the northern colonies, the population was found to double itself in 25 years'.[113] Interestingly, Xu Guangqi also did some similar work, making him, perhaps, the only economic thinker who comment on the population numerically, stating that 'the population doubles every thirty years approximately'.[114] It may be considered as a real coincidence.

5.4 Limited Outlook on Foreign Trade: State Defender

It can be seen that economic thinkers in the Ming dynasty only treated foreign trade as a special problem in some coastal areas, and did not consider it from the perspective of the overall national economy; it still considered agriculture to be the 'root' and foreign trade only served as a supplement to people's lives where coastal geographical conditions were not suitable for agriculture. Therefore, the thoughts regarding foreign trade still belonged to the category of traditional Chinese economic thought.

In Ming China, especially during the later period, a rise in the thought of supporting overseas trade was not only a challenge to traditional overseas trade policies, but also a fundamental challenge to ancient Chinese traditional concepts. Thinkers who supported trade openness had developed the idea of passively preventing piracy and foreign invasion since the opening of the ban into the idea of using trade openness to strengthen coastal order and promote national defence construction.

In particular, from the perspective of 'making profit is human nature', the thinkers affirmed the importance of overseas trade to the economic development of the country and the people, reflecting the impulse of merchants seeking overseas markets. However, in discussing the relationship between trade openness and the state economy, thinkers still mainly

[112] Malthus (1966 [1798], p. 324).

[113] Malthus (1966 [1798], p. 105).

[114] Hu (1998 [1965], Vol. 3, p. 426).

focused on the increase of state fiscal revenue. The use of foreign trade to develop the coastal economy, open up overseas markets, and make up for shortfalls through trade were considered to be one of the important means of increasing national fiscal revenue. Therefore, unfortunately, the starting point of their thinking was still not from the perspective of merchants.

Nonetheless, the thought of opening overseas trade that appeared in the middle and late Ming dynasty, although not vigorously promoted nationwide by the ruling class as a guiding principle, was closely linked with the rapid development of commerce in the middle and late Ming dynasty and the contemporary Age of Discovery in Europe 'led by explorers such as Vasco da Gama, Christopher Columbus and Ferdinand Magellan'[115] and the formation of the world market.

Although the rulers of the middle and late Ming dynasty still stubbornly adhered to the economic policy based on agriculture and only treated overseas trade as a special problem in some coastal areas, the idea of overseas trade in the middle and late Ming dynasty broke through to a certain extent in ancient China.

The idea of 'taxation of agriculture as the main source of national finance' saw the important role of foreign trade in the finance of Zhejiang, Fujian, Guangdong, and other coastal provinces, and played a driving role in finally making Ming China abandon the sea ban policy. It can be said that the idea of opening overseas trade in the middle and late Ming dynasty was closely related to the commercial development at that time and the situation of international trade in China's surrounding areas, and it was significantly different from the traditional foreign trade thinking before the Mongolian's rule (such as *Guanzi*, Sang Hongyang, Han Yu, mentioned earlier, etc.).

5.5 The Maritime Merchants' Role and Status in Ming China

As Richard Wilhelm stated in his *Chinesische Wirtschaftspsychologie*, 'In all the high periods of Chinese power, not only domestic but also foreign trade played a large part'[116] (my transl.). This statement was

[115] Shen (1996, Vol. 3, pp. 55–56).

[116] Wilhelm (1930, p. 70).

confirmed in the Ming dynasty, especially in the middle and late Ming dynasty. Although the Ming dynasty's relatively unfavourable foreign trade thoughts negatively affected China's private maritime merchants and set up many obstacles to their development, China's private merchants were still seeking development in the cracks, and had played a very active role in global trade, especially in trade in Southeast Asia.

In this section, I split the timeline into three, respectively 1368–1500, 1500–1567 and 1567–1644. 1500 was the partition of fifteenth and sixteenth century, while 1567 was the year when Emperor Longqing officially abolished the sea ban policy.

5.5.1 Merchants in Early Ming Foreign Trade: 1368–1500

As mentioned above, in 1374 Emperor Hongwu put forward the policy of *Haijin* (sea ban), prohibited private merchants from engaging in overseas trade, although some trade was allowed under a highly regulated system of tributary relations with foreign rulers. The ban on private maritime trade would last until the late sixteenth century.[117]

Thus, under the strict sea embargo policy, Ming China 'retreat[ed] from direct trade in the region',[118] and tributary trade became the only legal trade channel prior to the sixteenth century. In order to break this situation, the merchants first realized that they must be careful in finding a breakthrough deadlock under the maritime embargo policy of the Ming dynasty in order to continuously strengthen their power. Before the sixteenth century, they chose to rely on the framework of the tributary trading system to find opportunities for survival and development, which I call 'flexible penetration' of the tributary system. The merchants chose to use the favourable conditions in this system as much as possible instead of transforming or resisting the system.

Specifically, first, they tried to make use of the conflict between the central and local governments of the Ming dynasty and 'cooperate with' the local government. Although the sea ban policy was more stringent, the interests of the local government and the Ming central government were often inconsistent. As Prof. Deng pointed out, 'economic interests provided Chinese maritime activities with a lasting impetus,

[117] Von Glahn (2016, p. 287).

[118] Kaur and Isa (2020, p. 28).

and the private sector, obviously market-driven, played an irreplaceable role regardless of the pro- or anti-maritime merchant positions of the establishment'.[119] As long as local income could be increased, local governments were still willing to petition the central government to abolish the sea ban policy. This situation provided favourable conditions for the penetration of Chinese merchants. By bribing merchants, the local government offices often turned a blind eye to merchants trading overseas. There were countless records like this in the 1470s and 1480s.[120] Even some local officials and soldiers along the coast themselves would also take advantage of their power to engage in overseas trade.

Second, private merchants sometimes served as ambassadors and coordinators in the tributary trade. Unlike previous Tang and Song China, 'the effect on the Southeast Asia trade was not automatic because of repeated prohibitions on overseas trade by Ming rulers'.[121] However, due to the huge profits from engaging in trade between China and Southeast Asia and the 'not uniformly effective'[122] nature of sea ban policy, some merchants endeavoured to promote tributary trade and were willing to serve as members of tributary missions for the purpose of entering Southeast Asia through tributary trade channels to obtain exotic goods.[123] It was a circuitous way for them to engage in commerce. Thus, the infiltration of merchants made the tributary trade system serve the interests of merchants to a certain extent.

Some other merchants played fair and followed the envoys and engaged in private trade activities. According to the long-established system of the Ming dynasty, envoys were allowed to recruit merchants and private ships that were familiar with the ocean before going to sea. There was also a case in which merchants and ambassadors conspired to conduct commercial activities together[124].

In addition, some Chinese merchants who had gone abroad actively acted as envoys or ambassadors to come to China with the foreign mission in order to seek out trade opportunities. Although the Ming court may

119 Deng (1997, p. xix).

120 Liu (1962 [1491], Vol. 259, p. 4376).

121 Reid (1993, p. 12).

122 Reid (1993, p. 12).

123 Liu (1962 [1491], Vol. 97, p. 1850).

124 Zhang (1974 [1739], Vol. 325, p. 8418).

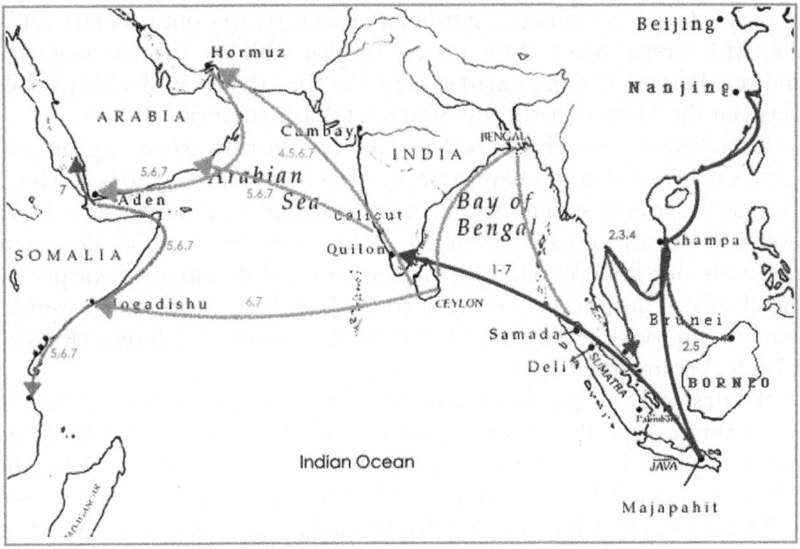

Fig. 5.1 A concise illustration of voyages led by Zheng He (1405–1431) (*Source* Routes depicted by the author. I consulted some original records and at least ten versions of maps in both English and Chinese. All of them show different routes. I tried my best to make my version as accurate as possible, to give my readers a general picture. The numbers in the illustration stand for the sequence. There were seven voyages in total, chronologically 1405–1407, 1407–1409, 1409–1411, 1412–1415, 1416–1419, 1421–1422, 1430–1431)

not fully agree with the Chinese serving as ambassadors of other countries, it usually did not make enquiries. Generally speaking, there were two types of Chinese merchants in Southeast Asia participating in the tributary trade system. The first type was the merchant who drifted overseas in the event of a shipwreck and later became a foreign envoy. The other type included Chinese merchants who 'had been living in Southeast Asia for a long time'.[125] For instance, some of them 'lived there since the era when Zheng He voyaged across the ocean' (see Fig. 5.1).[126] They tried

[125] Li (1962 [1509], p. 2277).

[126] Yang (1962 [1424], p. 1876).

to persuade and encourage the tributary states to carry out tributary activities with China. Most of them were familiar with the Chinese language and regulations, as well as market laws.[127] They thus played a bridge role between the Ming dynasty and Southeast Asian countries.

However, the merchants had to take certain risks when engaging in such activities and could have been arrested if not careful enough. Moreover, as the tribute system became more stringent, the number of tributes overseas was also greatly restricted. Relying on this method alone was obviously not good enough for the survival and development of private merchants. Thus, some of them tried their best to develop overseas markets without the backing of the tribute system, and *liuqiu* (Ryukyu Islands) became their priority.

'Pirates raids on the east coast caused the founder to ban all foreign merchants except Ryukyu and some South Asian ones'.[128] The Ming dynasty initiated contact with the Ryukyu Islands in 1372.[129] After the tributary relationship was established between the two sides, Ryukyu and China began a highly profitable tributary trade. However, since 'the cost of the imperial voyages together with the lavish treatment given to foreign envoys bearing tribute put a serious strain on China's economy',[130] the official tribute trade was called to an end by the Ming court in 1433. Ryukyu encouraged the original Fujian merchants who resided then in Ryukyu to trade with Fujian local merchants.[131] The boom took place from the 1430s to the early sixteenth century, and Chinese merchants in Ryukyu played a key role in the region's trade network. For instance, during the period of 1358–1487, the amount of Chinese porcelain, considered as 'complementary products',[132] exported overseas dropped sharply and was replaced by ceramic products from Vietnam, Thailand, and other places in Southeast Asia.[133] In this way, during the severe sea embargo period, porcelain that was shipped out

[127] Zhang (1974 [1739], Vol. 324, p. 8400).

[128] Chou and Edward (1974, p. 132).

[129] Chen (1986, Vol. 4, p. 2113).

[130] Kaur and Isa (2020, p. 30).

[131] Chen (1986, Vol. 4, p. 2115).

[132] Hengstmengel (2019, p. 77).

[133] Liu (2012, p. 85).

to Southeast Asia, which was even further 'flowed through' 'the difficult gateway to the Red Sea',[134] often required Chinese merchants to live in Ryukyu to do the work. And after the rise of Melaka, 'one of the key nodes in Asian maritime trade linked to China and eastern Indonesia',[135] since the 1410s, Chinese merchants in Ryukyu also maintained important trade relations with them. 'Melaka's rise to become the most important kingdom in the Straits of Melaka was linked to the support given by the Ming emperors'.[136] In this way, a trade circle centred on Ryukyu and connecting China, Japan, and Southeast Asia was formed. Chinese merchants not only played an important role in it, but also found an external channel for the sustainable development of trade via Ryukyu.

During the period from the establishment of the Ming dynasty to the end of the sixteenth century, the biggest crisis for the private maritime merchants was that the Ming court deliberately suppressed the power of private trade, which in turn made this factor gradually become the largest unstable factor within the regional trading system. Although private merchants adopted a flexible and penetrating approach to the tributary trade system, and the form of the Ryukyu trade network continued to promote the development of the trade network between China and Southeast Asia, this also lacked the support from the central government. On the contrary, the Ming court took increasingly severe measures to suppress this trade behaviour. Smuggling trade was thus beginning to take a new form. From the era of Emperor Chenghua,[137] the smuggling trade had gradually grown. In the 1550s, merchants such as Yan Qisheng conducted overseas trade activities along the coast of Guangdong. Due to the strong suppression of the Ming government, this new commercial force that did not comply with the tributary trade had a small volume, but it had developed to a certain extent. The scale of private overseas trade during this period was relatively small, and most of them were scattered. This situation would change in the next century.

[134] Braudel (1972, p. 550).

[135] Subrahmanyam (2012, p. 15).

[136] Kaur and Isa (2020, p. 30).

[137] Emperor Chenghua reigned from 1465 to 1487.

5.5.2 *Merchants in Mid-Ming Foreign Trade: 1500–1567*

From the end of the fifteenth century to the beginning of the sixteenth century, several important merchant groups were active in China and Southeast Asia: Chinese, Arab, Indian, and native Malay merchants. The merchants cooperated and competed with each other, but they basically adopted a peaceful approach. However, with the inflow of European merchants such as those from Portugal, the rules of peaceful trade were broken. As Sombart pointed out, 'Sea-robbery in the old style was, until well into the seventeenth century, a most important branch of the business of these companies'.[138] After Portugal took control of Melaka,[139] relying on its monopoly on Eastern routes, it established various commercial premises and trading posts from Melaka to Macao[140] (Sovereign power over Macao was nevertheless retained in Chinese hands),[141] becoming the most powerful Western commerce empire in the region. In a short time, the Europeans almost eliminated all the local large merchant forces (also their ships). Traditional merchants such as Chinese merchants were impacted to varying degrees.

However, the arrival of European merchants was also of great significance to the development of private Chinese merchants. As Tang pointed out, 'Of course, without the external stimulation from the world market, capitalism could still sprout from China's traditional society. Yet, the process would have undoubtedly been significantly postponed'.[142] First, they promoted closer links between Chinese merchants and China and Southeast Asia. Portugal's blockade of Melaka made China's official maritime forces quickly withdraw from the Indian Ocean region, and China's commercial power was limited to China and the surrounding areas. This, in turn, helped private Chinese merchants concentrate on activities throughout the entire South China Sea region. Second, with the decline of the traditional tributary system, the European merchants enabled Chinese merchants to have the opportunity to participate or even try to establish new trade rules, and 'high silver prices in China created

[138] Sombart (1967 [1915], p. 73).

[139] Clunas (1991, p. 58).

[140] Wen (2001, p. 294).

[141] Chou and Edward (1974, p. 133).

[142] Tang (2017, p. 139).

prodigious profit opportunities for all entrepreneurs participating in the East–West trade'.[143]

After the Portuguese's occupation of Melaka, Portugal tried to start direct trade with China after 'opening of a new sea route to China'.[144] However, since Portugal was not a member of the tributary system of the Ming Empire, and due to its resistance to the tributary system and rules, Portugal was not welcomed by the Ming court at first. Portuguese merchants thus began to keep in touch with private Chinese merchants, especially those along the Guangdong coast, in the form of smuggling trade.

But meanwhile, Portuguese merchants also actively bribed the eunuchs in charge of Guangdong sent by the Ming emperor. Through him, although after many setbacks, Tomé Pires, the head of Portuguese merchants, and his translator Huozhe Yasan[145] finally got the opportunity to meet the emperor in Nanjing (the emperor was then handling the noble rebellion in Nanjing). The emperor who was ruling at that time was just the young Emperor Zhengde; the emperor with the most open mind throughout the Ming dynasty mentioned earlier. According to Portuguese documents and the memoirs of some members of the mission, the Portuguese mission met Emperor Zhengde in May of that year. The emperor treated them with great respect, and even played checkers with Pires many times. In addition, Emperor Zhengde invited them to a banquet. Emperor Zhengde showed a keen interest in Portuguese. This nonconformist emperor even learned some Portuguese with Huozhe Yasan.

However, the preferences of the emperor himself could not change the preferences of the court headed by the government. After Emperor Zhengde passed away in 1521, the succeeding Emperor Jiajing, resumed the hostile policy towards Portuguese merchants and expelled them and

[143] Ma (2016, p. 34).

[144] Menudo (2020, p. 69).

[145] Huozhe Yasan (1473–1521) was a Chinese residing abroad in Melaka. In 1519, Tomé Pires and others (including Huozhe Yasan) arrived in the Ming Dynasty and established a relationship with Jiang Bin (?–1521), the allegedly male-concubine of Emperor Zhengde. Because Huozhe Yasan could speak Portuguese, he became a favorite of Emperor Zhengde. In 1521, Emperor Zhengde suddenly died in his well-known 'leopard house' (*baofang*). Jiang Bin was killed right after, and Huozhe Yasan was quickly put in jail (and died soon after). Some scholars assert that Jiang Bin was plotting to rebel, and Huozhe Yasan was responsible for contacting Portuguese to obtain weapons.

their merchant ships off the coast of Guangdong. Coupled with the gradual decline of trade between Chinese merchants and local merchants in Southeast Asia, smuggling trade between Chinese merchants and Portuguese merchants became the main form of trade within regional trading during this period. With the cooperation of Chinese and foreign merchants like the Portuguese, the smuggling trade system developed into a major form of trade adopted by Chinese merchants abroad.

Compared with straitlaced sea ban, smuggling was like 'the Wild West', becoming more frequent from the end of the fifteenth century, even though the central government repeatedly ordered local governments to strengthen smuggling controls, and merchants were prevented from going abroad. But local governments did not fully follow the central government's logic due to their fiscal needs. For example, Guangdong's local government was trying to legalize the rising smuggling trade. In 1511, Guangdong began to allow foreign ships to come to trade and pay certain taxes.[146]

The flourishing development of smuggling trade gradually led to the formation of *Haishang* (maritime merchant groups), which 'dominated China's exporting business even under the alleged bans of Ming-Qing times'.[147] Some previous studies have tended to regard the forming of these overseas trade groups as being forced by Ming government pressure. This is not the whole picture, though. More importantly, the appearance of these merchant groups was also inseparable from the competition between different merchants, not only between Chinese, but also between foreign merchants and Chinese merchants. The mode of 'trade and cum-plunder' brought by European merchants definitely affected the local merchants.[148] However, after suffering losses, records of Chinese merchants bullying or cheating foreign merchants can often be seen as well. And finally, Chinese merchants were forced to expand their power in the form of further organization.

The emergence of the *Haishang* group illustrated two changes: first, the original smuggling network of horizontal division of labour with multiple parties began to move towards a vertical division of labour, and the position of the *Haishang* group thus rose accordingly. Secondly,

[146] Fei (1962 [1525], Vol. 113, p. 2297).

[147] Deng (1999, p. 9).

[148] Zhang (1962 [1577], Vol. 350, pp. 6326–6327).

the *Haishang* group changed from a peaceful trade method to a form of armed trade, which means that they had the ability to challenge the existing order of the regional trade system under the tributary trade system and build a trade system that was more in line with their own interests.[149]

And the big *Haishang* group was even used by the local government. For example, Wang Zhi, the head of a giant *Haishang* group at the time, established a cooperative relationship with the local government in Zhejiang and was allowed to trade, while officials used Wang Zhi's strength to maintain maritime security. And for Wang Zhi, he could also take advantage of his official power to combat his maritime opponents.[150]

This looks like a win–win situation. However, this trading system had one of the biggest problems: it did not get the consent of the central government. Therefore, the cooperative relationship between the *Haishang* group and the local government was quite fragile, and subject to the response of the central government. For instance, in 1552, Emperor Jiajing dismissed Wang Zhi's local collaborators and reassigned Wang Yu and Yu Dayou, officials who insisted on being tough on maritime merchants, to eliminate the *Haishang* groups[151] such as the one led by Wang Zhi, which 'were eventually defeated by state fores over the period 1557–61'.[152]

Without the acquiescence and support of local governments, this newly established smuggling trade system quickly became unstable. The rupture of this relationship prompted the Chinese and foreign maritime groups to unite and forced them to transform into *daoshang* ('pirate merchants').[153] Most of the pirates during the fourteenth to fifteenth centuries were Japanese, while most of the pirates in the sixteenth century were Chinese. 'In the later period, at least, they were in fact mostly Chinese whose main interest was in the overseas trade which the Ming government had made

[149] Zhang (1974 [1739], Vol. 325, p. 8432).

[150] Zhang (1974 [1739], Vol. 325, p. 8433).

[151] Zhang (1974 [1739], Vol. 205, p. 5405).

[152] Subrahmanyam (2012, p. 20).

[153] Zhang (1962 [1577], Vol. 384, p. 6789).

illegal'.[154] 'The foreign pirates only account for at most one-tenth or two-tenths of them all'.[155]

However, the official annihilation of the *Haishang* groups and 'pirate merchants' did not mean the disappearance of the smuggling trading system. Syndicates of large merchants were suppressed, but the successive smuggling activities were not cut off. Rather, there was a growing trend. From the perspective of local interests, local governments advocated for the opening of the sea ban, which, they believed, could increase local fiscal revenue and, by doing so, eliminate the merchant's rebellion. The powerful forces of smuggling merchants forced local governments to make concessions first, and finally the pressure then spread back to the central government. Since then, proposals for lifting the sea ban continued to increase. And with Emperor Longqing ascending to the throne in 1567, the sea ban was completely abolished.

5.5.3 *Merchants in Late Ming Foreign Trade: 1567–1644*

The opening of the sea in 1567 finally enabled private merchants to gain the right to freely trade overseas. However, the credit for this progress cannot all be given to Emperor Longqing. It can be traced back to Emperor Zhengde, one of his late predecessors. During the sixteen years when Emperor Zhengde ruled Ming China, he reformed the coastal Department of Shipping. He took the first step to entirely lift the sea embargo by tacitly consenting to some private overseas trade along the coast. It expanded the government's tax sources and thus increased state income, although this received strong opposition from the high-level civil servants in the central government.[156]

After the opening of the sea, as the large *Haishang* groups were weakened before, the protagonists who went to sea became scattered merchants, along with merchants engaged in maritime transport. The number of merchants who traded overseas increased significantly.[157] Among them, some were only forced by the pressure to survive, while some others were aiming for profits, especially in coastal areas. For

[154] Elvin (1973, p. 91).

[155] Yan (1993 [1574], Vol. 9, p. 324).

[156] Fei (1962 [1525], Vol. 113, p. 2297).

[157] Li (1995, p. 350).

instance, in Fujian, the trade of Wuyi Mountain black tea began to be prosperous, which remains active until the beginning of twentieth century.[158] At that time, the evaluation of merchants was already based on whether they were engaged in overseas trade, and whether they had the ability to master foreign languages. Accordingly, they were divided into three groups, respectively the 'upper merchants', 'middle merchants', and 'lower merchants'. Those who operated successfully overseas and understood foreign languages were envied and respected by the commoners domestically.

However, when the court felt threatened by foreign 'pirates' again, the sea embargo was again put on the agenda. Like before, this promoted the merchants to form some large maritime merchant groups again. In this second round, the group headed by Zheng Zhilong was most famous. Just like Wang Zhi before, the Zheng group accepted amnesty and pledged loyalty to the local government in Fujian. However, the Ming court could not control them. Zheng kept his private armed forces and still had a great deal of independence. The two parties were more similar to a cooperative relationship than a superior–subordinate relationship. Thus, gradually, the Zheng group began to have an even stronger legally acknowledged armed force, transforming the group into a military-commercial group, 'rather than merely a big pirate group like before'.[159]

This was not good news for scattered maritime merchants. The other maritime merchants who previously competed with these big groups, like the Zheng group, were unable to match Zheng's power at all, so the living environment of scattered merchants also changed accordingly. They were then forced to rely on Zheng's protection to obtain safe trading opportunities. Accordingly, the Zheng group collected protection fees.[160]

As Wilhelm pointed out, 'The European and American trade had penetrated China since the sixteenth century, and from that time on the active element in this trade was no longer the Chinese but the foreign merchant' (my transl.).[161] It was mostly true. However, despite the seemingly immoral behaviour, on the whole, the strength of Chinese maritime

[158] Huang (2019, p. 49).

[159] Liu (2015, pp. 8–9).

[160] Chen (1962 [1638], p. 4333).

[161] Wilhelm (1930, p. 71).

merchants became so powerful that Japanese scholar Matsuura believed that, in modern East Asian trade, especially the silk trade, Chinese merchants and Chinese sea vessels played a leading role, while the Dutch East India Company played a supporting role. And from the beginning of the seventeenth century to the collapse of Ming China in 1644, 'the cross-strait trade dominance changed between the private maritime merchants of the Ming dynasty and the Dutch settlers at different stages'.[162] In fact, Taiwan 'was first settled by the Dutch with the aid of several illicit Chinese merchants'.[163] Matsuura's view can also be confirmed by Chou's work: 'Chinese merchants traded profitably with other parts of the Philippines, Borneo (which also served as a refuge for Chinese pirates), and other parts of the Indonesian archipelago. At that time the power of the Chinese people greatly exceeded that of the Europeans'.[164]

After the abolishment of the sea ban, the large number of Chinese merchants going abroad led to a rapid increase in Chinese merchants and trading diaspora in Southeast Asia. The number of sailing vessels increased from 50 in 1567 to 88 in 1589, and to 137 in 1597.[165] At that time, Southeast Asia also allowed polygamy, and the relatively high status of Chinese merchants who settled in the locality were quite attractive to local Malay women, who were generally willing to marry the Chinese. This deeper integration of Chinese merchants with local ethnic groups promoted the expansion of Chinese merchants' trade and social networks, thus Chinese merchants may play a more essential role in promoting China's regional trade system with Southeast Asia. Although from the Ming court's perspective, these localized merchants were nothing but, as Scott phrased, 'self-barbarianization',[166] the social status of these localized Chinese merchants enjoyed relatively higher status than merchants from China.

To sum up, during the last century of Ming China, the maritime merchants transitioned from a loose informal organization to a more formal organization (either a military-commercial group such as the Zheng group or trading diaspora settled in Southeast Asia). Accordingly,

[162] Matsuura (2016, p. 410).

[163] Chou and Edward (1974, p. 133).

[164] Chou and Edward (1974, pp. 133–134).

[165] Er (1887, pp. 26–27).

[166] Scott (2009, preface X).

they gained a greater voice. Although the thoughts regarding foreign trade in Ming China did follow traditional Chinese economic thinking, emphasizing the state's role in foreign trade, the reality and the shock brought by European countries unavoidably brought private merchants to the forefront of foreign trade, no matter if it coincided with the willingness of the Ming court or not. Accordingly, the thoughts regarding foreign trade and merchants' role in it became more positive and had more supporters among scholars. Even though their main purpose was still to increase state revenues or make people's lives more peaceful, these thoughts and the active role of merchants in reality did reinforce each other, enabling the Ming merchants more or less to show off their strength and importance in regional trade.

References

Reference in German

Wilhelm, R. (1930). *Chinesische Wirtschaftspsychologie.* Deutsche Wissenschaftliche Buchhandlung.

Reference in English

Balazs, E. (1967). *Chinese civilization and bureaucracy: Variations on a theme.* Yale University Press.

Baldanza, K. (2016). *Ming China and Vietnam negotiating borders in early modern Asia.* Cambridge University Press.

Braudel, F. (1972). *The Mediterranean and the Mediterranean world in the Age of Philip II, Volume I. Translation from the French by Sian Reynolds.* Harper & Row.

Brook, T. (1999). *The confusions of pleasure: Commerce and culture in Ming China.* University of California Press.

Calder, K. (2012). *The new continentalism: Energy and twenty-first-century Eurasian geopolitics.* Yale University Press.

Chou, C., & Edward, H. K. (1974). *An economic history of China.* Center for East Asian Studies, Western Washington University.

Clunas, C. (1991). *Superfluous things: Material culture and social status in early modern China.* Polity Press.

Deng, K. G. (1997). *Chinese maritime activities and socioeconomic development, c. 2100 BC–1900 AD.* Greenwood Publishing Group.

Deng, K. G. (1999). *The premodern Chinese economy: Structural equilibrium and capitalist sterility.* Routledge.

Elvin, M. (1973). *The pattern of the Chinese past*. Stanford University Press.
Hengstmengel, J. (2019). *Divine providence in early modern economic thought*. Routledge.
Hu, J. (1984). *Chinese economic thought before the seventeenth century*. Foreign Language Press.
Hu, J. (1988). *A concise history of Chinese economic thought*. Foreign Languages Press.
Kaur, M., & Isa, M. (2020). *Between the Bay of Bengal and the Java Sea: Trade routes, ancient ports and cultural commonalities in Southeast Asia*. Marshall Cavendish.
Li, K. (2010). *The Ming maritime trade policy in transition, 1368 to 1567*. Harrassowitz Verlag.
Ma, D. (2016). *Textiles in the Pacific, 1500–1900*. Routledge.
Malthus, T. R. (1966 [1798]). *First essay on population 1798*. Palgrave Macmillan.
Menudo, J. M. (2020). *The economic thought of Sir James Steuart: First economist of the Scottish enlightenment*. Routledge.
Reid, A. (1993). *Southeast Asia in the age of commerce 1450–1680* (Vol. 2). Princeton University Press.
Scott, J. C. (2009). *The Art of not being governed: An anarchist history of upland Southeast Asia*. Yale University Press.
Shen, F. (2009). *Cultural flow between China and outside world throughout history*. Foreign Language Press.
Smith, A. (1979 [1776]). *The wealth of nations: An inquiry into the nature and causes of the wealth of nations*. Clarendon Press.
Sombart, W. (1967 [1915]). *The quintessence of capitalism: A study of the history and psychology of the modern business man* (M. Epstein, Trans. and Ed.). Howard Fertig.
Subrahmanyam, S. (2012). *The Portuguese empire in Asia 1500–1700: A political and economic history* (2nd ed.). Wiley-Blackwell.
Vaggi, G. (1987). *The economics of François Quesnay*. Palgrave Macmillan.
Von Glahn, R. (2004). *The sinister way: The devine and the demonic in Chinese religious culture*. University of California Press.
Weber, M. (1951 [1915]). *The religion of China: Confucianism and Taoism*. Free Press.

Reference in Chinese

Chen, X. (1986). *Huangming Shifa Lu*. Taiwan Student Press.
Chen, Z. (1962 [1638]). *Compile of memorials to the emperor in the Ming Dynasty (Ming jingshi wenbian)*. Zhonghua Publishing House.
Er, E. (1887). *Zhupi Yuzhi*. Dianshi Zhai.

Fei, H. (1962 [1525]). *Ming Shilu, record of Emperor Zhengde*. Institute of History and Language.

He, Q. (2015 [1631]). *The collected work of Jingshan (Jingshan Quanji)*. Fukien Renmin Press.

Hu, J. (1998 [1965]). *History of Chinese economic thoughts* (Vol. 1–3). Shanghai University of Finance and Economics Presss.

Huang, H. (2019). *Tea village livelihood: The space and social changes of a tea village in Fujian Province*. Guangming Daily Press.

Li, D. (1962 [1509]). *Ming Shilu, record of Emperor Hongzhi*. Institute of History and Language.

Li, J. (1995). *The history of overseas trade in ancient China*. Guangxi Renmin Press.

Liu, J. (1962 [1491]). *Ming Shilu, record of Emperor Chenghua*. Institute of History and Language.

Liu, M. (2012). The export of porcelain under the sea ban policy in early Ming China. *Archaeological Studies, 4*, 84–91.

Liu, Q. (2015). *The maritime merchant empire: The official-merchant relations and the origin of the Zheng group*. Zhejiang University Press.

Matsuura, A. (2016). *The research on overseas trade in Qing China*. Tianjin Renmin Press.

Qiu, J. (1986 [1487]). *Daxue Yanyi Bu*. Taiwan Commercial Press.

Shen, M. (1996). *History (Lishi)* (Vols. 1 and 3). Shanghai Education Press.

Sun, S. (2009). *Matteo Ricci and Xu Guangqi*. China International Broadcasting Press.

Tang, L. (2017). *Merchants and society in modern China: Rise of merchant groups*. London: Routledge.

Wen, P. (2001). *The Western history*. Baihua Wenyi Press.

Wen, T. (1962 [1630]). *Ming Shilu, record of Emperor Wanli*. Institute of History and Language.

Wu, H. (2004). *Chinese commerce history*. The Finance and Economics Press.

Xie, J. (1962 [1411]). *Ming Shilu, record of Emperor Hongwu*. Institute of History and Language.

Xu, G. (1984 [1633]). *Xu Guangqi Ji*. Shanghai Ancient Books Publishing House.

Yan, C. (1993 [1574]. *Shuyu Zhouzi Lu*. Peking: Zhonghua Publishing House.

Yang, S. (1962 [1424]). *Ming Shilu, record of Emperor Yongle*. Institute of History and Language.

Zhang, R. (1962 [1577]). *Ming Shilu, record of Emperor Jiajing*. Institute of History and Language.

Zhang, T. (1974 [1739]). *The history of Ming*. Institute of History and Language.
Zhou, Q. (1987 [1626]). *The research on Eastern and Western Trade (Dongxiyang Kao)*. Shanghai Ancient Books Publishing House.

CHAPTER 6

Consumption: Two Pairs of Thought Involving Merchants

The above three chapters discuss the status of merchants and their relationship with the state, respectively regarding state monopoly, commercial taxation, and foreign trade. This chapter and Chapter 7 will then focus on the relative position of merchants among the four occupations from the perspective of economic thought.

Regarding the theory of four occupations proposed by *Guanzi*, no matter whether some scholars thought that the merchants were juxtaposed with the other three occupations, or that some other scholars believed that the merchants stay at the end, the fact is that after Qin unified China, the status of merchants has always been regarded very low. We must then be curious about whether, under the rapid development of commerce in Ming China, the status of merchants improved or they continued to be despised by society. We shall examine this by starting with the debate over two core issues in ancient Chinese economic thought: righteousness vs. profits, and thrift vs. luxury.

T. Hua, *Merchants, Market and Monarchy*,
Palgrave Studies in the History of Economic Thought,
https://doi.org/10.1007/978-3-030-77189-8_6

6.1 The Debates Over Righteousness and Profits

6.1.1 Qiu Jun and Thought Before His Age

As one of the most prominent economic thinkers in Ming China, Qiu Jun, in his *Daxue Yanyi bu*, expounded on righteousness and profits of the monarch, state, and commoners. From this, we can find out more about Qiu Jun's view on the relationship between righteousness and profits and the corresponding merchants' existence. Qiu Jun believed that seeking profits was the natural instinct of man and the need for social survival, especially for merchants.[1] However, Qiu Jun criticized merchants, for 'they often just [saw] profits but not righteousness',[2] and 'profits should be put below righteousness but above scourge'.[3] Qiu still emphasized that, when the state and merchants sought 'profits', they should use 'righteousness' as the criterion.[4] The most ideal state, in his opinion, was that under the principle of 'righteousness', the monarch, the state, and the merchants 'obtain[ed] their own benefits respectively and [did] not invade each other'.[5]

Qiu Jun's thoughts were quite consistent with, and can be traced back to, mainstream thinkers before Ming. The debate about righteousness and profits was one of the core propositions in the Confucian ideological system, and it was also a pair of very important objects for analysis in the history of ancient Chinese economic thought, which often extended to another pair of concepts: gentleman and villain. Since Confucius, Confucian culture had put morality above wealth and commerce. In *The Analects of Confucius*, it stated that 'The mind of the superior man [was] conversant with righteousness, while the mind of the mean man [was] conversant with gain'.[6] It was a representative assertion showing the opposition of the scholars against making profits, which was considered to be the antithesis of behaving as a righteous man. Nevertheless, Confucius himself did not despise merchants. He affirmed that 'the physical desires were uncontrolled... the merchant transported goods which were difficult

[1] Qiu (1986 [1487], p. 522).

[2] Qiu (1986 [1487], p. 530).

[3] Qiu (1986 [1487], p. 530).

[4] Qiu (1986 [1487], p. 532).

[5] Qiu (1986 [1487], p. 547).

[6] Hu (1998 [1965], Vol. 1, p. 86).

to obtain for the getting of money'.[7] Zigong, one of his favourite pupils, 'engaged in business instead of being an official, and he can forecast the market correctly every time',[8] and Confucius spoke highly of this.

Mencius, Dong Zhongshu, and even Confucians in Tang and Song generally inherited Confucius' thoughts on righteousness and profits. Mencius went one step further than Confucius' 'profits should be rarely talked about', advocating for 'why should we talk about profits?'[9] He said that 'When the chickens call[ed] in the morning, those who [rose] up and [did] good deeds [were] disciples of Shun[10] (the second of the three ancient sage kings), while those who pursued benefits [were] disciples of Zhi'.[11] This complete opposition between 'profits' and 'kindness' showed that Mencius was deeply disgusted by the behaviour of seeking profit.[12] However, Mencius also believed that economic conditions had a role in determining people's thinking. He said that people must have enough food to eat first before they can speak about courtesies.[13] In other words, Mencius actually acknowledged that people's moral values should be based on economic interests. On this basis, Mencius had a deep understanding of the functions of commerce, the exchange of commodities, and the necessity of the existence of merchants than previous thinkers (including Confucius).

Xunzi, although belonging to the Confucian School, believed that everyone, no matter gentleman or villain, had two tendencies, respectively righteousness and profits. But as a Confucian, Xunzi still advocated for 'using the good side (righteousness) to make rules to curb the evil side (profits)'.[14] Thus, he did not yet have any idea close to the emphasis of both righteousness and profits. However, while Confucius and Mencius acknowledged that people had the desire to pursue wealth but regarded desire as a negative thing, Xunzi took a positive attitude

[7] Chen (1911, p. 173).

[8] Hu (1998 [1965], Vol. 1, p. 90).

[9] Hu (1998 [1965], Vol. 1, p. 231).

[10] Shun was the second of the three ancient Sage Kings (Yao, Shun, and Yu).

[11] Zhi was a famous gangster in period of Spring and Autumn.

[12] Hu (1998 [1965], Vol. 1, p. 231).

[13] Hu (1998 [1965], Vol. 1, p. 230).

[14] Hu (1998 [1965], Vol. 1, pp. 418–419).

towards desire.[15] After affirming desire, the next step for Xunzi was to consider how to satisfy desire, and he claimed that 'circulating goods' can 'enable people in all walks of life to get what others produce[d] and what they need[ed]'.[16] The merchants were thus indispensable. However, Xunzi believed that although merchants belong to the necessary division of society, the number of merchants should be limited to some extent.[17]

During the Western Han dynasty, Dong Zhongshu, a well-reputed Confucian, particularly encouraged avoiding discussing financial gains and completely transformed the idea of 'righteousness' into an ethical dogma.[18] Starting from the 'Human beings [were] an integral part of nature', Dong Zhongshu regarded righteousness and profits as the two major elements in life.[19] In the choice between righteousness and profits, he stated categorically that 'Morality and utilitarianism cannot coexist, and nobles must seek righteousness and abandon profits'.[20]

At the famous debate over salt and iron, Sang Hongyang and Confucian scholars also had different views on righteousness and profits. The literati believed that Sang's policy of the state competing with the people for benefits not only caused poverty and displacement of the commoners, but also more importantly created a bad social atmosphere in society that 'people tend[ed] to pursue fame and fortune and [lost] their morality',[21] which corrupted folk customs and, in turn, caused everyone to not observe etiquette. The literati thus firmly believed that righteousness was the foundation of the country.[22]

On the contrary, Sang Hongyang believed that if the country did not pursue material gains, it would be impossible to realize the prosperity of the country. If only righteousness was pursed, the governors at the court would like 'armchair strategists',[23] which would not help solve the real issues relating to the state's destiny. It is obvious that Sang

[15] Hu (1998 [1965], Vol. 1, p. 419).

[16] Hu (1998 [1965], Vol. 1, pp. 438–439).

[17] Hu (1998 [1965], Vol. 1, p. 439).

[18] Hu (1998 [1965], Vol. 2, p. 36).

[19] Hu (1998 [1965], Vol. 2, p. 38).

[20] Hu (1998 [1965], Vol. 2, p. 39).

[21] Hu (1998 [1965], Vol. 2, p. 110).

[22] Hu (1998 [1965], Vol. 2, p. 111).

[23] Hu (1998 [1965], Vol. 2, p. 80).

Hongyang's thinking on righteousness and profits was completely based on the standpoint of national income, and he said nothing about the individuals pursuing interests. Therefore, we dare to assert that, at the level of individuals, Sang Hongyang was, just like other Confucian scholars, still an advocate of 'righteousness before benefit'. The reason is obvious: only under the premise that ordinary people followed this point, merchants would not 'compete with the country for profit', thus ensuring that the state was 'profitable' and had stable fiscal revenue.

When it came to the Song dynasty, the argument about righteousness and profits was heated up. The philosophers of neo-Confucianism, which were then mainstream, had pushed the theory of putting righteousness in opposition to benefit to a new high level. For example, Cheng Hao proposed that 'righteousness and profits [were] mutually exclusive' and were 'utterly incompatible like water and fire'.[24] Zhu Xi, the great master after Confucius, made a new definition of righteousness: 'righteousness [was] the right thing for heaven'.[25] In Zhu Xi's ideology, heavenly principles and human desires were a pair of opposing concepts, so any factors related to 'profits' should be discarded.[26]

The train of thought laid out above can greatly validate the thoughts of Qiu Jun. However, in Song, there were also some thinkers who had raised their views in 'emphasis on both righteousness and profits'. Representative thinkers were Li Gou (1009–1059), and Ye Shi (1150–1223) of the Southern Song dynasty. Li Gou pointed out that refusing to speak about profits and desires would 'deprive people of their right to live and violate human nature'; 'this [was] why people increasingly dislike[d] Confucianism'.[27] He criticized Mencius' view of 'why should we talk about profits', saying that Mencius's view was too extreme.[28] He made a tit-for-tat claim, asserting that 'righteousness itself [was] a kind of profit'.[29] Ye Shi[30] said, 'the righteousness and profits should be simultaneously

[24] Hu (1998 [1965], Vol. 3, p. 168).

[25] Hu (1998 [1965], Vol. 3, p. 210).

[26] Yu (2004, p. 269).

[27] Hu (1998 [1965], Vol. 3, p. 20).

[28] Hu (1998 [1965], Vol. 3, p. 20).

[29] Hu (1998 [1965], Vol. 3, p. 21).

[30] Ye Shi (1150–1223) was a famous Song scholar and the representative of Yongjia school.

emphasized, with righteousness being prioritized'.[31] As a then essential school, it showed the trend that making profits was no longer considered to be disgraceful behaviour, although righteousness was still to be put in the first place for an upright gentleman. These thoughts can be considered to be a harbinger of the similar or even more advanced thoughts after mid-Ming.

6.1.2 *Wang and His Yangming School*

From mid-Ming, the Yangming School started to become one of the most mainstream ideological schools, which influenced many senior court officials, including Xu Jie, Zhang Juzheng, and many other cabinet ministers, and ordinary people as well. The founder, Wang Yangming was a well-known thinker and philosopher. He was good at commanding war as well, and was among the main contributors to putting down Prince Ningwang's rebellion during Emperor Zhengde's reign. His thoughts derived essence from various schools such as Confucianism, Taoism, Buddhism, and Song-Ming Neo-Confucianism.[32] His ideas even spread to Japan, the Korean Peninsula, and Southeast Asia.

In terms of righteousness and benefit, Wang Yangming still followed the traditional Confucian views, just like other thinkers in Ming who worshiped the views and comments made by Zhu Xi and Lu Jiuyuan, the greatest masters in Neo-Confucian thought. He did not discuss the issue of righteousness and benefit directly, but in the last paragraph of '*Responding to Dongqiao*' in his well-known work *Chuanxi Lu*, he rebuked the traditional views on righteousness and profit.[33] In the Ming dynasty, he was not the one who held the view that 'the righteousness and profit can be combined'. But indeed, he was the first one to clearly encourage equality among different occupations.[34] By conveying this thought, he blatantly defeated the traditional theory of four occupations, which will be elaborated in the next chapter.

It was Wang Yangming's most famous disciples who first proposed the combination of righteousness and profit, including He Xinyin, Yan Jun,

[31] Hu (1998 [1965], Vol. 3, p. 172).

[32] Chang (1962, pp. 51–55).

[33] Wang (1978 [1525], p. 42).

[34] Wang (1978 [1525], p. 92).

and Li Zhi. All of them belonged to the Taizhou school, the left wing of the Yangming School after Wang Yangming's death. The thought of 'maintaining the heavenly principles and eradicating human desires' ruled from Zhu Xi's era all the way to the mid-Ming dynasty when Wang Yangming lived. Although there were a few thinkers during this period, such as Qiu Jun's belief that the motive of 'letting people deal with each other' was the pursuit of profit and wealth, but it was not until Wang Yangming and his disciples that the thought of 'eradicating human desires' was completely eliminated. These representatives of the Taizhou School demonstrated a hypothesis similar to that in Western economics when demonstrating their economic thoughts, that is, man is selfish by nature. For example, He Xinyin, by quoting Confucius and Mencius, contended that 'such human desires as the "desire for music and beauty, flavours and tastes, ease and comfort" must be properly satisfied',[35] thus criticizing the theory of 'eradicating human desires' put forward by Zhu Xi and advocating utilitarianism.[36] Yan Jun, his teacher, believed in the purity of the original nature of man and hence in the spontaneity of action unbridled by conventional morality.[37]

Among them, the thoughts of Li Zhi were the most famous. His published books were said to have reached even women and children in the big cities, as well as in the small villages. Li Zhi emphasized that 'everything in life, industry, and other things in the world' was a 'common good' shared and 'learned, known and spoken together' by people.[38] He further pointed out that 'it [was] completely impossible to say that sages [did] not want to be rich and wealthy', and criticized the traditional dogma of 'avoiding discussing profits'.[39] Some thinkers of the Tang and Song dynasties admitted that the saint might talk about 'good fortune', but that was for the sake of 'people of the world', rather than for their own selfish motive. Li Zhi, however, believed that the saints themselves could also aim for wealth. He stripped the sacred vestments of the sages and put them on the same level of lust as the 'philistine'.[40] Therefore,

[35] Hu (1988, p. 463).

[36] He (1960 [1579], p. 46).

[37] Yan (1996 [1596], p. 134).

[38] Li (2000 [1602], p. 231).

[39] Li (2000 [1602], p. 231).

[40] Li (2000 [1602], p. 232).

he regarded 'loving goods', 'accumulation of gold and jade', 'fondness of purchases of fields and houses', etc. as natural phenomena for the whole population.[41]

Due to the commerce booming during mid-Ming period, Li Zhi's thoughts would inevitably lead to an affirmation of the commodity exchange relationship between private individuals who '[had] both private goods and private selfish desires'. Therefore, he not only specifically encouraged the exchange of goods between merchants and other commoners, but even said that 'every relationship between people in the world [was] a certain relationship of exchange of goods'.[42]

Therefore, based on the above-mentioned ideas, further, Li Zhi had a clear positive attitude towards the profit-seeking nature of merchants. He stated,

> How can merchants be considered vulgar? They carr[ied] tens of thousands of goods, experience[d] the risk of land or sea, withst[ood] the humiliation of bureaucrats, and work[ed] so hard. They even ha[d] to make friends with some high level officials in order to gain income and avoid danger. Thus it [was] not easy for them to gain something.[43] (my transl.)

He rejected the Neo-Confucian view, which stated that man's salvation lied in the elimination of human desire. On the contrary, he felt that it was not immoral to desire wealth, to achieve social status, or to gratify the sexual impulse, and it was natural for men to be selfish.[44] He expressed great sympathy for merchants and found no justification for regarding them as inferior. He explained that merchants had to undertake long and hazardous journeys and to endure humiliation from customs officials and buyers. Their burden was heavy, and their occupation could not be considered to be 'substance' (*moye*).[45]

[41] Li (2000 [1602], p. 234).

[42] Li (2000 [1602], p. 238).

[43] Li (2000 [1602], p. 243).

[44] Li (2000 [1602], p. 243).

[45] Li (2000 [1602], p. 244).

6.1.3 Combining Righteousness and Profit: Han, Li, and Gu

After the sixteenth century, not only in the Yangming School, but also widely among scholars in general, the concept of 'righteousness and profit' underwent subtle changes in the same way as 'rational and desire' and 'public and private'. Here were some other examples: Han Bangqi had some related comments in his work. The main purpose of his argument was to show that the argument of righteousness and profit was not exclusive to scholars, and was applicable to merchants as well.[46] A merchant named Jiao Ge in the Zhou dynasty was taken by him as an example[47] in order to explain that, in the ancient times, the righteousness was not exclusive to the scholar class, and even more so in the Ming dynasty. He claimed that when scholars were 'in the time of recitation, the profit can be seen in it', while when the merchants were 'in the time of trading, the righteousness can be seen in it'.[48] Here, Han Bangqi expanded the social meaning of debate on righteousness and profit, and the merchants who acknowledged that they were 'focusing on interests' were also able to keep themselves in line with the spirit of 'righteousness'. This was obviously a new interpretation of the traditional concept of righteousness and profit.

But this new theory did not start with Han Bangqi, and some scholars earlier than him already held similar opinions. In one of the epitaphs he wrote for some merchants, Li Mengyang asserted the following:

> The merchants and the scholars ha[d] different skills, but they ha[d] the same pursuit of the Tao. Although business-savvy people live in money and goods all day, they also practice[d] noble behaviour. Therefore, although the merchants pursue[d] profit, they [kept] their integrity. Therefore, the (merchants') profit-making behaviour was still constrained by righteousness, and he stick[ed] to his profession like scholars.[49] (my transl.)

[46] Han (1973 [1556], p. 112).

[47] Han (1973 [1556], p. 112).

[48] Han (1973 [1556], p. 113).

[49] Li (1991 [1529], p. 142).

This new view of righteousness and profit did not happen by chance in the sixteenth century, but rather, it continued to develop. In the early seventeenth century, Gu Xiancheng[50] wrote an epitaph for one of the merchants in his own county, Ni Cheng (1530–1604), in which he asserted that

> The righteousness expel[led] the profits, and the profits also expel[led] the righteousness, so the two [were] separated from each other and hostile towards each other. (There was also another case,) righteousness [was] used to support profits, and profit [was] used to support righteousness. The two complement[ed] each other. The ordinary people only [saw] the separation of profits and righteousness, while Ni Cheng [saw] the merger of profits and righteousness. This [was] something that scholars cannot measure.[51]

The significance of the thoughts embodied in Gu Xiancheng's epitaph was that it directly pointed out the difference between the traditional view and the contemporary view of profits and righteousness. The former emphasized the 'separation of profits and righteousness', while the latter emphasized the 'combination of profits and righteousness'. His new thought may be based on the words of his predecessors (for instance, he may have read articles written by Han Bangqi and Li Mengyang), but more importantly, his own life experience. His father, Gu Xue, was a successful merchant. His elder brothers Gu Xingcheng and Gu Zicheng also assisted his father in business. So he grew up in a merchants' family, and he knew the issues of profits and righteousness also existed in the commerce world. Now he blatantly abandoned the old Confucian interpretation of 'separation of righteousness and benefit' and advocated the new theory of 'combination of righteousness and benefit'. We cannot but attach great importance to this important ideological turn.

[50] Gu Xiancheng (1550–1612) was a famous scholar, one of the representatives of the Donglin School, and once served as the Grand Secretary.

[51] Gu (1997 [1612], p. 119).

6.1.4 Human Nature and Profit-Seeking: Huang Zongxi and Gu Yanwu

Huang Zongxi's commerce thought was based on the theory of human nature of 'self-interest', asserting that people's pursuit of interests was in line with human nature. He criticized the autocratic monarchy system only for the monarch himself, not for ordinary people to pursue their own interests.[52] For the monarch to treat the country as his own property, while the ordinary people were not allowed to pursue their own wealth; he saw this as a system that violated human nature. He said that 'not pursuing his own benefits' was not in line with the requirements of human nature. 'Everyone ha[d] his own self, and each ha[d] his own self-interest'.[53] Only in this way can everyone be in harmony with the world.

Based on this, Huang Zongxi made a fierce attack on the traditional notions of despising merchants, emphasizing righteousness and disregarding profits. He believed that the essence of this kind of thought was to deprive the majority of merchants and thus monopolize the interests of the world.[54] The monarch 'left all the best things to himself, while he left the bad things to the merchants, making the merchants of the world predestined to not consider self-interest'.[55]

Bentham's thought is like the 'more fundamental version' of Huang's. At the beginning of his masterpiece *Principles of Morals and Legislation*, he defines principle of utility as 'principle which approves or disapproves of every action whatsoever, according to the tendency which it appears to have to augment or diminish the happiness of the party whose interest is in question'.[56] For the merchants, he believed that 'however strong the empire of fashion and imitation may be, he will not be able to rid himself of that disposition to accumulate which, to a greater or less degree, seems to be inseparable from his mode of life'.[57] In other words, it is natural

[52] Huang (1975 [1695], p. 82).
[53] Huang (1975 [1695], p. 82).
[54] Huang (1975 [1695], p. 83).
[55] Huang (1975 [1695], p. 83).
[56] Bentham (1823 [1780], p. 2).
[57] Stark (2005, p. 82).

for the merchants to 'at all times insist on the best price he can get'[58] or 'add to the mass of their respective capitals',[59] which is exactly what Huang tried to express.

Gu Yanwu believed that ancient rulers since the 'Xia, Shang and Zhou dynasties' all made personal gains for themselves, and used this kind of private gain to achieve the so-called 'righteousness'.[60] This 'righteousness' was just a guise of the monarch, and, in fact, the monarch refused to let people 'make a single day's worth of profit'.[61] Gu said, 'People in the world ha[d] their own families, and it [was] normal for them to pursue a profit. Instead of working with heart and soul in the interests of the people, it [was] better for the monarch to let the people make their own profits. This ha[d] already been the case during the Xia, Shang and Zhou Dynasties'.[62] Therefore, in his opinion, in order to facilitate people's personal gain, developing agriculture and commerce at the same time became an inevitable choice. Therefore, the private merchants were to play important roles, because he believed that all production and development depended on the effective circulation of goods and basic resources. It was thus not in the national interest to crack down on merchants: 'the merchant's self-interest and profit seeking, although not laudable qualities in themselves, were nevertheless essential to the empire'.[63]

Confucianism has long occupied the mainstream of the ideological circle in ancient China, and upholding righteousness or profit-seeking based on Confucian value judgments became a basic value for distinguishing *junzi* (gentlemen) from *xiaoren* (villains) in ancient society. The merchants were easily branded as 'villains'. The personality opposition between gentlemen and villains was the most basic personality type of ancient China and, to some extent, a reflection of social status.

In the history of ancient Chinese economic thought, the 'disputation of righteousness and benefit' had a strong anti-personal utilitarian connotation. It complemented the thoughts of 'inhibiting merchants' pursued by the dynasties from the ideological level, thus enabling the scholar class and

[58] Stark (2005, p. 20).

[59] Stark (2005, p. 81).

[60] Gu (1985 [1682], p. 94).

[61] Gu (1985 [1682], p. 94).

[62] Gu (1985 [1682], p. 96).

[63] Lufrano (1997, p. 46).

the merchant class to form some degree of opposition. The dominance of this idea was slightly challenged in the Ming dynasty. The idea of 'emphasizing both righteousness and profit' represented by Qiu Jun, the Yangming School, Huang Zongxi, and Gu Yanwu was also quite appealing in society. However, so far we have not been able to draw any conclusions as to whether this thinking had changed the status of merchants. Even Gu Xiancheng, who advocated for the pursuit of personal self-interest, once said that 'morality [was] beyond the rich and the poor, and the moral level can never be measured by the level of wealth at all'.[64] For scholars who studied Confucian classics throughout their lives, even if they gave an affirmative nod to selfish desire and were even willing to emphasize both righteousness and profits, deep in their mind, scholars seeking truth and merchants seeking profit was a fundamental ideological clash. Even if they did not despise merchants, they did not admire merchants either.

6.1.5 *Extension: Thoughts on Usury in Ming China*

After discussing the debate about righteousness and profits and the thoughts acknowledging the necessity of the merchants in Ming China, as an interesting (although meagre) supplement, this section will discuss the thoughts on merchants' usury behaviour, and thereafter the actual position of merchants in usury in the Ming dynasty.

In the history of Western economic thought, 'The debate about usury played a decisive role in the origin of this theory or, rather, chain of theories, for the debate about usury led to the question of how incomes could be justified in ways other than by work'.[65] However, in ancient China, 'scholars rarely engage[d] in hair-splitting scholastic discussions about usury'.[66] Nevertheless, some clues about the evaluation of merchants' usury activities can still be found in some scholars' thoughts.

In Western feudal society, lending and receiving interest has long been attacked by the church and has been considered illegal and immoral. The Church maintained an organicist idea of society based on three orders of men: clergymen, noblemen, and labourers: 'God made the clergy, knights,

[64] Gu (1997 [1612], p. 94).

[65] Schefold (2016, p. 368).

[66] Schefold (2016, p. 368).

and labourers but the Devil made burghers and usurers'.[67] Even afterwards, moneylending was still considered to be 'of a cold, calculating nature'.[68] Although operating usury and collecting interest in ancient China did not encounter any religious obstacles, there were ethical obstacles. This obstacle was reflected in thoughts exactly as the aforementioned debate about whether the righteousness and profits can be combined.

'Perhaps at no time did money have greater symbolic import than in the late Ming period, when domestic economic growth and the infusion of foreign silver engendered a rapid expansion in its use'.[69] And the merchants constituted the main force, although not the only force, in usury activities in Ming China. Since the thought of 'combining benefits with righteousness' became popular in the Ming dynasty, as discussed previously, attitudes towards merchants' usury also began to differ. Qiu Jun lived in the mid-early period of the Ming dynasty, and it was not yet time for the commercial blowout of Ming China. However, as the grand secretary, he had expressed a completely different idea about usury than the previous dynasties. In contrast to Sang Hongyang's resolute support for the country's usury behaviour and opposition to individual usury, Qiu resolutely 'opposed the government's money-lending activities, condemning it as unrighteous',[70] so he naturally attacked Wang Anshi's (Sang Hongyang's heir in the Northern Song dynasty) Law of *Qingmiao* (the government lending usury to peasants, also called 'the Green Sprouts policy').[71] He believed that 'It [was] the thing of ordinary men to collect interest by lending money, not what the country should do … Emperor Shenzong of the Song dynasty appointed Wang Anshi to implement this, and this misfortune caused difficulties in people's livelihoods and the country's ruin'.[72] This showed that he was firmly opposed to the government participating in usury activities.

Qiu repeatedly emphasized that government lending usury and grasping interests were an 'injustice'.[73] So what was his opinion regarding

[67] Poettinger (2019, p. 4).

[68] Sombart (1967 [1915], p. 44).

[69] Von Glahn (2004, p. 222).

[70] Hu (1988, p. 452).

[71] Hymes and Schirokauer (1993, p. 86).

[72] Hu (1998 [1965], Vol. 3, p. 351).

[73] Hu (1998 [1965], Vol. 3, p. 352).

the usury activities of private merchants? Qiu believed that merchants participating in usury was not only an 'injustice' but also reasonable and should be protected by the government. The government should make a ruling based on the 'deed' to protect the rights of merchants. He even cited ancient evidence to prove the rationality of private moneylending and interest-collection activities. He said,

> Lending money for interest ha[d] been available even in the Xia, Shang and Zhou dynasties, and there [was] a receipt stipulating the interest rate and the lender [could] not obtain more interest than stipulated. Even after the debtor dies, as long as there [was] evidence, it must be repaid. In current times, there [were] fraudulent powers who instigate[d] the government to prohibit all private money lending, which [was] meant to inhibit merchants from becoming too wealthy. However, they [did] not realize that the poor thus ha[d] nowhere to borrow money, and more ha[d] to wait and die.[74] (my transl.)

Lu Shen[75] also discussed the inevitability of merchants' usury business:

> Private money lending among the people in the Jiangnan region created more possibilities for local land mergers. This [was] indeed a major drawback. But why can't we abolish private money lending either? The rich [were] the mothers of the poor. When the poor need[ed] to borrow money in an emergency, they must find someone with more money to borrow. The poor and the rich [were] like left and right hands, and we should guarantee to raise one hand to help the other.[76] (my transl.)

Some thinkers opposed the merchants' usury activities. Song Yingxing[77] believed that usury would promote debtors' laziness. He said that 'if there [was] no way to borrow', people [would] make up their minds to make a living. Borrowing a loan 'facilitates laziness', and 'once the left hand

[74] Qiu (1986 [1487], p. 91).

[75] Lu Shen (1477–1544) was a famous scholar in Songjiang (part of current Shanghai) during Mid-Ming.

[76] Lu (1987 [1544], p. 160).

[77] Song Yingxing (1587–1666) was a Chinese scientist and encyclopedist who lived during the late Ming Dynasty. He was the author of *Tiangong Kaiwu*, an encyclopedia that covered a wide variety of technical subjects, including the use of gunpowder weapons. The British sinologist and historian Joseph Needham called Song Yingxing 'The Diderot of China'.

got the loan, the right hand immediately paid for wine and meat'.[78] As a result, the debtors '[would] finally even fail to drink porridge'. Even if the borrower's acres had a harvest, the money would 'flow into the merchant's house' in order to pay the heavy interest.[79]

Hai Rui,[80] a well-known unusual official and thinker in mid-Ming, always considered issues from the angle of the poor. Naturally, he was also opposed to the usury of merchants. During his term in Chun'an County, Hai Rui issued a notice, criticizing usurers:

> I learned from a close visit that families who ha[d] accumulated grain often exploit[ed] the poor by taking advantage of barren years, forcing collateral in kind, and doubling their interest. Even though it [was] apparent that they [were] impoverished and obviously unable to repay, the interest rate double[d] and the usurers still, nevertheless, len[t] usury to them. When the harvest [was] not good, the crops in the farmers' fields [was] very weak. The wives and children [were] crying. Few people can see this situation without feeling compassion. However, those usurers [didn't] have the compassion to this extent![81]

Interestingly, he still told rich merchants to 'lend money to the poor', but 'no interest should be charged'.[82] Although this kind of thinking seemed to consider the interests of the poor, it was actually an obvious 'robbing the rich and helping the poor'. Gao Gong,[83] the grand secretary at the time, completely dismissed Hai Rui's thoughts: 'Hai Rui [did] not abide by our country's existing practice and attempt[ed] to ban private usury. If the debt borrowed today [did] not charge interest, future borrowing [would] be blocked. Next time when the poor need[ed] to borrow money, no one want[ed] to lend them money anymore'.[84] As local officials, Song Yingxing and Hai Rui's vision and ability to see the

[78] Song (2010 [1637], p. 96).

[79] Song (2010 [1637], p. 96).

[80] Hai Rui (1514–1587) was a Chinese scholar-official and politician during the Ming dynasty. He is remembered as a model of honesty and integrity in office.

[81] Hai (1962 [1587], p. 167).

[82] Hai (1962 [1587], p. 167).

[83] Gao Gong (1512–1578) was a Chinese politician of the Ming dynasty. He once served as the Grand Secretary.

[84] Gao (2006 [1578], p. 199).

bigger picture were naturally far inferior to Gao Gong, who served as grand secretary. Based on the actual needs of the people's lives, Gao Gong highlighted and supported the economic inevitability of merchants' usury activities, just like Lu Shen did.

Different from the ideas and policies of the Western Han dynasty and other dynasties that supported state-owned usury and restricted private usury, the Ming dynasty pursued a 'dual-track system' of both private usury and national usury. Under the above-mentioned support of senior court officials like Qiu Jun and Gao Gong on private usury, the role of Ming merchants was quite conspicuous in usury activities. Despite the diversity of the source of money flowing into usury, such as the profits of merchants and shops, rents of landlords, government salaries of bureaucrats and sergeants, and the properties of various clans and temples, the majority and the most notable among them were the itinerant merchants.[85] The merchants here included not only wealthy merchants who also had senior official status, but also ordinary small and medium-sized merchants. In particular, the regional merchant groups (such as Huizhou merchants and Jin merchants, as previously mentioned) formed during the Ming dynasty carried out local or cross-regional lending of money or, in kind, formed a national capital and currency flow.[86]

Of course, private merchants were not without competitors in usury activities. Among the competitors, state usury was still clearly the most powerful one. An important constraint was the policy controlling the interest rate, which formulated and implemented by the state, although this policy was not always strictly enforced. Moreover, merchants were not without advantage compared with the state. A major disadvantage of state usury was that it was difficult for the state to penetrate into underdeveloped areas and rural areas (forced by cost considerations caused by too large of territory and relatively inconvenient transportation), while the scattered merchants could relatively easily do it.[87]

The small and medium-sized merchants who worked alone or in groups of two or three were dominant in these two areas. It is not difficult to understand that, geographically speaking, the rate in more developed areas of the commodity economy was generally lower than other relatively

[85] Liu (2000, p. 32).

[86] Liu (2000, pp. 32–33).

[87] Liu (2000, p. 221).

less developed areas, and that of the urban area was generally lower than that of the rural area. Small and medium-sized merchants were thus able to make a sizeable income from it.[88]

6.2 The Views on Thrift and Luxury

6.2.1 *Equal Emphasis on Thrift and Luxury*

As the increasingly extravagant lifestyles of some merchants since the middle of the Ming dynasty started to be followed by other classes, some thinkers in the Ming dynasty re-evaluated traditional Chinese (mainly Confucian) values of frugality. Some thinkers suggested that both luxury and frugality should be emphasized. Among them was the representative Wang Fuzhi.

'The Confucian documents also [were] full of warnings addressed to princes against the use of rare and expensive goods'.[89] On the basis of criticizing and inheriting the traditional Confucian philosophy of advocating frugality and exclusion of luxury, Wang put forward a new consumption concept for the consumption behaviour of people in his era (that is, the late Ming dynasty), and transformed the traditional worship of frugality and exclusion of luxury into the thought of 'temperate frugality and temperate luxury'.[90] He still advocated frugality, but opposed being stingy. He encouraged proper and reasonable consumption while opposing extravagance and waste. He believed that only by adhering to such ethical value orientation of consumption could it be beneficial to social and economic development.[91]

Wang despised merchants, not because of the wealth of merchants, but because of the wealthy merchants easily becoming extravagant and profane, thus corrupting the thrift of society.[92] Therefore, to restrain merchants was not to restrain merchants' trade in goods or the amount of wealth of merchants, but to curb the excessive extravagance of merchants. Wang Fuzhi thus greatly appreciated the measures taken by Emperor Han Gaozu and Emperor Hongwu to restrict the dress of merchants and their

[88] Liu (2000, p. 230).

[89] Wilhelm (1930, pp. 69–70).

[90] Wang (1975 [1692], p. 195).

[91] Wang (1975 [1692], p. 195).

[92] Wang (1975 [1692], p. 180).

daily expenses.[93] He believed that this was a manifestation of knowing 'the root of ruling'.[94] The ruler should eliminate the arrogance of the merchants originated from his wealth, and avoid the merchants being unkind. In Wang's view, prohibiting wealthy merchants from crossing social status and stipulating certain etiquette were essential for rulers.[95]

Other thinkers who were not very mainstream, such as Guo Zizhang,[96] also proposed similar thoughts. Guo believed that too much luxury and too much thriftiness were both unnecessary, and the harm of being too frugal was greater than the harm of being too extravagant.[97]

6.2.2 *The Thoughts Pro Luxury*

Lu Ji,[98] who was the thinker who admired luxury the most in the Ming dynasty, went further. This was a ground-breaking economic thought not only in Ming China, but also throughout the whole of ancient China, which is thus worth a detailed introduction.

Lu Ji 'came from a wealthy official-and land-holding family based in the lower Yangtze Valley city of Songjiang'[99] (currently part of Shanghai). Lu Shen, Lu Ji's father, was also a well-known literati at the time.[100] In Lu Ji's work '*The Excerpt of Jianjia Tang*', there was a large paragraph on economic thought that criticized the prohibition ofluxury. This idea ofLu can be traced back to *Guanzi*, who held the same view as Lu Ji that luxury was better than thrift. *Guanzi* started with confirming 'it is human nature not to refrain

[93] Wang (1975 [1692], p. 181).

[94] Wang (1975 [1692], p. 181).

[95] Wang (1975 [1692], p. 181).

[96] Guo Zizhang (1543–1618) once served as the governor of Chaozhou and the military governor of Guizhou. He was famous for putting down several rebellions.

[97] Hu (1998 [1965], Vol. 3, pp. 432–433).

[98] Lu Ji (1515–1552) was a famous thinker and scholar.

[99] Clunas (1991, p. 146).

[100] His father Lu Shen (1477–1544) was a famous literati during Mid-Ming. Although never serving as a high-level official in the court, Lu Shen had quite a few close connections with high-level officials and famous scholars. Lu Shen's own epitaph was written by Xia Yan, a student of Lu Shen and the Grand Secretary during the early Emperor Jiajing years. The epitaph of Lu Shen's wife Mei Shuren was written by Xu Jie, a even more famous Grand Secretary during late Emperor Jiajing and early Emperor Longqing. Xu Jie, like Lu Shen, is also Shanghainese.

from going after profit',[101] and developed a unique idea that advocated for the encouragement of luxury consumption, with its obvious purpose of increasing wealth, controlling the macroeconomic situation, and ensuring a smooth economic operation. In *Guanzi*, it said that,

> In the case of insufficient production, it [was] necessary to control excessive consumption, but when there [was] more production, it [was] necessary to increase consumption. Under certain conditions, luxury consumption also ha[d] a positive effect on production.... Roads should be repaired, and the measurements should be unified, so that it provide[d] convenience for merchants to engage in exchange activities... Merchants must be honest. The four occupations must all get average profits, so there [would] be no treacherous people.[102] (my transl.)

In *Extravagance,* the thirty-fifth chapter of *Guanzi,* the author stated,

> Duke Huan of Qi asked how to increase wealth and goods that go with the change of time and conditions. Guan Zhong replied that 'there [was] no better way than implementing extravagant consumption. Despising practical things and respecting useless things [would] compel people to obey.' Therefore, people [would] disregard food and cherish jewellery, take pleasure in ritual and look down upon production.[103]

Guan Zhong also said in the same chapter that, 'for the purpose of increasing wealth, surplus food should be used for extravagant consumption, the cart and horse should be decorated before being driven, and tasty wine should be brewed for enjoyment. In that way, poverty and begging [wouldn't] come into being in a thousand years, which [was] called the fundamentality of wealth accumulation'.[104]

To more fully illustrate extravagant consumption, *Guanzi* mentioned 'carving and painting the egg before eating, enchasing the firewood before burning'.[105] The reason is that the 'extravagant consumption of

[101] Hu (1984, p. 39).
[102] Hu (1998 [1965], Vol. 1, p. 315).
[103] Hu (1998 [1965], Vol. 1, p. 315).
[104] Hu (1998 [1965], Vol. 1, p. 316).
[105] Hu (1998 [1965], Vol. 1, p. 317).

rich people can create jobs for poor people, while people's livelihoods should be formed by mutual help between the rich and the poor'.[106]

Similarly, Lu said, 'I didn't see that the luxury makes the world poor'. When analysing the positive effects of luxury on society, Lu Ji said that the luxury of the rich can increase the means of livelihood for the poor (this was basically a copy of the idea of the *Guanzi*), 'the rich merchants' cart drivers, chefs, tailors, etc. can obtain profits from them'.[107] 'The heavy spending on food by rich merchants and powerful families benefit[ed] the farmers; the heavy spending on clothes benefit[ed] the weavers'.[108] Therefore, he believed that the epicurean[109] lifestyle of merchants was quite beneficial to ordinary people. He took the people of Suzhou and Hangzhou, which were located near Shanghai county, as an example.[110] Here, many people 'made a living without farming and weaving',[111] and they could solve their daily life problems through *moye* (commerce). Lu believed that instead of 'wasting the wealth of the world', the luxury of merchants could play the role of 'enriching the world and averaging commoners' wealth',[112] so it should not be banned at all.

Lu also argued that, as we all know, the merchant class was mostly typically utilitarian and '[would] not get up early if there [was] no profit'.[113] However, luxury goods usually had high profit margins, which were very popular among merchants, and, naturally, the merchants spared no effort in the transaction process.[114] However, the premise of profit-seeking by merchants was that consumers had a potential consumption ability and desire. From a macro perspective, the luxury consumption climate had contributed to the prosperity of the market. The existence of a prosperous

[106] Hu (1998 [1965], Vol. 1, p. 317).

[107] Lu (1985 [1552], p. 103).

[108] Clunas (1991, p. 146).

[109] The luxurious lifestyle encouraged by Lu Ji easily reminds us of a famous ancient Greek philosopher, Epicurus (341–270 B.C.). 'Epicurus's name entered many languages in adjectival form as a tribute to his interests (in a pleasurable lifestyle)'. For more details, please refer to de Botton (2000, pp. 49–52).

[110] Clunas (1991, p. 146).

[111] Lu (1985 [1552], p. 103).

[112] Lu (1985 [1552], p. 104).

[113] It is a famous ancient Chinese saying, in Chinese, *wuli bu qizao*.

[114] Lu (1985 [1552], p. 104).

market was also a necessary condition for luxury life, and it was also an inevitable requirement for luxury culture. Lu Ji used Shanghai County as an example to demonstrate what he meant.[115] Shanghai County in the Ming dynasty 'was in a relatively remote location near the sea, and was not a traffic route or strategic place for boat and car traffic'; thus, the local economy was also relatively lagging behind the Yangzhou, Suzhou, and Hangzhou at the time.[116] However, even in Shanghai at the time, 'the number of merchants was much higher than one hundred thousand, and the people lived in peace'.[117] And Ningbo, Shaoxing, Jinhua, and Quzhou, which were also not far from Shanghai, became counterexamples to Lu's argument. He said that the customs of these cities were 'mostly advocating frugality', but the people 'cannot guarantee their lives, and half of the population roam from place to place for food'.[118] Therefore, he said that frugality did not make the people rich, while people in the Wuyue region (Suzhou, Hangzhou, Shanghai, etc.) advocated for luxury consumption, and the local economy and commerce were very prosperous[119].

Lu Ji's idea of luxury consumption cannot help but be reminiscent of the thoughts of Mandeville approximately 100 years later. In 1705, Mandeville wrote an allegory poem, *The Fable of the Bees*, which told the history of the rise and fall of a group of bees. At first, they were extravagant because of their pursuit of prosperity and vanity. In this way, the whole society flourished and all were able to find employment.[120] Later, the bees changed their original habits, gave up their extravagant lives, and advocated for frugality. As a result, the palace was deserted, commerce

[115] Lu (1985 [1552], p. 105).

[116] To illustrate more vividly for readers who are unfamiliar with China, the geological location and comparative standing of Shanghai to Suzhou in Ming China is similar to that of Pompeii to Rome during the two centuries before its complete annihilation. I went to Pompeii with my close friend SJH in 2016. Even with only relics remained, we can still see its prosperity and luxury life style at the time, which is very similar to that of Suzhou and Shanghai in middle and late Ming China. For details, please refer to Beard (2008, p. 162).

[117] Lu (1985 [1552], p. 106).

[118] Lu (1985 [1552], p. 106).

[119] Lu (1985 [1552], p. 106).

[120] Mandeville (2017 [1723], pp. 1–4).

was depressed, and the bees' livelihoods withered away.[121] Mandeville also commented that he '[could not] help dissenting from the received notion' 'that luxury [was] as destructive to the wealth of the whole body politick, as it [was] to that of every individual person who [was] guilty of it, and that a national frugality enriche[d] a country in the same manner as that which [was] less general increase[d] the estates of private families'.[122] Lu also said that frugality may make a family rich, but certainly not a country. Mandeville's view was very similar, and German economist Sombart also promoted the positive value of luxury consumption in his *Luxus und Kapitalismus*.[123]

Lu Ji's thoughts were considered by some scholars to be a signal of the mainstream ideological community's appreciation of the wealthy class in the middle and late Ming dynasty, which was represented by merchants. In fact, this interpretation was much too forced. Based on ancient China's long withstanding traditional economic thought of advocating for frugality, it is unlikely that Lu Yong's thoughts suddenly jump to the same level as Western luxury related ideas (such as the luxury thoughts in seventeenth century Britain). He still believed that 'the total money in the world [was] constant'.[124] This statement was first used by early thinkers to illustrate that taxes should not be too heavy. Lu, however, used this thought to show that the loss of one family was the benefit of another family, which had a different meaning from the original. He believed that thrift was only good for individuals and families, and it was harmful from a social perspective. Since the loss of one family was the benefit of another family, the 'ruler of the world' should not only seek the wealth of one person and one family (and not a single merchant of course), but must achieve 'all the world becoming rich'.[125] This meant that Lu Ji's thoughts were only a modification of traditional Chinese thoughts, such as the thoughts of egalitarianism, which combined together with the current state of commercial development in the Jiangnan region, but not to completely overthrow it. So his thought did not include a desire for promoting merchants' social status.

[121] Mandeville (2017 [1723], pp. 12–22).

[122] Mandeville (2017 [1723], p. 110).

[123] Sombart (1913, pp. 71–76).

[124] Lu (1985 [1552], p. 82).

[125] Lu (1985 [1552], p. 84).

There was another point that can prove this assertion, that is, he explained his thoughts completely based on the current situation of the society without quoting the classics. The reason may be that although his thoughts, as analysed above, partly come from *Guanzi*, it was difficult for him to find a clear basis in any previous Confucian classics, including Ming works. Moreover, although his father Lu Shen was also a famous scholar, his great-grandfather was a merchant who abandoned Confucianism, and his grandfather was also good at managing money. Thus, the background of this family was also descriptive of why Lu had such thoughts. Even if he did not engage in commerce himself, at least part of his life overlapped with commerce.

6.2.3 The Thoughts Against Luxury

As mentioned above, in Chinese traditional culture, the advocacy of thrift was the ideology that held a predominant position. For thousands of years, both the government and civilians were proud of frugality and felt ashamed of luxury. Thus, despite the development of commerce, the prohibition of luxury was still the mainstream idea pursued by thinkers in the Ming dynasty. For example, He Tang said,

> People who own[ed] extra wealth like to compare with each other. In this comparison, the previous boundary between upper and lower levels of the class (scholars, peasants, artisans and merchants) [were] gone. The luxury customs [were] established, the people's hearts [were] bewildered, resulting in more poor people on the streets. Whether it [was] a wedding or a funeral, people tr[ied] their best to show extravagance, and even borrow[ed] money to do so, just because they [were] afraid of being laughed at by relatives and friends if the extravagance was not enough.[126]

During the Emperor Jiajing period of the Ming dynasty, Lu Shen (Lu Ji's father) also opposed luxury. He was anxious about the day-by-day declining public moral, and felt that all he could do was restrain his family. Therefore, he wrote to his son 'to be frugal ... not to learn the extravagance and luxury of a merchant'.[127] He hoped that Lu Ji would maintain the style of frugality.

[126] He (1985 [1536], p. 186).

[127] Lu (1993 [1544], p. 121).

Although Xu Jie, the grand secretary serving during the final years of Emperor Jiajing and early years of Emperor Longqing, was a big corrupt official known in the Ming dynasty and had a luxurious lifestyle, he also advocated for the prohibition of luxury in his memorial. He insisted that luxury should be prohibited, and he even carefully planned and outlined obstacles that may be encountered in the implementation of prohibiting luxury.[128] When Xu Jie was a young, low-level official at the Hanlin Academy,[129] he claimed himself to be a follower of Lu Shen,[130] so it is not surprising that he held this view. Besides Lu Shen's influence, it was also difficult for Xu Jie to avoid the accusation of him speaking for the court: if society was pervaded with an extravagant lifestyle, it was obviously not conducive to the governance of the country.

Even in the late Ming dynasty, there were still thoughts like those of Li Xianfang,[131] who believed that no matter whether it was a merchant or a peasant, only thrift and modesty could make them rich, and people would certainly become even more stingy after getting rich.[132] He said that he truly realized that 'the stingier a merchant [was], the more real the benefits he [saw]'. In his view, the fact that merchants can get rich lay in their stinginess, and the premise of stinginess was to maintain their own wealth.

Lü Kun, another great Confucian in the Ming period, also expressed his worries towards luxury. Lü Kun criticized the influence of an extravagant social atmosphere on academics and culture. He pointed out that the 'fashion' of luxury and flashy life had eroded the essence of traditional cultures such as pragmatism, frugality, and education. The words such as '*binggen* (cause of trouble)' and '*bing* (illness)' often appeared in Lü Kun's works. For instance, he said that 'This cause of "illness" was human desire. Snobbishness of lust after women and pursuing goods and fame were manifested in "pursuing luxurious things" in human actions'. And among them, merchants were the representatives. However, in contrast to

[128] Xu (2009 [1583], p. 158).

[129] Hanlin Academy was the institution that trained future senior officials in the imperial court.

[130] Xu (2009 [1583], p. 134).

[131] Li Xianfang (1510–1594) was a middle level official in Ming China, who mainly served some trivial positions.

[132] Li (1997 [1594], p. 161).

the brashness of Hai Rui, the thinker who was mentioned in the section on usury, Lü's thoughts stayed 'within the conventional boundaries'.[133]

6.2.4 *Fancy Dress: Merchants in the Apparel Regulations*

After discussion of the thoughts on thrift and luxury, we may now investigate some related facts in the history, to see whether the thoughts had any influence on (or were influenced by) the merchants' behaviour. Let's start with the merchants in the dressing regulations. In ancient China, the definition of official and civilian clothing according to the different social stratum was usually originated from the need of the ruling class to use state power in order to control members of society and maintain order. It can be traced back to the early Western Han dynasty, when merchants' clothing was restricted in the form of national law for the first time ever:

> Emperor (Han) Gaozu ordered that merchants [were] not allowed to wear silk-made clothes and [could] not ride in a horse-drawn carriage, and he also levied an extortionate tax on merchants, thus humiliating them. By the time of Emperor Huidi[134] and Empress Dowager Lü[135]'s reign, the whole country had been settled, thus the ban on merchants was abolished. Nevertheless, the law still stipulated that the descendants of the merchants could not become officials.[136] (my transl.)

When Emperor Gaozu established the Western Han dynasty, the masses were impoverished, and the whole country was eager to be rebuilt out of the ruins, while the wealthy merchants still led luxurious and dissipated lifestyles. This could be considered the wherefore of Emperor Gaozu's ban on merchants.[137] However, when Empress Dowager Lü started to

[133] Handlin (1983, p. 119).

[134] Emperor Han Huidi (210–188 B.C.), the son of Emperor Han Gaozu and Empress Dowager Lü, reigns from 195 to 188 B.C.

[135] Empress Dowager Lü (241–180 B.C.) was the empress of Emperor Han Gaozu. After Gaozu passed away in 195 B.C., their son Emperor Huidi ascended the throne, and Empress Lü was the real leader of the empire until her death 15 years later. After Emperor Huidi died in 188 B.C., she act as regent. However, she never ascended the throne herself. Empress Wu Zetian (624–705, r. 690–705) was the only female emperor in ancient China.

[136] Sima (1959 [86 B.C.], Vol. 30, p. 1418).

[137] Wang (1984 [1936], p. 51).

hold the reins of power, the ban on merchants was relaxed under the guidance of the thoughts of Huang Lao,[138] and thus the merchants' power developed quite rapidly. 'When it came to Emperor Wendi's era, the emperor and the empress' costumes were ridiculed by the merchants, and it was not long after that the ban on the merchants was abolished'.[139] At that time, 'the law which despised merchants failed to stop the trend of merchants becoming rich, while the law which respected farmers also failed to prevent farmers from becoming poor',[140] which seems to be ironic. Emperor Hongwu (r. 1368–1398) once said,

> In the Western Han dynasty, merchants could not wear silk clothes and ride in horse-drawn carriages. I ha[d] been thinking about it for a long time, but still do not get what Emperor (Han) Gaozu intended. From ancient times, the active market during the day ha[d] always been indispensable, and all merchants [were] members among ordinary people. Thus it [was] really difficult to understand the reason for humiliating these merchants.[141]

Despite his thoughts, Emperor Hongwu, just like Emperor (Han) Gaozu, ordered that 'members from the peasant families were allowed to wear clothes made of silk and crepe, while those from the merchant families were only allowed to wear linen clothes. Even if only one member in the peasant family was engaged in commerce, the whole family had to abide by the merchant family regulations'.[142] Qiu Jun commented on this, arguing that it [was] feasible to promote frugality among merchants, but it [was] unnecessary to use harsh laws to humiliate. He said that 'the Western Han dynasty was not far away from the more ancient times. The policy it adopted to restrain merchants followed the policy of its predecessor. Regarding merchants' clothing and daily expenses, it [was]

[138] The thoughts of Huang Lao are the combination of Yellow Emperor (Huangdi)'s learning and Laozi's ideology. It can be mainly divided into three themes: self-cultivation (including alchemy), statecraft (recuperation, inaction, etc.), real application (technological invention, etc.), which is based on the Tao of metaphysical ontology, combined with way to maintain good health, numerology, art of war, strategy, etc.

[139] Song (2010 [1637], Vol. 2, p. 19).

[140] Ban (1962 [92], Vol. 24, p. 1133).

[141] Zhu (1986 [1398], Vol. 10, p. 1223).

[142] Zhu (1986 [1398], Vol. 10, p. 1223).

reasonable to not allow them to be extravagant, but policies to make merchants feel miserable [were] a bit excessive'.[143]

The social environment in the early Ming dynasty was very similar to that of the early Western Han dynasty. Therefore, Emperor Hongwu followed the example of Emperor Han Gaozu. He did have the practical consideration of cultivating the national strength and advocating for frugality, which was lacking during the Mongolian's rule. At the time, in addition to the clothing restrictions mentioned above, 'when accessing the market, civilians who [were] not related to agriculture [were] not allowed to wear a *douli*,[144] while peasants [did] not fall into this category'.[145] This was often decoded as evidence of the traditional thought of 'emphasizing the root (agriculture) and restraining the branch (commerce)'. However, another potential interpretation of this article could be, to a greater extent, that Emperor Hongwu focused on the economic recovery and ordered stability in the society at that time, and asked the four categories of people to stay in their proper places. His combative and strengthening supervision was actually targeting vagrants and treacherous people, rather than the merchant class. After all, merchants [were] still quite useful for social development and daily life.

Collected Statutes of the Ming Dynasty mentioned that, 'in the first year of Emperor Zhengde (1505), merchants, servants and actors [were] not allowed to wear mink or fur clothes. And monks, yamen runners and sergeants [were] not allowed to wear clothes made of silk, yarn or cotton'.[146] Although this showed that the merchants were juxtaposed with the servants and actors, it also reflected the fact that the extravagant atmosphere in the society at that time (the middle and late Ming dynasty) had cropped up so that the government had to readjust the stipulations on the standards of clothing for all classes of people. The change that can be seen here is that, during the Emperor Zhengde years, the monks and the bailiffs in *yamen*[147] were forced to follow the strictest of dressing codes, while ordinary merchants were not restricted by their restrictions.

[143] Qiu (1986 [1487], Vol. 2, p. 53).

[144] *Douli* is a cone-shaped bamboo hat in traditional China.

[145] Zhang (1974 [1739], Vol. 67, p. 1649).

[146] Shen (1989 [1587], Vol. 61, p. 394).

[147] *Yamen* refers to government office in feudal China.

He Mengchun,[148] a high-level official at the time, noted that, 'for today's merchants, regarding the dressing, no one [wore] clothes made of coarse cloth any more'.[149]

When it came to the late Ming period, the merchants began to flout the sumptuary laws. Few people wore the styles and colours of clothing appropriate to their status as prescribed by law. The plain dress prescribed for the daily wear of Confucian students in government schools was considered to be the garb of the poverty-stricken. The dress for the official class, indiscriminately worn by low-ranking officers and government clerks, was discarded by higher ranking officials who were in favour of a more fashionable costume worn by the merchants.

Interestingly, even without the restrictions decreed by the court, the merchants themselves would choose to wear plain clothing in public, especially for travelling traders. 'If the merchant's journey was to take him to unfamiliar places, … traveling clothes were to be chosen with care. Expensive-looking clothes would make him a target of the highwaymen and river pirates who preyed upon wealthy travellers. Plain clothing should thus be worn for both convenience and safety'.[150] However, merchants were also advised 'not to dress too drably, which would be inappropriate to their status'.[151] The mid-level merchant had to maintain a certain reputation for respectability and reliability if he was to do business successfully.

6.2.5 Books and Arts: Merchants and Bibliophiles

Another interesting example is the merchants' attitude in purchasing arts and books. The trend of the merchant class becoming more 'literate' and 'elegant' was not the natural result of a long history of their own culture and aesthetic cultivation, but in the form of obtrusive and rude 'material things', forcibly intervening with the vulgarity and exaggeration inherent in the secular and underlying society. This was what the orthodox scholars

[148] He Mengchun (1474–1536) was a scholar and official (his highest position was Minister of Civil).

[149] He (1985 [1536], p. 3).

[150] Lufrano (1997, p. 158).

[151] Lufrano (1997, p. 158).

were unable to stand for, and it shook the social identity, power, and dignity of the scholars to some extent.

Some scholars believed that 'paintings during the Song dynasty should be valued instead of others' and 'Ge Kilns and Ru Kilns during the Song dynasty should be valued instead of others',[152] but the people of the Ming dynasty valued the present over the past. Goods for entertainment were in short supply, resulting in the popularity of counterfeit products in the market. It was difficult to distinguish between true and false, which seriously damaged morals and customs. What was more serious was that this chaotic situation disrupted the established artistic and cultural patterns. Orthodox scholars were concerned that 'their vulgarity [was] more than enough'.[153]

The Huizhou merchants were considered to have played a vital role in fuelling the flames of 'fashion and monsters sweeping the world'.[154] Suzhou, the core city in the Jiangnan area at the time, was considered to be the place where 'fashion' and 'witches' originated. Shen Defu[155] claimed that commercial capital's involvement in the cultural market raises prices, making intellectuals with real appreciation unable to purchase and collect antique cultural relics, calligraphy and painting instruments, and squeezing them out of cultural circulation.[156]

Moreover, due to the lack of deep cultural accumulation, artistic accomplishment, and true aesthetic appreciation among the merchant class, they participated in the antique and art trade only for the sake of hoarding and profiteering. It made up the dominant force of the circulation and trade of antiques, and art transformed from traditional elites (scholars) to merchants. Correspondingly, cultural 'arts' such as antiques and works of art faded in terms of their cultural and artistic connotations, evolved into symbols of power and wealth, and became

[152] Yuan (2010 [1610], pp. 730–731).

[153] Shen (2007 [1642], Vol. 26, p. 653).

[154] Shen (2007 [1642], Vol. 26, p. 654).

[155] Shen Defu (1578–1642) was a scholar who never became an official, since he only obtained *juren* title. He was famous for his interesting work *Wanli Yehuo Bian*, which involves miscellaneous topics such as Ming regulations, anecdote, disputes within the ruling class, ethnic relations, foreign relations, mountains and rivers, classics and history collection, technology, gods and ghosts, etc. He was greatly influence by his father, who was an official historian.

[156] Shen (2007 [1642], Vol. 26, p. 654).

'snobbish'.[157] The fashionable pursuit of precious items in the late Ming dynasty brought 'the culturally connotative items, such as antiques, calligraphy and paintings, which were spread among only a few elite figures' during the early Ming period, to 'the money world of the moral vacuum' during the mid and late Ming period.[158]

The motivation of merchants to participate in cultural transactions and competition was not purely for profit. Those merchants who were satirized by Shen Defu for not discerning the true meaning and for spending a lot of money to buy fake antiques, calligraphy, and painting fakes hunger for 'culture'. In other words, merchants eagerly hoped to decorate the facade by purchasing cultural 'material things', imitating the elegant and leisurely lifestyle of the upper class, especially the class of scholars, in order to shape the new image of 'being civilized' and that of 'leisure elegance' and to get rid of crazy profits, as well as vulgar, stingy, lascivious, and other negative social critiques. This implied that the Huizhou merchants had become a unique social label that was generally regarded as insulated from life taste, cultural heritage, and aesthetic appreciation. In the late Ming period, Zhan Jingfeng, a Huizhou native, recorded events in his work of appreciating paintings and calligraphy, which can show the world's prejudice towards Huizhou merchants, as well as the resistance against them.[159]

Only when a merchant strived to approach the scholar class in terms of values, lifestyles, and social communication could he be recognized and respected by the latter. Meanwhile, the merchant class was eager to receive recognition from scholars in the cultural sense mentioned above. However, in most cases, not all of the merchants' dedication to civilized and elegant actions could get a positive response. Most people who tried to 'stand up to the entry as an equal' received only ruthless mockery and contempt.[160]

Collecting books was obviously another unique symbol of the scholarly tradition. In fact, before the middle of the Ming dynasty, contrary to our potential conjecture, books were extremely scarce and 'access to

[157] Yuan (2010 [1610], p. 642).

[158] Yuan (2010 [1610], p. 642).

[159] Lu (1992, Vol. 4, p. 38).

[160] Tang (1922 [1560], Vol. 4, pp. 70–71).

private collections was often restricted'.[161] 'Acute shortages of books were widely reported both inside and outside of the delta in the fifteenth century'.[162] At the start of sixteenth century, Lu Shen (1477–1544), whom I mentioned above, 'had to go to Nanjing and Beijing to see many books (and even then could afford only incomplete, cheap copies)'.[163] Even when it came to the late Ming period, according to Gu Yanwu (1613–1682), 'as for what circulated among the people, it was no more than the Four Books, the Five Classics, the Comprehensive mirror for government, and books on moral nature. If any other books were printed, then they were stored up only by families who were fond of the past'.[164]

However, this 'privilege' enjoyed by scholars only had to be shared by some philistines, including merchants,

> Social change in the ranks of the literati, however, became common in the latter half of the Ming dynasty, when the ranks of literati official authors and book collectors were joined by many men who never held an official post and yet now created, consumed, transmitted, and added to literati book culture.[165]

What was harder for scholars to accept was that many people who were 'stained by copper odours' (i.e. merchants who dealt with money all the time) entered the officialdom through some special ways other than the orthodox imperial exams, and thus more easily became the main force of collecting books due to their abundant financial resources. Therefore, scholars showed full contempt but had no alternative when facing the emergence of the merchants, while it also showed the bumpiness and embarrassment of the merchant class in their attempt to become more literate and elegant through behaviours such as art and the collection of books.

Nonetheless, fortunately for the scholars, I find an interesting characteristics among the most influential Ming bibliophiles: all of them came from Jiangnan region or southern coastline area, and none of them had

[161] Lin (2013, p. 272).

[162] McDermott (2006, p. 58).

[163] McDermott (2006, p. 99).

[164] McDermott (2006, pp. 57–58).

[165] McDermott (2006, p. 104).

connection with merchants or merchant families. The generally recognized Ming book collectors with richest book collection[166] were Song Lian,[167] Ye Sheng,[168] Fan Qin,[169] Wang Shizhen,[170] Hu Yinglin,[171] Huang Juzhong,[172] Qi Chengran,[173] Mao Jin,[174] and Qian Qianyi.[175] They were all scholars. We may infer that individuals in the Jiangnan region, the richest area in Ming, had better advantage of collecting books, corresponding to its commerce development. And we may also safely infer that despite the richness of merchants, the right to speak in book collection was still controlled in the hand of scholars.

References

References in German

Sombart, W. (1913). *Luxus und Kapitalismus*. Duncker & Humblot.

Wilhelm, R. (1930). *Chinesische Wirtschaftspsychologie*. Deutsche Wissenschaftliche Buchhandlung.

[166] Jiao (2011, pp. 93–101).

[167] Song Lian (1310–1381), a Shaoxing (in Zhejiang) native, was a well-known scholar and official during Emperor Hongwu era. His book collection was over 80,000 volumes.

[168] Ye Sheng (1420–1474), a Kunshan (in Jiangsu, near current Shanghai) native, was an official. His book collection was over 22,700 volumes.

[169] Fan Qin (1506–1585), a Ningbo (in Zhejiang) native, once served as the Vice Minister of Military during Emperor Jiajing era. His book collection was over 70,000 volumes.

[170] Wang Shizhen (1526–1590), a Taicang (in Jiangsu, near current Shanghai) native, was a high-level official in Nanjing. His book collection was over 30,000 volumes.

[171] Hu Yinglin (1551–1602), a Lanxi (in Zhejiang) native, was a scholar who did not obtain any official position. His book collection was over 42,384 volumes.

[172] Huang Juzhong (1562–1644), a Jinjiang (in Fujian) native, was a high-level official in Nanjing. His book collection was over 60,000 volumes.

[173] Qi Chengran (1565–1628), a Shaoxing (in Zhejiang) native, was a scholar who did not obtain any official position. His book collection was over 100,000 volumes.

[174] Mao Jin (1599–1659), a Changshu (in Jiangsu) native, was a scholar who did not obtain any official position. His book collection was over 84,000 volumes. Please also refer to McDermott (2006, p. 109).

[175] Qian Qianyi (1582–1664), a Changshu (in Jiangsu) native, once served as the Vice Minister of Ritual during late Ming period. His huge book collection, thanks to a thoughtless servant, went up in flames in 1650. Please also refer to McDermott (2006, p. 140).

References in English

Beard, M. (2008). *Pompeii: The life of a Roman town*. Profile Books Ltd.

Bentham, J. (1823 [1780]). *Principles of morals and legislation*. Clarendon Press.

Chang, C. (1962). *Wang Yang-ming: Idealist philosopher of sixteenth-century China*. St. John's University Press.

Chen, H. (1911). *The economic principles of confucius and his school*. Columbia University, Longmans, Green & Company, Agents.

Clunas, C. (1991). *Superfluous things: Material culture and social status in early modern China*. Polity Press.

De Botton, A. (2000). *The consolations of philosophy*. Vintage Books.

Handlin, J. F. (1983). *Action in late Ming thought: The reorientation of Lü Kun and other scholar-officials*. University of California Press.

Hu, J. (1984). *Chinese economic thought before the seventeenth century*. Foreign Language Press.

Hu, J. (1988). *A concise history of Chinese economic thought*. Foreign Languages Press.

Hymes, R. P., & Schirokauer, C. (1993). *Ordering the world: Approaches to state and society in Sung dynasty China*. University of California Press.

Lin, H. (2013). Intersecting boundaries: Manuscript, printing, and book culture in late Ming China. *Oriens Extremus, 52*, 263–304.

Lufrano, R. J. (1997). *Honorable merchants: Commerce and self-cultivation in late imperial China*. University of Hawaii Press.

Mandeville, B. (2017 [1723]). *The Fable of the Bees; or, private vices, public benefits*. Georg Olms Verlag.

McDermott, J. (2006). *A social history of the Chinese Book*. Hong Kong University Press.

Poettinger, M. (2019). The Medici Pope, Jacob Fugger and the new catholic view on the economy: Johann Eck and the problem of usury. In *International Conference at Forschungskolleg Bad Homburg 2019*.

Schefold, B. (2016). *Great economic thinkers from antiquity to the historical school: Historical school, old and young*. Routledge.

Sombart, W. (1967 [1915]). *The quintessence of capitalism: A study of the history and psychology of the modern business man* (M. Epstein, Trans. and Ed.). Howard Fertig.

Stark, W. (2005). *Jeremy Bentham's economic writings: Critical edition based on his printed works and unprinted manuscripts* (Vol. III). Routledge.

Von Glahn, R. (2004). *The sinister way: The devine and the demonic in Chinese religious culture*. University of California Press.

References in Chinese

Ban, G. (1962 [92]). *Book of Han*. Zhonghua Publishing House.

Gao, G. (2006 [1578]). *The collected work of Gao Gong (Gaogong quanji)*. Zhongzhou Guji Press.

Gu, X. (1997 [1612]). *Xiaoxin Zhai Zhaji*. Qilu Press.

Gu, Y. (1985 [1682]). *Tianxia Junguo Libing Shu*. The Commercial Press.

Hai, R. (1962 [1587]). *Collected work of Hai Rui* (Vol. 1). Peking: Zhonghua Publishing House House.

Han, B. (1973 [1556]). *Yuanluo Ji*. Taiwan Commercial Press.

He, M. (1985 [1536]). *Yudong Xulu Zhaichao Neiwai Pian*. Zhonghua Publishing House.

He, X. (1960 [1579]). *Collected work of He Xinyin (He Xinyin Ji)* (Vol. 3). Zhonghua Publishing House House.

Hu, J. (1998 [1965]). *History of Chinese economic thoughts* (Vols. 1–3). Shanghai University of Finance and Economics Press.

Huang, Z. (1975 [1695]). *Songyuan Xue'an*. Heluo Tushu Press.

Jiao, S. (2011). *History of ancient Chinese book collection*. China International Broadcasting Press.

Li, M. (1991 [1529]). *Kongtong Ji*. Shanghai Ancient Books Publishing House.

Li, X. (1997 [1594]). *Dongdai Shanfang Shilu*. The Phoenix Press.

Li, Z. (2000 [1602]). *Li Zhi Wenji*. China Social Science Literature Press.

Liu, Q. (2000). *Usury capital of Ming-Qing period*. China Social Science Literature Press.

Lu, F. (1992). *The collection of Chinese painting and calligraphy*. Shanghai Shuhua Press.

Lu, J. (1985 [1552]). *Jianjia Tang Zazhu Zhaichao*. Zhonghua Publishing House.

Lu, S. (1987 [1544]). *Yanshan Waiji*. Shanghai Ancient Books Publishing House.

Lu, S. (1993 [1544]). *Jintai Jiwen*. Shanghai Ancient Books Publishing House.

Qiu, J. (1986 [1487]). *Daxue Yanyi Bu*. Taiwan Commercial Press.

Shen, D. (2007 [1642]). *Wanli Yehuo Bian* (Vol. 26). Zhonghua Publishing House House.

Shen, S. (1989 [1587]). *Ming Huidian*. Zhonghua Publishing House.

Sima, Q. (1959 [86BC]). *Records of the grand historian*. Zhonghua Publishing House.

Song, Y. (2010 [1637]). *Tiangong Kaiwu*. Shanghai: Shanghai Ancient Books Publishing House.

Tang, S. (1922 [1560]). *Jingchuan Xiansheng Wenji*. The Commercial Press.

Wang, F. (1975 [1692]). *Discussion on Zizhi Tongjian (Du Tongjian Lun)*. Zhonghua Publishing House.

Wang, X. (1984 [1936]). *Chinese commerce history.* Shanghai Bookstore Publishing House.

Wang, Y. (1978 [1525]). *Chuanxi Lu.* Shanghai: Shanghai Ancient Books Publishing House.

Xu, J. (2009 [1583]). *Shaohu Xiansheng Wenji.* Qilu Press.

Yan, J. (1996 [1596]). *Yan Jun Ji.* China Social Science Press.

Yu, Y. (2004). *Confucian ethics and merchant spirit.* Guangxi Normal University Press.

Yuan, H. (2010 [1610]). *Pinghua Zhaiji* (Vol. 3). Shanghai Ancient Books Publishing House.

Zhang, T. (1974 [1739]). *The history of Ming.* Institute of History and Language.

Zhu, Y. (1986 [1398]). *Ming Taizu Wenji.* Taiwan Commercial Press.

CHAPTER 7

Ranking: Scholars, Merchants, Craftsmen, and Peasants

As early as Western Han, Sima Qian said in his *Records of the Grand Historian*, 'If a poor man wants to become rich, it is better to be an artisan than a farmer, better to be a merchant than an artisan'.[1] And with the unusual expansion of commerce in the Ming dynasty, especially during the middle and late Ming periods, the consumer demand grew, the domestic and foreign markets enlarged, and merchant groups began to appear. Meanwhile, the number of people who abandoned farming and Confucian study gradually increased. This seems to be, as also reflected in ideology, a change in the traditional theory of four occupational groups, which was first put forward in *Guanzi*. Compared with the other three occupations, did the status of the merchants substantially improve in the Ming dynasty, especially during the middle and late Ming period? This is what this chapter aims to analyze.[2]

[1] Hu (1984,, pp. 41–42).

[2] This Chapter was modified to my paper titled 'Underdevelopment of Commerce in the History of Ancient Chinese Economic Thoughts: An examination of the status of merchants in Ming China (1368–1644)', which was selected as one of the 2020 winners of the Young Scholar Seminar at ESHET annual conference (European Society for the History of Economic Thought). For those who are interested, please refer to https://www.eshet.net/eshet-grants/265-1683/2020-winners-of-the-young-scholar-seminar.

T. Hua, *Merchants, Market and Monarchy*,
Palgrave Studies in the History of Economic Thought,
https://doi.org/10.1007/978-3-030-77189-8_7

7.1 Merchants Relative to Scholars

7.1.1 New Theory of Four Occupational Groups: Cliché or Coinage

It is widely recognized by many scholars that in the history of Chinese economic thought, the very first scholar putting forward the so-called 'new theory of four occupational groups' was Wang Yangming (1472–1528), the founder of the Yangming School. As a great Confucian of the Ming dynasty, he insisted on writing an epitaph titled *Inscription mourning Fang Lin*[3] to a merchant named Fang Lin in Kunshan,[4] which was considered to have epoch-making significance.

An extremely well-known Confucian writing an epitaph for a merchant was something absolutely unimaginable in previous dynasties or before the mid-Ming period. This inscription was written three years before Wang Yangming's death. Fang Lin was originally a scholar. He married the daughter of a merchant and thus gave up imperial examinations and engaged in commerce. He actively participated in public service, while training his two sons to study as Confucian students who later became officials. He was thus locally considered as a sage. In the inscription, Wang wrote that a friend once asked Fang, 'Why don't you become a Confucian and become a merchant instead?' Fang replied, 'How do you know that a Confucian can't engage in commerce, and a merchant can't be a Confucian?' Then, Wang Yangming expressed his own thought:

> The ancient sages proposed the theory of four occupational groups, but people from different occupations actually follow the same path. Scholars cultivate themselves by studying Confucian and govern the country, farmers use tools and plough the fields, craftsmen polish their work pieces and make utensils, and merchants are responsible for the circulation of goods. People with different professions do their work diligently. Although they belong to different industries, they have fulfilled their respective responsibilities, and there is no difference. All men, regardless of their occupation, can become sages Yao or Shun, once they grasp the essence of their philosophy.[5] (my transl.)

[3] 'Inscription mourning Fang Lin', *Jie Fang AnGong Mubiao* in Chinese, was written in 1525.

[4] Kunshan, belongs to Jiangsu province, is a neighbouring city of Shanghai.

[5] Wang (1978 [1525], p. 454).

Compared to the fact that Wang Yangming wrote an epitaph for a merchant, this view was undoubtedly more striking. Wang Yangming's words clearly put the merchants at a similar social status level as that of scholars and peasants, 'four occupations share the same pursuit and no occupation has superiority over others, despite different work content'.[6] Wang pointed out that the professionalism and ability of merchants in 'circulating goods' should be equally respected just like the painstaking work of scholars and farmers. This view was later developed by Huang Zongxi during the late years of the Ming dynasty, who transferred it into the thought that[7] 'both the craft and commerce are root industries'.[8]

However, do Wang Yangming's words really show that the relative status of merchants and scholars have been completely reversed? These thoughts of Wang Yangming have always been regarded as important expositions of the fundamental change of merchants' social status after the mid-Ming period. Even the famous Ming expert Yu Ying-shih,[9] in his work, pointed out that the traditional theory of four occupational groups came to an important change during late Ming and early Qing period, and quoted the epitaph written by Wang Yangming as 'an epoch-making document'.[10]

However, there clearly existed two issues here. First, even if some opinions appeared during the middle and late Ming periods that the status of merchants was equal to that of other professions, we cannot easily conclude that the traditional theory of four occupational groups has been overturned. We may boldly infer that the meaning of 'only the son of a merchant can become a scholar' is that scholars cannot afford the necessary material foundation for the next generation because of their living pressure, so engaging in commerce has become a last resort. This choice is not an initiative of the scholars themselves, but is forced by economic pressure. Once merchants become wealthy, they still want themselves or their children to 'gain a decent social status by studying Confucianism

[6] Li (2013, p. 10).

[7] 'both the craft and commerce are root industries' is, in Chinese, *gong shang jie ben*.

[8] Huang (1975 [1695], p. 132).

[9] Yu Ying-shih (1930–) is a Chinese-born American historian, sinologist, and was a tenured professor at Harvard University and Yale University before his time at Princeton. His major research interest lies in synthesis of Chinese history and philosophy.

[10] Yu (1987, pp. 118–119).

and taking part in the imperial exams'.[11] This phenomenon existed not only in ancient China or the Ming dynasty, but also in current times. Ming Merchants always 'sought official positions and meritorious names through donation and by actively carrying out charitable activities'.[12] The purpose was nothing more than to promote their social status.

In the imperial examination system, the scholars who couldn't pass the exam and get the official positions actually occupied the vast majority of the scholars. Meanwhile the success of the Ming dynasty merchants seduced the scholars. The young people who had not gained anything in the imperial examinations had only two options: to farm or to do business. In the era of quickly developing commerce, even though engaging in commerce still requires excellent talents compared to 'ten years of hard studying', it is still relatively easy to make profits by engaging in business. In the middle and late Ming periods, a folk saying spread: 'Only one of the ten scholars can succeed, while nine of the ten merchants can succeed'.[13] During Mongolian's Yuan China, a famous scholar named Xu Heng put forward a theory of 'earning living', in which he claimed that 'scholars should live by engaging in agriculture'.[14] While accepting the adoption of other methods to 'earn living', the scholars in Ming leaned towards becoming merchants instead of 'engaging in agriculture'. And, in addition to basic survival issues, the profit-seeking climate in social reality has also changed scholars' views on merchants.

Even officials who were regarded as successful people among scholars also engaged in commerce and, in most cases, it was not due to corrupt intent, but rather for a living as well. As early as the Northern Song dynasty, Wang Anshi pointed out: 'The salaries of most officials nowadays are very low'.[15] It is for sure that the salaries of officials in Ming China were much lower than those in the Northern Song. Thus, official-scholars in Ming had an even stronger incentive to operate commerce due to their meagre salaries. But this is certainly not due to merchants suddenly gaining more respect from the scholar class.

[11] Hua (2019, p. 5).

[12] Handlin (1998, p. 419).

[13] Yu (1987, pp. 92–93).

[14] Xu (1983 [1281], pp. 288–292).

[15] Wang (1961 [1086], Vol. 39, p. 222).

Second, at least as early as the Tang and Song dynasties, the era long before Wang Yangming lived, scholars' needs for commerce and the changes of their perceptions of merchants had led to scholars' expressions of sympathy for merchants or 'the four occupations being equal'. For example, some Tang scholars praised the righteous deeds of some merchants and described their activities in a fair manner. Liu Zongyuan[16] even thinks that Song Qing, a Chang'an drug dealer who, 'using his own money to rescue poor people, was more noble than the scholars who pursued profit in the officialdom'.[17] Fan Zhongyan[18] of the Song dynasty wrote in his work, 'Merchants engaging in commerce is good for the country, and nice for their own livelihood as well'. 'Merchants had their normal registrations just as other occupations since the Zhou dynasty. Why should they be considered as engaging in the "branch" occupation?'.[19]

Fan Zhongyan expressed profound sympathy to the merchants in his verse. In other verses, it also showed a strong criticism of 'the moral loss of scholars'.[20] Sima Guang, another famous Song Confucian, also regarded peasants, craftsmen, and merchants as equal in status, and affirmed their respective value and contribution. Sima Guang said: 'The labour of peasants, craftsmen, and merchants are all the source of wealth ... The merchants are responsible for the circulation of goods. Some have excess goods while others want to buy them. There is nothing to blame to become the intermediary.'[21]

Fan Zhongyan and Sima Guang's attitude towards merchants illustrates that some Confucians' views on merchants in the Song dynasty are already quite different from the traditional theory of four occupational groups. And such a view is more clearly illustrated in some scholars' work in the succeeding Southern Song. For instance, Huang Zhen[22] asserted

[16] Liu Zongyuan (773–819) was a famous poet, writer, and politician in Tang China.

[17] Li (2013, p. 13).

[18] Fan Zhongyan (989–1052) was a philosopher, writer, military strategist, and a well-known scholar-official in Northern Song China.

[19] Fan (1919 [1052], Vol. 1, p. 9).

[20] Yu (1987, pp. 81–82).

[21] Sima (1919 [1086], Vol. 23, p. 223).

[22] Huang Zhen (1213–1280) was a scholar and official in Southern Song, who was a local in Cixi, Zhejiang.

that scholars, peasants, and merchants 'are among the same class' and 'have no distinction'.[23]

Thus, we can say that Wang Yangming's theory of four occupational groups stated in the epitaph did not exceed his predecessors. I agree with Li's assertion that as a master of Confucianism, 'the fact that Wang Yangming affirmed the equal social status of the four occupations is naturally some thought that cannot be ignored, but we cannot overemphasize its impact'.[24] It seems that Wang Yangming's thought of the four occupations has spread or at least developed during the Tang and Song period. The thoughts reflected in the first-hand literature of Tang and Song thinkers that are quoted above are representative, and we will be sure to find more evidence if we dig deeper into more primary materials.

From the thoughts stated above, we can see that, when the Confucians reassessed the status of merchants, they were all in a time when commerce was more developed and merchants and scholars were in close contact. Regarding the thought of equality among scholars, farmers, workers, and merchants, there may be internal thought changes in Confucianism, but the external factors of the socio-economic environment may have a deeper impact on it.

We may find some other evidence that the traditional theory of four occupational groups has not been overturned. Tang Shunzhi,[25] another great Ming Confucian who lived later than Wang Yangming, wrote the following paragraph in a letter, mocking Wang Yangming's writing of the epitaph for the merchant,

> As for Wang Yangming writing the epitaph, it is ridiculous. But in fact, if you really get used to it, it is not so ridiculous. After all, even those people who are engaged in slaughtering animals and selling wine will die and must have someone to help them write an epitaph ... This kind of thing was absolutely absent before the Xia, Shang and Zhou dynasties, not to mention the era before the Tang and Han dynasties.[26]

[23] Zhu (1986, p. 133).

[24] Li (2013, p. 15).

[25] Tang Shunzhi (1507–1560) was a Confucian scholar, military strategist and mathematician.

[26] Tang (1922 [1560], p. 223).

It obvious here that Tang Shunzhi turned up his nose at people who were 'slaughtering animals and selling wine', who he thought did not deserve an epitaph written by a Confucian, especially a well-known Confucian like Wang Yangming. And writing an epitaph for a merchant, from Tang's view, was something unimaginable regarding scholars' deemed behaviour. And, unfortunately, Tang's attitude might still be the mainstream even in the late Ming period. Just as Brook pointed out, 'The presence [of scholars' writing] on the stele was hardly a major concession to the rising status of merchants within gentry culture, inasmuch as both groups of merchants were licensed agents of the state and enjoyed a status far above that of ordinary merchants'.[27] And in the succeeding Qing China, the Emperors continuously proclaimed clear decrees of the orthodox status of the traditional theory of four occupational groups and the idea of *zhongnong yishang*. Thus, we may safely conclude that Wang Yangming's new theory was neither new nor long-lasting.

7.1.2 *Yangming School and Donglin School: Overturning Illusion*

The above analysis can also be confirmed from the viewpoints of the descendants of Wang Yangming. Following Wang, some of the most well-known thinkers in the Yangming School continued to develop Wang Yangming's thoughts regarding the four occupations, but none of their thoughts could prove that the status of merchants was considered higher than that of scholars in the middle and late Ming period. Since Yangming School concentrated on 'cultivating the mind' instead of 'reading classics', thus their thoughts regarding merchants either came from the reality or originate from their cultivation.[28]

Specifically, the left side of the spectrum of the Yangming School collected students almost all from lowest rung, quite a few of whom were small merchants.[29] Its representative Li Zhi stated in general terms that 'all skills that can be used to make a living can be learned'.[30] He considered that all useful occupations, surely also including the traditional four

[27] Brook (1993, p. 220).

[28] Ji (2013 [1943], p. 141).

[29] Ji (2013 [1943], p. 175).

[30] Li (2001 [1602], p. 38).

occupations, can be regarded as equal, but did not highlight the relative status of merchants and scholars.

He Xinyin, who also belongs to the Taizhou School, rearranged the traditional order of the four occupations, asserting that 'the role of merchants is greater than that of peasants and craftsmen, and the role of scholars is greater than that of merchant'.[31] He made it clear that the status of merchant was below that of scholars:

> He moves the merchant to second place in the traditional ranking system. In another instance, he placed merchants and scholars together in contrast to the lower orders, and in a similar vein he wrote, 'Moreover, if a merchant understands the status of scholar, and relies on it, then this is to transcend the status of merchant, and become a scholar…can we not say that he has mastery over the scholar status.'[32] (my transl.)

By the end of the Ming dynasty, Huang Zongxi of the Jiangyou School, generally considered as the right-wing of the Yangming School, starting from the theory of human nature, lashed out at the contempt of merchants in the previous dynasty, arguing that taking commerce as the 'branch' was a 'Confucian delusion'. He pointed out that the nature of the ruling class to restrain merchants is 'aiming at monopolizing the interests of the whole world'. He denied the thought of merchants as the most inferior occupation and proposed that craftsmen who 'had been desired by the capable and virtuous monarchs', and merchants 'who had been considered necessary for trade', were 'both essential'.[33] However, meanwhile, he pointed out that the commercial nature of services for production and non-production is different. From his view, the circulation of goods serving the production sector was reasonable and could increase national wealth, while the circulation of luxury goods serving non-production sectors was not conducive to the growth of national wealth and was to thus continue to be regarded as the 'branch'. He clearly stated that 'commerce activities outside the cloth, cotton, and silk should all be prohibited'.[34]

[31] Lufrano (1997, p. 44). Also may refer to He (1960 [1579], Vol. 3, p. 76).

[32] Lufrano (1997, pp. 44–45).

[33] Huang (2011 [1662], p. 29).

[34] Huang (2011 [1662], pp. 29–30).

Huang's thought shows that only the non-luxury commerce can be excluded from the 'branch'. And he attaches certain importance to merchants based on the fact that 'merchants had been considered necessary for trade'. Therefore, he does not respect the commerce activities and merchants from the heart. There is also nowhere in his thought to find the way in which the status of merchants is compared with scholars, and we may safely presume that he did not overthrow the status of the merchants among the traditional four occupations.

The thoughts regarding the four occupations in the Donglin School, the school generally considered as supporting merchants, also only played the same old tune. For instance, Zhu Guozhen,[35] who served as the vice grand secretary, said, 'Agriculture and commerce are the foundation of the country and the lifeblood of the people'.[36] Zhao Nanxing[37] said that 'The scholars, peasants, craftsmen and merchants are all eligible occupations for those who want to make a living'.[38] None of them seems to have had the intention to overturn the traditional order of the four occupations.

7.1.3 The Prerequisite for the Recognition of Merchants

Scholars' acknowledgement and praise of merchants appear more frequently among Ming scholars. However, after taking a closer look, the appreciation often comes with some prerequisites. First of all, although engaging in commerce was recognized as a normal occupation like agriculture and crafts, scholars believed that the only legitimacy of becoming a merchant was to pursue profit. In other words, if a merchant cannot make profits, there were no longer any reasons to consider being a merchant as a decent occupation. For instance, Liu Daxia[39] a prominent official, taught his children that 'commerce is only honourable when you want to become richer'.[40] This was actually a widespread phenomenon: 'the elders of the group chose those young men whom they regarded as qualified for

[35] Zhu Guozhen (1558–1632) was a historian and writer in Ming China.

[36] Zhu (2012 [1632], Vol. 9, p. 69).

[37] Zhao Nanxing (1550–1628) was politician, one of the leaders of Donglin School.

[38] Zhao (2000 [1627], Vol. 4, p. 72).

[39] Liu Daxia (1437–1516) was poet and once served as Minister of Military.

[40] Yin (2000 [1631], pp. 5–6).

study and met the costs of preparation, examination and the purchase of office'.[41]

And in the opposite direction, from scholars' views, merchants were considered to have the necessity to become officials, that is, to learn from scholars' career paths. By using Needham's word, 'In every age the sole ambition of the sons of even wealthy merchants was to get into the official bureaucracy; such was the prestige value of the world-outlook of the scholar-gentry that every channel of advancement led through it and every young man of whatever origin wanted to get into it'.[42] Some scholars even suggested that officials should be picked up not only from traditional civil service examinations, but from merchants as well. The proposal came from Chen Yiqin[43] Minister of Rites during the Emperor Longqing era. He asserted that the state should not select officials from the official Confucian schools or from the imperial examinations alone.[44] He believed that talents may also be found among the butchers, wine-sellers, or even fortune tellers.[45] However, this precisely reflects that the scholars still believed that if a merchant wanted to truly reflect his value (and be respected), it was by far not enough to be a merchant alone. Only after becoming an official could they receive real respect.

Secondly, merchants being publicly envied and appreciated is based on their financial resources, their contribution to charity, and their respect for their ancestors (through activities like repairing ancestral temples), rather than the accomplishment in their commerce activities or the legality of engaging in commerce. For instance, Wu Kuan[46] asserted that 'the state could benefit financially if the court honoured a man like Tang Jin, a successful merchant from Suzhou who is well-known for his charitable activities'.[47] This kind of thought obviously follows 'the teachings of Confucius, as recorded in the Mencius, also advocated benevolence',[48]

[41] Weber et al. (1978, pp. 320–321).

[42] Needham (2005 [1969], p. 39).

[43] Chen Yiqin (1511–1586) once served as Minister of Rites. He was one of the descendants of Chen Yaozuo (963–1044), a prime minster during Northern Song period.

[44] Zhang (2000 [1598], pp. 14–15).

[45] Zhang (2000 [1598], p. 62).

[46] Wu Kuan (1435–1504) was a poet, essayist and calligrapher in Ming China.

[47] Wu (1929 [1504], p. 10).

[48] Reda (2018, p. 193).

which can also be found similar expression in other culture, such as Islamic economic thought.[49]

However, without 'contribution to charity', the wealth itself cannot win the praise from scholars. As Brook pointed out, 'The late-Ming gentry represented themselves collectively as the highest elite in local society. That identity conformed with ancient notions regarding the social elevation of the scholar above the merchant and hence could not be predicated on wealth alone'.[50]

One may even suspect that some epitaphs written by Confucians, just like the one Wang Yangming wrote for Fang Lin, are not out of the Confucians' own intent. Instead, some wealthy merchants hired famous scholars to show praises for their philanthropic activities, because the praise to some merchants is a bit blatantly exaggerated.[51] For example, Chen Jiru[52] fiercely criticized that 'some scholar-officials of spending too much money decorating their own homes, while merchants like Fang Liqi helped renovate the ancestral temples'.[53]

7.2 Merchants Relative to Peasants

7.2.1 Deep-Rooted Pro-Agriculture Predisposition

In Chapter 2, I have elaborated the supreme standing of agriculture in ancient China. Interestingly, not only this kind of pro-agriculture thought is not rare in the West, but the Physiocracy and Ming economic thinkers might have interacted with each other already. Prof. Klump suggests that the thought during Ming has influenced French Physiocracy, according

[49] As Reda (2018) stated, '... the Persian empire [who] had established programs of public philanthropy by means of which surplus foods were periodically distributed to the poor...' (p. 197). I paid a visit to Iran with my close friend HHQ in 2018. I saw such kind of relics during my visit not only in Tehran, but in Esfahan and Yazd as well. This is exactly the same thing that many emperors in ancient China (including Ming China) did. For more details regarding the study of economic thought in ancient China and Persian, I recommend Reda (2018), and Wittfogel (1957).

[50] Brook (1993, p. 222).

[51] Lu (1993 [1551], pp. 21–22).

[52] Chen Jiru (1558–1639) was a famous scholar, writer and painter in late Ming.

[53] Chen (2010 [1639], p. 8).

to Poivre, and 'Quesnay himself was probably much more influenced by Chinese thought than is evident from quotations in his woks alone'.[54]

'Food is the first necessity of the people', a famous old saying that originated from *Records of the Grand Historian*, has become popular among the commoners for thousands of years. The importance of diet in the lives of ordinary people in ancient China is self-evident. And since agriculture and the people's diet were inseparable, from this perspective, some thinkers in the Ming dynasty, just like their predecessors, still emphasized the importance of farmers and agriculture. For example, Ma Yilong[55] said, on the basis of the above statement, that 'agriculture is the first necessity of governance, since food is the first necessity of the people'.[56] Similarly, Xu Guangqi said, 'The monarch takes the commoners as the most important issue, the commoners take the diet as the priority, the diet is based on agriculture, and agriculture is based on the power of farmers'.[57] The importance of peasants in their thoughts is quite obvious.

Wang Fuzhi agreed that commerce and commodity circulation were inseparable from people's production and life, and it played an important role in the process of social and economic development. He pointed out that 'merchants and peddlers who engage in trade are indispensable, and the circulation of gold and corn enables people to survive and become richer'.[58] Wang also opposed the government's policy of lowering food prices and the policy of 'driving the merchants thousands of miles away'.[59] He believed that the circulation of commodities was inevitable.[60] Quesnay, as the representative of French Physiocrats, believed that 'merchants are the necessary links between farmers and artisans, who produce the commodities, and landlords and other consumers who want to buy them'.[61]

However, Wang's contempt for merchants was everywhere in his thoughts. For example, reiterating the traditional concept of suppressing

[54] Klump (2004, p. 180).

[55] Ma Yilong (1499–1571) is an agronomist and calligrapher in Ming China.

[56] Ma (1985 [1571], p. 80).

[57] Xu (1984 [1633], p. 9).

[58] Wang (1975 [1692], p. 98).

[59] Wang (1975 [1692], p. 886).

[60] Jiang (1990, pp. 288–289).

[61] Vaggi (1987, p. 67).

merchants, he believed that merchants were exploiters who 'made themselves rich by making others poor'.[62] 'Peasants work hard to accumulate wealth, while merchants use tricks to obtain wealth'[63]; 'Merchants are richer than the country, while the country is becoming poorer'.[64] He fully affirmed the policy of suppressing merchants, as conducted by Sang Hongyang in Western Han, and proposed that 'merchants were the objects that the monarch must suppress'.[65] Likewise, Quesnay also believed that 'then the increase in the fortunes of these merchants represents a deduction from the circulation of the revenue, which is detrimental to distribution and reproduction'.[66]

Wang even believed that merchants were the factors of social unrest just like *yidi* (ethnic minority in the border area). The logic of Wang's argument was as follows: 'The greatest calamity in the world is *yidi* and *xiaoren* (villains)'. The nomads, the representatives of *yidi*, had more 'spirit of commerce', while the nature of merchants was also 'profit-only'. Therefore, Wang believed that if 'minority aristocrats seized the right to control some areas of the Central Plains', it would further promote the development of commerce, thus *yidi* and merchants would be two of a kind, and 'merchants could be more profitable'. The merchants would become villains who relied on the power of *yidi*. On the contrary, if there was no temptation of 'profit' in commerce, merchants would not 'aid and abet an evildoer', and the society would be much more stable.[67] In the history of Chinese economic thought, Wang Fuzhi was among the thinkers who most 'looked upon the merchants as the most wicked among the so-called inferior men, equating them with barbarians'.[68] Wang arbitrarily equated merchants with *yidi* (barbarians) simply because of his profit-seeking nature, which reflected Wang's profound disdain for merchants. Such thoughts may find its parallel in medieval Europe when

[62] Wang (1975 [1692], p. 22).

[63] Wang (1975 [1692], p. 81).

[64] Wang (1975 [1692], p. 56).

[65] Wang (1975 [1692], p. 432).

[66] Vaggi (1987, p. 67).

[67] Wang (1975 [1692], p. 22).

[68] Hu (1988, p. 488).

'Pietism and humanism moved the consciences of scholars and people alike against the wealth displayed by the merchant classes'.[69]

Wang also criticized merchants for bullying peasants. Wang pointed out that tyrants often colluded with merchants to exploit peasants[70] As an enlightened central government, commerce or merchants should not be encouraged. If the government supports merchants, it will lead to 'a society dominated by merchants, where the energy of farmers will wither'.[71]

Therefore, on the issue of the relationship between agriculture and commerce, Wang was a staunch supporter of 'supporting farmers and suppressing merchants'. For example, with regard to the grain trade, Mencius once said, 'As long as there is as much corn as water or fire, people will become full of righteousness'. Wang disagreed. He believed that 'if there is as much corn as water and fire, the merchant will become more treacherous and hoard the corn'. In this way, 'although the farmers are superficially valued, the corn produced by the farmers is becoming increasingly worthless; although the corns are superficially valued, the actual situation is that the gold held by merchants becomes more valuable'. Thus, the farmers were still subject to crafty merchants. Quesnay, on the other hand, confirmed some positive role of merchants to the farmers, 'in years of scarcity, stocks allow tradesmen to limit their demand and to prevent the establishment of even higher current prices, which would be more profitable to the farmers'.[72]

Therefore, Wang resolutely opposed the possession of a large amount of food in the hands of merchants, and advocated the price of gold and silver lower and the value of corn higher through the regulation of grain prices by the state, thereby transferring the interests of merchants to the agricultural sector. Someone asked Wang, 'the rising price of corns will harm the welfare of merchants, while the decreasing price of corns will harm the welfare of peasants. How can we balance these two?'[73] Wang explicitly replied that it was better to hurt the merchants than hurt the farmers.

[69] Poettinger (2019, p. 12).

[70] Wang (1975 [1692], p. 56).

[71] Wang (1975 [1692], p. 56).

[72] Vaggi (1987, p. 68).

[73] Wang (1975 [1692], p. 44).

Xu Guangqi had a similar pro-agriculture inclination with Wang Fuzhi. However, the essence is not the same. He again followed the pragmatism here, just like his thought regarding solving the pirates issue. Xu Guangqi's basic view on wealth was that only corn and cloth (crop production) were the most basic wealth (since they can be directly produced and consumed), while currency was not in the scope of wealth.[74] In fact, Xu's most well-known masterpiece was *Nongzheng Quanshu*,[75] a book discussing.

Since wealth comes from agriculture, Xu advocated *wunong guisu* (emphasis on food production and corn). He pointed out that during the period when state financial resources were exhausted, most of them were among the period when 'less than three in ten are farmers' and 'less than one in ten are hard-working farmers'. So, 'one person farms and dozens of people enjoy it' was the root cause of the depletion of wealth. He said that once the production of food was valued, 'the price of food will definitely fall'. When the price reduced to half, the soldiers in the border town who bought food with silver could now get twice as much food as before. And when the price was reduced by two-thirds, the soldiers could get three times as much food as before.[76]

For the purpose of developing agriculture, Xu believed that it was necessary to restrain merchants. He said, 'Today there are too many people working in the branch (commerce) while too few people in the root (agriculture). It is best (for the government) to make some regulations to drive most people in the branch to engage in agriculture. Peasants should further be respected'.[77]

Based on Sima Qian's division of the *benfu* (people who get rich by cultivating in fields), *mofu* (people who get rich by engaging in commerce), and *jianfu* (people who get rich by crafty skills), Xu pointed out,

> Currently there are hustling and bustling individuals in the south. If you want to cultivate, there are not enough fields; if you want to participate

[74] Xu (1984 [1633], p. 237).

[75] *Nongzheng Quanshu* is a book written by Xu Guangqi, summarizing the previous agriculture techniques and recording new techniques at the time. Please refer to Wen et al. (2001, p. 22).

[76] Xu (1984 [1633], p. 8).

[77] Xu (1984 [1633], p. 9).

> in the imperial examinations, there are not enough places. Then many people can only abandon the agriculture and engage in commerce. Most of the *mofu* have not become a scourge of society, but the *jianfu* are surely becoming a major worry for the society.[78] (my transl.)

Meanwhile, he said, 'Although most of the *mofu* have not become the scourge of society, reducing the number of *mofu* is still necessary'. He also said, 'It is necessary to gradually move the population from the south to the north, so that both the *mofu* and *jianfu* will be *benfu*'.[79] Xu believed that this could make 'the folk customs increasingly simpler and the state wealth more abundant'.[80]

Despite these seeming cliché, in many ways, Xu's work is considered as 'remarkable for its fight against the traditional doctrine'.[81] For instance, while the Confucian doctrine asserted that all plants had their own favourable region and should not be transferred to other areas, Xu 'rejected this view and pointed out that he saw no reason why the fitness of land for a given plant should be fixed and should never be changed'.[82] Thus, as a scholar-official, he appeared more like a modern scientist, regardless of his clear dislike towards merchants for the aim of strengthening the state. His thought therefore certainly cannot be simply categorized in the traditional sphere.

7.2.2 Equalizing Agriculture and Commerce

As mentioned above, the thought of *zhongnong yishang* is deeply engrained in the Chinese subconscious, which was still quite marketable in the Ming dynasty. However, the thought of 'equal emphasis on peasants and merchants' has gradually been recognized by more thinkers (before the Ming dynasty, the idea of equal emphasis on farmers and merchants was very sporadic).

78 Xu (1984 [1633], p. 229).

79 Xu (1984 [1633], p. 227).

80 Xu (1984 [1633], p. 228).

81 Klump (2004, p. 182).

82 Klump (2004, p. 182).

Following the consistent idea of being thrifty in the history of Chinese economic thought, Zhang Juzheng also believed that the country's financial management should give top priority to saving financial expenses. He praised the literati in the salt and iron debate in Western Han, and argued that 'though their remarks may seem pedantic, their thoughts were implemented by Emperor Zhaodi of Western Han and eventually achieved splendid results'.[83]

From this, he concluded, 'the people who managed the country's finances perfectly in ancient times all saved unnecessary expenses and did not increase the channels of profit at will'. And even when the country was lacking, 'it is still necessary to plan for a long time and develop the economy in a direction that benefits the people'.[84]

To achieve this, Zhang proposed a new theory on the relationship between agriculture and commerce. He said that since the Warring States period, thinkers who advocated *zhongnong yishang* had always emphasized that there was a contradiction between commerce and agriculture, asserting that over-development of commerce hindered agricultural production. Although many thinkers affirmed the positive role of commerce and merchants before, no one has come to understand the relationship between the two from the side of mutual promotion between agriculture and commerce.

Zhang said that in the past, when the central government encountered financial difficulties, it often levied more taxes from merchants to obtain income, and the Ming dynasty was no exception. He criticized this approach, arguing that agriculture and commerce were interdependent and mutually beneficial, and damage to either party would affect the other. He said,

> People who governed the country should focus on keeping merchants' goods flowing. If the merchants do not conduct commerce smoothly, the situation of the farmers will be worse. And if the farmers have insufficient financial resources to buy goods, the situation of the merchants will also become worse.[85] (my transl.)

[83] Zhang (1937 [1582], p. 360).

[84] Zhang (1937 [1582], p. 790).

[85] Zhang (1937 [1582], p. 360).

To be more specific, Zhang believed that both agricultural and commercial taxes need to be reduced to alleviate the burden on both farmers and merchants.

> In order to let people have enough food and enough energy for work, then it is no better than reducing agricultural taxes to treat farmers kindly, so that they have enough money to buy merchants' goods; In order to let people have enough daily necessities, then it is no better than reducing customs duties to treat merchants kindly, which is ultimately good for peasants.[86] (my transl.)

As a result, agriculture and commerce developed in a mutual promotion.

Hai Rui was also a supporter of the traditional theory of emphasizing agriculture. He believed that the fundamental way for the commoners' living was to develop agriculture, and considered agriculture as 'the top priority of the four occupations'. However, he also said that 'below the scholar class, farmers are the most important', which is inconsistent with his statement that the farmers are 'the top priority of the four occupations'. Nevertheless, his emphasis on agriculture was unquestionable. He criticized that some officials asserted 'emphasizing agriculture' while in fact 'despising agriculture'.[87] The peasants had 'no wealth and no ability to give the officials any benefit'. 'They can't speak nice words, and their taste is vulgar'.[88] Therefore, rulers often didn't take them seriously. This caused many peasants to 'run away from the root and become reckless and cunning'.[89] He demanded a change in this situation of undervaluing agriculture and peasants. He sharply pointed out, 'I don't see that there is anything to talk about regarding government administration if agriculture is abandoned'.[90]

However, Hai Rui's thinking was different from traditional Confucianism: Hai Rui attached importance to peasants but did not restrain merchants. Although this may be related to his birth in Guangdong, or contribute to his long-term experience being an official in Jiangsu and Zhejiang where commerce was developing rapidly, it reflects to a

[86] Zhang (1937 [1582], p. 212).

[87] Ye (2003, p. 363).

[88] Ye (2003, p. 363).

[89] Hai (1962 [1587], p. 252).

[90] Hai (1962 [1587], p. 252).

certain extent that the Ming dynasty Confucian thinkers like Hai Rui, who called themselves 'orthodox successors of Confucianism', were obviously different from the Confucians in previous dynasties. He truthfully believed that commerce promoted agriculture. Merchants, just like peasants, were 'labours that are conducive to society', and they adopted 'survival strategies' that could 'support themselves as a living'.[91] He not only treated merchants justly, but also proceeded with his thought that 'merchants can provide funds to the whole country'.[92] He believed that more *xushi* (villages or places that were once populated by people and now deserted) needed to be re-established to 'provide places for merchants to trade', thus making 'the market thrive'.[93]

7.2.3 *Talented Merchants, Dumb Farmers*

Merchants and the three other occupations were all means of livelihood and were different options people chose for life. In Sect. 7.1, it has been pointed out that becoming officials, i.e. the main method of making a living for scholars, was recommended to merchants. There is no doubt that this method of 'making a living' was fully affirmed. So, what did the thinkers of the Ming dynasty think about the other two ways of making a living, namely merchants 'doing business' and peasants 'cultivating land'?

Dating back to the Western Han dynasty, Sima Qian, in his *Records of the Grand Historian*, said, 'If a man is not a gentleman of talent who has deliberately sought retirement, and if he grows old in poverty and lowliness, and still insists upon talking about "benevolence and righteousness", then he ought to be ashamed of himself'.[94] In other words, what Sima Qian is criticizing is 'not the fact that people grow old poor, but the fact that, having failed to make any money'.[95]

Accordingly, he summed up the thoughts of how merchants make a living (*zhisheng*), which should be the first time ever in the history of Chinese economic thought. Sima Qian believed that, in order to 'make a living', the merchants needed to have the following four abilities: 'getting

[91] Hai (1962 [1587], p. 249).

[92] Hai (1962 [1587], p. 249).

[93] Hai (1962 [1587], p. 249).

[94] Watson (1958, p. 151).

[95] Watson (1958, p. 151).

wealth through the branch industry (commerce) and then protecting the wealth through the root industry (agriculture)'; mastering the timing of decisions in commerce activities (very similar with Sombart's saying, 'the undertaker must be able to do the right thing at the right time'[96]); the ability to get reasonable profit rates; and personal qualities. The personal qualities can also be understood by using Sombart's words, 'Intellectual elasticity, mental energy, and intensity and constancy of will'.[97]

However, similar thoughts like Sima Qian's were not mentioned again for a long time until the mid-Ming dynasty when merchants making a living became one of the main concerns again. Quite a few scholars observed that, compared with engaging in agriculture, only people with rare ability, ingenuity, and insight could become successful merchants.

For instance, Xie Zhaozhe[98] emphasized that 'if some commoner can become rich and lead a good life through engaging in commerce, then this person must have extraordinary abilities'. It was from this perspective that he fully understood Sima Qian's insistence on writing a full section of biographies for 'people engaging in commerce' in *Records of the Grand Historian*.[99]

Xie divided the more successful merchants into three categories: merchants like Tao Zhugong and Ji Ran belonged to the first class, who had a sense of time, and a keen business mind and insight; merchants like Zhuo Shi and Cheng Zheng belonged to the second class, who got rich by working hard in living rough or on the market; the third class included people like Shi Chong and Wang Yuanbao, who were corrupt officials engaging in commerce by using their power in hand. Xie believed that most of the merchants in Ming belonged to the first and second class. Their ability to pursue *mofu* was higher than the ability of farmers in pursuing *benfu*, so it was worthy of respect.[100]

Another example is Gu Dashao, who believed that the peasants' pursuit of wealth mainly depended on thrift, while the success of merchants was not frugality. Instead, insight was the key to a merchant's success. He said, for example, if a merchant has great interest for an item, in order to

[96] Sombart (1967 [1915], pp. 55–56).

[97] Sombart (1967 [1915], p. 53).

[98] Xie Zhaozhe (1567–1624) was a famous scholar in late Ming.

[99] Xie (2001 [1624], pp. 90–91).

[100] Xie (2001 [1624], pp. 90–91).

get it, he depended on two qualities, namely '*lüe*' and '*cha*'. The so-called '*lüe*' stands for strategy and talent; the so-called '*cha*' means investigating, making clear observations, and grasping the latest market changes in a timely manner.[101] Therefore, he believed, compared with peasants, the talents of successful merchants were just enough for them to make great amounts of money.[102]

These Ming thinkers just praised the merchants for their extraordinary talents compared to the peasants. Some other thinkers not only emphasized the merchant's ability, but also pointed out that the farmers were stupid in comparison. For example, Gu Yanwu argued that doing business was considered to require excellent capabilities. He indicated that 'the profit earned was proportional to the amount of labour and the degree of commerce ability the merchant showed'.[103]

Li Zhi expressed similar views. Li said that since the snobbery was the natural endowment of people, it was natural for people to compete for chasing snobbishness or wealth, and to differentiate between the competition. He believed that although everyone had a snobbish heart, it was 'different by birth' for individuals to obtain wealth. Farmers did not possess such talents. Therefore, competition would inevitably lead to victory and differentiation. 'Strong people will annex the weak, and those who are in the minority will be dependent on the majority'.[104] Therefore, Li affirmed competition and acknowledged the law of market competition in which superiority prevailed, while the peasants lacked these abilities.[105]

Such ability of a merchant making a living was sometimes even considered to be better than some scholars. For example, Hai Rui believed that everyone who engaged in socially beneficial occupations, whether in agriculture or in other fields, should be respected by society. He believed that what was 'shameless' were those 'lazy people' who were parasitic and harmful to society. Among them, according to Hai Rui's classification, included 'the pedantic Confucians who indulge in empty talk' and 'decadent scholar-officials living extravagantly', both of whom actually belonged to the scholar class. Later, Li Wen also had a similar thought:

[101] Gu (1997 [1571], p. 65).

[102] Chen (2014, p. 256).

[103] Gu (1985 [1682], pp. 14–15).

[104] Li (2000 [1602], p. 35).

[105] Zhu (1957, p. 21).

'Previously vagrants were mostly treacherous and stubborn people, while today's vagrants are mostly Confucian students'. Although this kind of praise, as mentioned before, cannot be regarded as evidence that the merchant class surpassed the scholar class, at least it acted as a foil that the merchant's ability was sometimes even considered to be better than some scholars, not to mention 'stupid and rustic' farmers!

7.2.4 *Shifted Views on Wealth: Dampening the Peasant Class*

Shifted views on getting rich might be another major reason for the decline in the status of peasants in Ming. Men farming and women weaving were regarded as a 'holy monarch's system' in ancient China, and are also the main content of traditional life: 'Men do not weave but have clothes to wear, and women do not cultivate but have food to eat. Men and women exchange their gains for survival'.[106]

However, Ming China was actually very different from the previous dynasties. Due to the commerce development in Ming, while the life may be self-supporting and self-sufficient by being frugal previously, in Ming China, both diligence and wisdom seem to be prerequisites for a decent life, as 'diligence and application are the sources of wealth'.[107] Based on this, the status of peasants began to sharply decline. As Chen Yiqin said in his memorial to the emperor,

> During the last century, the interests of the branch (commerce) have flourished, and many farmers who have stayed in their hometown have developed the habit of laziness. Many fields are uncultivated, and many families are not able to leave a single penny of savings if they have many mouths to feed. The situation can get worse if levying exorbitant taxes occurs.[108] (my transl.)

This statement has clearly revealed the actual situation of life in the rural areas and the two major thoughts regarding the decline in the status of farmers. First, for the first time in history, laziness is considered to be one of the main reasons for the decline of the peasant's status, especially when society is stable and the court's taxation is relatively light (since

[106] Xu (1979 [1633], p. 44).

[107] Sombart (1967 [1915], p. 109).

[108] Zhang (2002 [1636], p. 50).

during the time when the court levied exorbitant taxes, both farmers and merchants were in a miserable situation, and there was no question of whose status was higher ...). In ancient China, it has always been believed that as long as you are frugal, you can keep your family surviving and even get rich. This is one of the fundamental economic thoughts in traditional China, and in fact it must have some reasonable element, but in the Ming dynasty, this thought may seem out of place.

The thought of Cai Yu[109] is very representative among the scholars in Ming. He believes that 'getting rich normally contributes to hard work, while poverty must originate from laziness'.[110] This view is certainly questionable, but such ideas were not even possible to appear before the Ming dynasty, since there has always been such a view among thinkers in Chinese history: if poverty occurs among peasants, then it must be due to the imperialist expropriation or exploitation of land owners (the annexation of well-connected families or wealthy merchants). Sang Hongyang in Western Han, Liu Yan in Tang, Wang Anshi, and Ouyang Xiu in Northern Song all have such thoughts. Regardless of their thoughts on state monopoly, they all want to simply adopt the strategy of 'robbing the rich and helping the poor' in order to benefit peasants, which will ultimately guarantee the stability of the state. These, in the view of Huang Guan, a Ming thinker, are undoubtedly inappropriate. He believes that 'Both merchants or peasants are people of the monarch and should be treated equally'.[111]

Second, the development of commerce in the Ming dynasty triggered a 'popularity of engaging in *moye* (commerce)'. Not only does Shen Bang agree with the principle that 'the key to earning a living is hard work', but he also sees the increasing diversity of paths to becoming rich in the Ming dynasty, rather than simply working hard on farming.[112] He believed that 'The noble families and government officials, who are rich because of their special status, can be taken for granted. However, even being a servant at the noble's house or a merchant who has a relationship with the rich is

[109] Cai Yu (?–1541) was a scholar, calligrapher and calligraphy theorist in Ming China.

[110] Zhang (2002 [1636], p. 61).

[111] Huang (1983 [1551], p. 45).

[112] Shen (1980 [1597], p. 8).

better than being a peasant'.[113] It can be seen here that commercialization has led to the differentiation of the rural population, and at least in some areas has formed a tendency to abandon farming and engaging in commerce.

Therefore, before the Ming Dynasty, the migration of most new refugees who were originally peasants was mostly from one agricultural area to another, or to an uncultivated remote area. Although some of them might entered the city, they all ended up with staying unemployed or wandering in the city. However, after the mid-Ming Dynasty, the situation changed significantly. Especially in many areas along the southeast coast, peasants who were forced by living purposefully entered cities and towns to engage in commerce or handicraft, or 'became merchants directly on the spot (in the countryside)'.[114]

7.3 Merchants Relative to Artisans

Unfortunately, it is almost impossible to find direct thoughts or direct historical facts about the relative position of merchants and craftsmen. After all, commerce and handicrafts were both regarded as the 'branch industries' in ancient China, or using Sombart's saying, 'The craftsman as an undertaker bears the mark of the trader; and both have much in common'.[115] It is thus understandable that scholars and thinkers were not interested in comparing the two groups at all. Therefore, in order to make a rough comparison of the relative positions of merchants and craftsmen, I first analyze the thoughts and attitudes of the scholars about the craftsmen, and then I will appraise the relative positions of the merchants and craftsmen by combining the thoughts and attitudes of the scholars on the merchants.

7.3.1 *Admiration and Sorrow for the Craftsmen*

Huang Zongxi, a famous scholar of the late Ming period, attacked the absurdity of a suggestion to restrict craftsmen and merchants. He pointed out that the intention of the ancient kings in restraining the 'substance'

113 Shen (1980 [1597], p. 8).

114 Sun (2001, p. 205).

115 Sombart (1967 [1915], p. 102).

(or 'branch') industry was to limit the production of useless goods, i.e. goods used by Buddhists, sorcerers, prostitutes, and entertainers. He indicated that those who suggested the restrictions had not examined the ancient rules carefully; thus, they falsely concluded that crafts and trade were 'substance', and recklessly proposed to restrain them. He concluded that craftsmen had been desired by the sage kings and that merchants had been considered necessary for trade; therefore, both craftsmen and merchants were of 'essence' (or 'root').[116]

Although Huang attached great importance to commerce, he believed that only necessary commerce related to people's lives was worth promoting, and any other commerce not related to people's lives should still be prohibited. He differentiated 'commerce served for production' from 'commerce served for circulation of luxuries'. The latter, in his view, was unfavourable to national wealth growth. He included 'machines and emerging workshops'[117] and some other technological innovation in the luxuries group, which thus stayed in the ranks of his firm opposition.

Scholars' attitudes towards artisans were sometimes not just 'emphasizing their importance' like Huang Zongxi. From the mid-Ming dynasty, the society was becoming increasingly extravagant. From the nobles to the commoners, they were all keen to decorate their facades. The importance of products made by artisans was raised to an unprecedented level. Some scholars were even envious of the craftsman class, and meanwhile looked at their shadow and lamented their lot. For example, Yuan Hongdao, who often wandered around street markets in Peking, depicted the grand occasion of the Lantern Festival in this capital city and various 'daily uses for the commoners made by artisans', and lamented himself 'as poor as he were still in the countryside',[118] expressing vividly the huge psychological gap between the aesthetic experience and the reality of his life.

Another example is Shen Meng, a Suzhou native who 'entered the capital for a sightseeing tour', describing his experience. Shen said that he planned to go to the town god's temple (*Chenghuang miao*). A long way before he reached his destination, he was already caught up in sudden and overwhelming 'miscellaneous artefacts made by artisans'.[119]

[116] Huang (2011 [1662], p. 29).

[117] Huang (2011 [1662], p. 30).

[118] Yuan (2010 [1610], p. 625).

[119] Liu (2010 [1636], p. 244).

And after visiting the wonders of the temple, in addition to his aesthetic experience of 'surprise, admiration, and indulgence', he felt helpless and sentimental: 'Confucian articles are not easy to write. Even if they are written, how can they be handed down from generation to generation like those gold and bronze objects'.[120] Among the 'gold and bronze objects' he refers to, a popular product at the time called 'Xuande Furnace' is something 'everyone can afford to buy except himself?',[121] which provokes his sentiment.

7.3.2 *Scholars' Contempt and Disdain of Artisans*

Did the above-mentioned thoughts and facts prove that the status of craftsmen surpassed the scholar class in the middle and late Ming dynasty? Similar to the status of merchants compared to scholars, the answer here is also negative.

Although the commercial prosperity after the mid-Ming dynasty led to the shock of artisan-made works, even life ideas, life tastes, and lifestyles on the established social order, in the face of a society filled with material, the late Ming orthodox intellectuals showed more tendencies towards panic and anxiety, rather than compromise.[122] The scholars overall did not intend to cater to the changes brought about by artisans and merchants, but intended to stick to their positions, at least on the ideological level.

First of all, the hostility of the scholars towards the craftsmen can be frequently seen from the words of the scholars used to describe the products made by craftsmen. Scholars in the middle and late periods of the Ming dynasty analyzed and criticized the phenomenon of social materialization. They often referred to fashionable clothing and utensils as 'clothing demon' (*fu yao*) and 'article demon' (*wu yao*), and others more detailed, such as 'ink demon' and 'fan demon', and so on.[123] For example, Wang Shixing said that 'During the Jiajing, Longqing and Wanli periods, small products randomly made by small pieces of bamboo or small stones can sell at a price of more than thousands of *wen*.

[120] Liu (2010 [1636], p. 244).

[121] Liu (2010 [1636], p. 244).

[122] Luo (2006, p. 153).

[123] Shen (2007 [1642], pp. 660, 663).

Examples are Lu Yukang's jade horse, Xiao Guan's fans, Zhao Liang-bi's silk goods.[124] Regardless of the outrageous price, the appearance of these objects alone is like some "article demon", and looks particularly vulgar'.[125] Shen Defu also said,

> In the previous dynasties, the object is rarer and with higher prices when it is more ancient. However, it is not the case in the Ming dynasty. The red lacquer ware made during Yongle, the heating furnace during Xuande, and the glazed kiln during Chenghua were more expensive than the antiques made in the previous dynasty ... Not only is it difficult to tell whether it is a fake, the degree of their appearance is also like a 'demon' and beyond description.[126]

Second, some artisans were economically rewarding because of their superb skills and exquisite creations, which had attracted the attention of some mainstream scholars. But being aware of this phenomenon does not mean that the scholars recognized the craftsmen. The names of some famous artisans were indeed recorded in history by some scholars such as Yuan Hongdao[127] and Zhang Dai,[128] as mentioned above, which was unthinkable before the Ming dynasty. And 'the conditions of production might also provided the ideal conditions for the recording of craftsmen's names, due to the common practice of workers in the capital-starved luxury trades often taking up residence in a patron's home and working there on expensive raw materials supplied by him'.[129] Nevertheless, the same Zhang Dai once stated explicitly that 'Even if an item is well-known, it is not enough to make the person who made the object enjoy a higher reputation. The person (who made the object) is still humble'.[130] And the same Yuan Hongdao also said,

> These days there are many people who are famous for some small technique. They only make small handiwork that only need nondescript

[124] Clunas (1991, p. 62).

[125] Wang (1997 [1598], p. 33).

[126] Shen (2007 [1642], p. 653).

[127] Yuan (2010 [1610], p. 731).

[128] Zhang (2010 [1684], pp. 20, 60).

[129] Clunas (1991, p. 67).

[130] Zhang (2010 [1684], p. 60).

> techniques. However, some people rushed to buy this stuff. This situation started in the Wuzhong area, the purpose of which is to deceive the wealthy people who can afford high prices. Later, this phenomenon spread to scholars, and thus gradually became a social atmosphere, even though some of the handicrafts are indeed of excellent workmanship, and other craftsmen can't make them. However, after thousands of years, who knows if these handicrafts can be passed on?[131]

While Zhang Dai's statement is relatively simple, Yuan Hongdao clearly pointed out that the market value of the artefacts the artisans made had no necessary relationship with their own social status. Zhang's thought can also be confirmed in Song Yingxing's thought. Song said that artisans were devoted to the practice of 'diabolic tricks and wicked craft', and even introduced Western technology, but these were still 'left out on the table by scholars' because they had 'nothing to do with fame or becoming officials'.[132]

More importantly, the decision of the reputation of artisans and the quality of handicrafts was still in the hands of scholars. As Yuan Hongdao said, 'people of the ancients and today have different preferences'. Although the craftsmanship itself was grasped by the artisans, it was also an entertaining function and thus its true value cannot be determined; this was also the case for the handicrafts. Thus, how can we ensure that skills can meet the 'preference' of the era? In other words, what is the criterion for judging that 'the skill of craftsmen has reached the extreme?' Yuan Hongdao's answer was: 'The scholars appraise the treasures among handicrafts while placing equal emphasis on poetry and painting'.[133] In other words, only if it met the scholars' aesthetic taste, can the handicrafts be recognized, accepted, and appreciated by the scholars, and the artisans can thus be regarded as having 'skills reached the extreme'. Zhang Dai held the same view. He argued that '... the thickness and lightness of the workpieces must be adapted to those of later connoisseurs' eyes. It is hard for a craftsman, since 'the technology must also conform to Tao'.[134] On the other hand, if the handicrafts didn't 'enter the connoisseurs' eyes', that is, the scholars' eyes, 'even if the craftsman has done good and hard

[131] Yuan (2010 [1610], pp. 730–731).

[132] Song (2010 [1637], p. 3).

[133] Yuan (2010 [1610], p. 731).

[134] Zhang (2010 [1684], pp. 20–21).

work and with all kinds of ingenuity, he is not qualified to become a valuable master yet'. On the contrary, in some cases, the craftsman had to bear the risk of becoming a laughingstock. For instance, there was a design named 'horse tail'. Its design and production technology were extremely skilful, but the shape was too exaggerated, not meeting the aesthetic taste of the scholar class, and it was thus mocked and accused.

Moreover, we can see that all well-known craftsmen who have been recorded by scholars have shown a strong scholar temperament in many aspects such as lifestyle and 'ways of getting on in the world'. As recorded by Wang Yingkui, three masters of bamboo products in Zhu family in Jiading[135] (part of current Shanghai) 'can read just like scholars and have noble morals as well'; a wood products maker Xiao Zhongsu 'is good at writing poetry, although he only writes poetry in his spare time'.[136] These words deliberately emphasized the scholarly qualities of craftsmen beyond their own occupation attributes. Similarly, pot master Shi Dabin, potter Wu Jiuzhai, and bamboo ware master Pu Zhongqian, etc., who were appreciated by Yuan Hongdao, all showed some 'traditional scholar style' such as 'being indifferent to fame and profit in nature' and 'treating with indifference when in poverty'.[137] Some individual artisans were even enshrined in temples because of their high moral devotion.[138] These noble behaviours were exactly what Confucianism spared no effort to admire.

To sum up, despite a new social lifestyle and interest in extravagant life in the Ming dynasty, it was still the scholars who mastered the right to speak in essential society and culture issues. Only when those craftsmen who intended to approach the scholar class actively cooperate, imitate their aesthetic taste and even lifestyle, can it be possible for them to obtain positive evaluation and recognition from scholars, and thus 'sit as equals with members of the gentry'.[139] In other words, in the middle and late Ming dynasties, only when some craftsmen in the artisan class showed a trend of 'behaving like scholars' can their status be finally recognized by scholars.

[135] Clunas (1991, p. 62).

[136] Wang (1983 [1759], p. 170).

[137] Gong (2010).

[138] Fu (1993, pp. 118–119).

[139] Clunas (1991, p. 62).

7.3.3 *Merchants and Craftsmen: Fellow Sufferers*

Based on the analysis above, in this section, I will roughly analyze three aspects regarding the status of merchants relative to craftsmen, which were, respectively, the attitude of the scholars towards the merchants and craftsmen, the state's management of the merchants and craftsmen, and the profitability of the merchants and craftsmen.

Scholars' attitudes towards merchants and craftsmen were similar. On the one hand, the envy of scholars towards the craftsmen mentioned above was very similar to the attitude of scholars towards merchants, such as 'Nine out of ten merchants can succeed'. On the other hand, the scholars' disdain for craftsmen were also similarly reflected in the attitudes of scholars towards merchants. 'A distrust of, and even a distaste for, the social role of artisans and their products has deep roots in traditional Chinese political economy'.[140] And this disdain can also be understood as a result of intellectuals thinking themselves morally superior to others. If these two classes want to win the favour of the scholars, their most feasible, if not the only, choice is to imitate the scholar class. Considering the merchants for whom Wang Yangming and others were willing to write epitaphs in Sect. 7.1, they either originally had academic backgrounds and later turned into merchants, or had habits, in terms of ethics and ideals, very close to the scholar class, with a tendency of 'behaving like scholars'. This was very similar to the scholars' views on craftsmen in the previous section as well.

The ability of state-managing merchants and artisans was also similar. In the traditional theory of four occupational groups, the status of craftsman was higher than that of the merchants. The main reason was that although craftsmanship and commerce were both regarded as '*moye*' in addition to '*benye*' (agriculture), travelling merchants, the majority of the merchant class, were always 'homeless wanderers'.[141] Thus it was very inconvenient for the country to manage and monitor them, and 'hence the commercial class was for long looked upon as occupying the lowest rung of the social ladder' (my transl.).[142] In contrast, artisans owned at least one fixed workshop, which would not easily change positions and thus facilitated state supervision. Before the middle of the Ming

[140] Clunas (1991, p. 141).

[141] Wilhelm (1930, p. 25).

[142] Wilhelm (1930, p. 25).

dynasty, craftsmen were all forced to register in some form of 'craftsman registration' (*jiang ji*), and inherited from generation to generation. Artisans worked shifts to serve the country, and this craftsmanship system obviously limited the autonomy of craftsmen. However, from the mid-Ming period, artisans started to resist the system by means of idle work, retreat, escape, etc. The Ming government was thus forced to formulate a substitution plan, which allowed artisans to pay silver instead of working shifts.[143] Therefore, after the abolishment of 'craftsman registration', merchants and craftsmen were similar in terms of freedom, and the state's management of craftsmen was therefore not as convenient as before.

Moreover, compared to the fact that scattered merchants were the main composition of the merchant class before the Ming dynasty, due to the expansion of the merchant gangs, merchants in Ming China have the relative fixed business scope and business areas in many regions. Therefore, it was easier for the state to supervise merchants in the middle and late Ming dynasty. Thus, overall, the feasibility of state-managing merchants and artisans can be considered alike.

In addition, the merchants and craftsmen had similar earning power. I mentioned the extravagant social atmosphere of the middle and late Ming dynasty, so it is not hard to imagine that the ability to make money became an important indicator of social status, which also influenced scholars' views on merchants. Except for the wealthy gentry and royal families, the income and daily life standard of merchants and artisans were close to or even surpassed that of ordinary scholar-officials. For example, the annual income of ordinary yamen runners was about 15 taels in silver, and the salary of the grooms was about 20 taels, which was close to that of the seventh-rank officials[144]; the annual income of artisans' helpers was about 14 taels,[145] while vendors who pushed carts to sell soy milk could have a balance of nearly 20 taels after deducting the daily usage of food and clothing.[146] In contrast, if only relying on salaries without other sources of income (such as contributions from relatives and friends,

[143] Shen (1989 [1587], Vol. 4, p. 273).

[144] Gao (2008).

[145] Jiang (2000 [1605], p. 207).

[146] Feng (1979 [1627], pp. 47–48).

bribery, etc.), being an official was considered to be a 'loss-making business'. In quite a few Ming biographies, we can often find materials stating that the officials often lived beyond their means, or some of them even had no money for interment after death,[147] etc.

To sum up, although the above comparisons were certainly not comprehensive, at least to a certain extent, a rough inference can be made as follows: in the Ming dynasty, especially in the middle and late Ming dynasty, the status of merchants relative to craftsmen can be considered as equal.

7.4 Short Summary

In the middle and late period of Ming China, the phenomenon of identity being changed or overlapped between scholars and merchants was indeed more frequent than before, and the line between scholars and merchants is more blurred. However, the scholars 'did not like to appear entirely easy in the presence of merchants and preferred to draw a disdainful line between the market and the study',[148] and the thought of suppressing merchants under scholars still turned out to be the mainstream.

As mentioned in the analysis in this section, ideological cognition and social phenomena similar to the theory of four occupational groups are not new things unique to the Ming dynasty, but are some diachronically shared facts that can be found throughout the history of ancient China, especially after Tang. At best, it can be said that after the middle of the Ming dynasty, there were more Confucian scholars who held positive views of merchants than before Ming. The social value of the merchant class got more affirmation from other members of the society. Even so, the so-called new theory of four occupational groups, if it existed, did not represent an irreversible trend at all. Even Yu Ying-shih, who believed that 'the merchant's status has begun to surpass scholars', after enumerating and interpreting much evidence, confirmed the emergence of the new theory of four occupational groups with reservations: 'Here we encounter a methodological difficulty: Of course we can find a lot of evidence from the Ming and Qing merchants to practice their moral creed, but how representative is this practice in the real world? According

147 Zhang (1974 [1739], Vol. 14, p. 4205).

148 Brook (1999, p. 211).

to my understanding of Ming and Qing historical materials in this regard, this question remains to be unanswerable'.

As shown by this chapter, in order to determine the relative status of the four occupations, two types of evidence are relied on: the economic thoughts and the actual social phenomenon. They are respectively derived from the expressions and observations of individual members, in most cases, scholars. As we saw, many thoughts were still quite hostile to merchants. And for those thoughts which turned to support the rise in the status of merchants, some contradictory facts can often be found at the same time.

For instance, the statement that 'the scholars are often mixed with merchants' were often mentioned by some scholars after mid-Ming such as Gui Youguang and many other scholars. However, the same Gui Youguang, with his scholar friend Wang Zhong, had witnessed a Confucian school student talking with a merchant. The scholar's humility and the merchant's arrogance caused their dissatisfaction, and Wang Zhong, who was extremely angry, came out and humiliated that merchant. Although we can't make any definitive assertions about this, at least the scholar class still subconsciously believed that such scholarly humility and merchant arrogance were unacceptable and was not in line with the positioning of the relative status of scholars and merchants determined by the traditional theory of four occupational groups. Thus, the scholars 'mixing with merchants' may be explained as scholars who had more interactions with scholars and farmers, with whom they began to share more hobbies. Or, it can also be interpreted as scholars not having avoided those profit-making activities, which were traditionally in merchants' expertise. But it is too far-fetched to interpret it as merchants' status exceeding that of scholars.

Although thoughts of emphasizing peasants and despising merchants still had its market in Ming, it is undeniable that the position of merchants relative to peasants did arise. Moreover, with the support of some evidence, although limited, we can thus safely conclude that, in Ming China, especially in the middle and late Ming dynasty, the relative positions of merchants and craftsmen were basically equal, ranking behind the scholars and before peasants. However, in reality, some discriminatory provisions on merchants, such as the most representative restrictions on the dress of merchants, were almost never abolished from the legal level (the only exception is during Emperor Zhengde's reign, who was considered a monarch of marked individuality in ancient China), regardless of the fact that the restrictions were not strictly observed throughout the Ming dynasty either. As long as the law, which represented the formal regime, did not remove the discrimination against merchants, the discrimination against merchants in the traditional theory of four occupational groups was not truly eliminated, even if the actual social role of merchants was undoubtedly far stronger than that of farmers.

Even with the emergence of the thoughts of equal emphasis on and interaction between agriculture and commerce, the emphasis on agriculture was always the core value of ancient dynasties, and it is still no exception in modern China. It was difficult to shake the orthodox economic thought that had been established for two thousand years with mere commercial development and some changes in some social customs, which was clearly reflected in a large number of economic thoughts and historical facts listed in this chapter. The main tune was still suppressing the development of commerce, and merchants as well.

References

References in German

Wilhelm, R. (1930). *Chinesische Wirtschaftspsychologie*. Deutsche Wissenschaftliche Buchhandlung.

Reference in English

Brook, T. (1993). *Praying for power: Buddhism and the formation of gentry society in late-Ming China*. Harvard University Asia Center.

Brook, T. (1999). *The confusions of pleasure: Commerce and culture in Ming China*. University of California Press.

Clunas, C. (1991). *Superfluous things: Material culture and social status in early modern China*. Polity Press.

Handlin, J. F. (1998). Social hierarchy and merchant philanthropy as perceived in several late-Ming and early-Qing texts. *Journal of the Economic and Social History of the Orient, 41*(3), 417–451.

Hu, J. (1984). *Chinese economic thought before the seventeenth century*. Foreign Language Press.

Hu, J. (1988). *A concise history of Chinese economic thought*. Foreign Languages Press.

Hua, T. (2019). Underdevelopment of commerce in the history of ancient Chinese economic thoughts: An examination of the status of merchants in

Ming China. In *2020 Young Scholar Seminar at ESHET annual conference (European Society for the History of Economic Thought)*.
Klump, R. (2004). The kingdom of Ponthiamas—A physiocratic model state in Indochina: A note on the international exchange of economic thought and of concepts for economic reforms in the 18th century. In I. Barens, V. Caspari, & B. Schefold (Eds.), *Political events and economic ideas* (pp. 173–183). Elgar.
Lufrano, R. J. (1997). *Honorable merchants: Commerce and self-cultivation in late imperial China*. University of Hawaii Press.
Needham, J. (2005 [1969]). *The grand titration: Science and society in East and West* (Vol. 1). Routledge.
Poettinger, M. (2019). The Medici Pope, Jacob Fugger and the new catholic view on the economy: Johann Eck and the problem of usury. In *International Conference at Forschungskolleg Bad Homburg 2019*.
Reda, A. (2018). *Prophecy, piety, and profits: A conceptual and comparative history of Islamic economic thought*. Palgrave Macmillan.
Sombart, W. (1967 [1915]). *The quintessence of capitalism: A study of the history and psychology of the modern business man* (M. Epstein, Trans. and Ed.). Howard Fertig.
Vaggi, G. (1987). *The economics of François Quesnay*. Palgrave Macmillan.
Watson, B. (1958). *Ssu-ma Chien: Grand historian of China*. Columbia University Press.
Weber, M., Runciman, W. G., & Matthews, E. (1978). *Max Weber: Selections in translation*. Cambridge University Press.
Wittfogel, K. (1957). *Oriental despotism: A comparative study of total power*. Yale University Press.

References in Chinese

Chen, B. (2014). *Social transformation and cultural changes in the Ming dynasty*. Chongqing University Press.
Chen, J. (2010 [1639]). *Bai Shijiao Zhengao*. Normal University Press.
Fan, Z. (1919 [1052]). *Collected work of Fan Wenzheng (Fan wenzhenggong ji)* (Vol. 1). The Commercial Press.
Feng, M. (1979 [1627]). *Stories to awaken the world (Xingshi hengyan)*. People's Literature Publishing House.
Fu, Z. (1993). *Jingdezhen pottery notes (Jingdezheng taolu xiangzhu)* (Vol. 8). Bibliographic Literature Press.
Gao, S. (2008). Prices and wages in Beijing during the Wanli period of the Ming dynasty. *Academic Journal of Tsinghua University (philosophy and Social Sciences), 3*, 45–62.

Gong, T. (2010). Discussion on the changes of craftsmen's status in the literati value system in the middle and late Ming dynasty. *Academic Journal of Shandong University, 1*, 45–48.
Gu, D. (1997 [1571]). *Bingzhu Zhaigao*. Peking Press.
Gu, Y. (1985 [1682]). *Tianxia Junguo Libing Shu*. The Commercial Press.
Hai, R. (1962 [1587]). *Collected work of Hai Rui* (Vol. 1). Zhonghua Publishing House House.
He, X. (1960 [1579]). *Collected work of He Xinyin (He Xinyin Ji)* (Vol. 3). Zhonghua Publishing House House.
Huang, W. (1983 [1551]). *Ming Daobian* (Vol. 4). Zhonghua Publishing House.
Huang, Z. (1975 [1695]). *Songyuan Xue'an*. Heluo Tushu Press.
Huang, Z. (2011 [1662]). *Mingyi Daifang Lu*. Yuelu Publishing House.
Ji, W. (2013 [1943]). *History of late Ming thought*. Zhonghua Publishing House.
Jiang, J. (1990). *History of Chinese commerce and economics thoughts*. China Financial and Economic Publishing House.
Jiang, Y. (2000 [1605]). *Xuetao Xiaoshuo*. Shanghai Ancient Books Publishing House.
Li, D. (2013). Suppressing before emphasizing the merchants. *Modern History Institute Collected Papers, 82*, 1–53.
Li, Z. (2000 [1602]). *Li Zhi Wenji*. China Social Science Literature Press.
Li, Z. (2001 [1602]). *Fen Shu*. Yuanfang Press.
Liu, D. (2010 [1636]). *Guide of landscape and articles in the capital city (Dijing Jingwu Lue)*. Shanghai Ancient Books Publishing House.
Lu, C. (1993 [1551]). *Lu Ziyu Ji*. Shanghai Ancient Books Publishing House.
Luo, Z. (2006). *A study of the mental state of scholars in the Late Ming dynasty*. Nankai University Press.
Ma, Y. (1985 [1571]). *Discussion on agriculture (Nong Shuo)*. Zhonghua Publishing House House.
Shen, B. (1980 [1597]). *Wanshu anthology (Wanshu Zaji)* (Vol. 1). Peking Ancient Books Publishing House.
Shen, D. (2007 [1642]). *Wanli Yehuo Bian* (Vol. 26). Zhonghua Publishing House House.
Shen, S. (1989 [1587]). *Ming Huidian*. Zhonghua Publishing House.
Sima, G. (1919 [1086]). *Wenguo Wenzhenggong Ji* (Vol. 23). The Commercial Press.
Song, Y. (2010 [1637]). *Tiangong Kaiwu*. Shanghai Ancient Books Publishing House.
Sun, H. (2001). *History of Chinese refugees, volume of ancient China*. Anhui People Press.
Tang, S. (1922 [1560]). *Jingchuan Xiansheng Wenji*. The Commercial Press.
Wang, A. (1961 [1086]). *Wang Linchuan Ji* (Vol. 39). World Publishing House.

Wang, F. (1975 [1692]). *Discussion on Zizhi Tongjian (Du Tongjian Lun)*. Zhonghua Publishing House.
Wang, S. (1997 [1598]). *Guangzhi Yi* (Vol. 2). Zhonghua Publishing House.
Wang, Y. (1978 [1525]). *Chuanxi Lu*. Shanghai Ancient Books Publishing House.
Wang, Y. (1983 [1759]). *Liunan Suibi*. Zhonghua Publishing House.
Wen, G., et al. (2001). *The local history of Shanghai*. Shanghai: Shanghai Education Press.
Wu, K. (1929 [1504]). *Paoweng Jiacang Ji*. The Commercial Press.
Xie, Z. (2001 [1624]). *Wuza Zu*. Peking: Shanghai Book Store Publishing House.
Xu, G. (1979 [1633]). *Nongzheng Quanshu* (Vol. 2). Shanghai Ancient Books Publishing House.
Xu, G. (1984 [1633]). *Xu Guangqi Ji*. Shanghai Ancient Books Publishing House.
Xu, H. (1983 [1281]). *Luzhai posthumous writings*. Taipei Commercial Press.
Ye, S. (2003). *History of ancient Chinese economic thoughts*. Fudan University Press.
Yin, S. (2000 [1631]). *Mingshi Qie*. Peking Press.
Yu, Y. (1987). *Religious ethics and merchant spirit in modern China*. Linking Publishing.
Yuan, H. (2010 [1610]). *Pinghua Zhaiji* (Vol. 3). Shanghai Ancient Books Publishing House.
Zhang, D. (2010 [1684]). *Memory of dreams in Tao'an (Tao'an Mengyi)*. Zhonghua Publishing House House.
Zhang, J. (1937 [1582]). *Zhang Wenzhonggong Quanji*. The Commercial Press.
Zhang, L. (2000 [1598]). *Jialong Shuchao*. Shanghai Ancient Books Publishing House.
Zhang, T. (1974 [1739]). *The history of Ming*. Institute of History and Language.
Zhang, X. (2002 [1636]). *Records of sights in the West Garden (Xiyuan Wenjian Lu)* (Vol. 32). Shanghai Ancient Books Publishing House.
Zhao, N. (2000 [1627]). *Zhao Zhongyigong Wenji* (Vol. 4). Peking Press.
Zhu, G. (2012 [1632]). *Yongchuang Xiaopin* (Vol. 9). Shanghai Ancient Books Publishing House.
Zhu, Q. (1957). *Li Zhi: Pioneer of anti-feudalism in China in the 16th century*. Hubei People Press.
Zhu, R. (1986). The social status of merchants in the Song dynasty and its historical role. *History Research, No. 2*, 127–143.

CHAPTER 8

Conclusion

This chapter summarizes the whole book and presents the main results. And after the conclusion, a little extension is discussed by comparing merchants in early modern China and contemporary Western Europe, which hopefully can together provide some more explanation for the discussion of great divergence.

8.1 Merchants in Early Modern China: Evidence from Economic Thought and History

In order to investigate the role and status of merchants in the Ming Empire, this book discusses, mainly from the perspective of economic thought, almost all the aspects that the merchants were related to: cooperation with the state, commercial taxation, foreign trade, usury activities, their relationship with other major occupations and stratum, etc. As we saw in this book, throughout the Ming period, other than the division of schools put forward in Chapter 1, the economic thoughts related to commerce and merchants may also be divided into the following three categories.

First, for scholars like Qiu Jun and Zhang Juzheng who often expressed sympathy for merchants, their economic thoughts included compassion for small and medium merchants because they along with farmers formed

T. Hua, *Merchants, Market and Monarchy*,
Palgrave Studies in the History of Economic Thought,
https://doi.org/10.1007/978-3-030-77189-8_8

the basis of stable rule, while large-scale merchants who could potentially compete against the state were considered to be subject to suppression. Although scholars like Qiu and Zhang were not members of the royal family, as high-level officials at the court, they either served the royal family directly or were spokespersons for royal interests. Meanwhile, since most of the scholars in this category were officials, often high-level officials, their thought usually shows a trend of pragmatism. They didn't rigidly adhere to accepted theories despite the fact that they received orthodox education in their youth.

A second type of economic thought was posited by scholars like Gao Panlong and Ye Xianggao, most of whom belong to schools like the Donglin School. Their theories centred primarily on trying to improve the status of small and medium merchants. While the ideological predisposition seems to be similar, unlike the first category, the economic thinking of these scholars was based in large part on their own positions because most of them came from merchant families. Naturally, their economic thoughts reflected the interests of their group. During the Ming era, the status of merchants remained at the lower end of the four occupation scale; therefore, it was of utmost importance to support the trend of 'abandoning Confucianism' to improve the reputations of merchants and perhaps even gain social respect for their contributions. It is also worth mentioning that most of these ideas appeared in the late Ming period parallel with the period of rapid commercial expansion.

The third type of economic thought came from scholars with traditional ideas that dominated the narrative during the Ming era. Representing this group were Lin Xiyuan, Li Wen, Wang Fuzhi, and many others who remained firmly committed to the idea of 'emphasising the root and restraining the branch'. They made no attempts to conceal their opinions that the engagement of too many merchants in commerce would diminish the number of farmers. This was understandable under the context of maintaining rule over a small peasant economy, but their economic thoughts undeniably inherited the contempt for the merchant class in ancient China as well. This did not change in the middle of late Ming when trends featuring exquisite lifestyle and luxury goods were introduced at least partly by merchants. Many were envious of the merchants' ability to make money; nevertheless, most sincerely believed that engaging in commerce itself was an essentially humble profession.

To sum up, the economic thoughts in Ming China encompassed the following prominent characteristics accordingly. First, economic thinking centred on propositions to 'make the state rich' for the sake of monarchy interests. Second, scholars often discussed commerce and merchants based on the potential benefits afforded to their own interest groups. Finally, while some changes were evident, economic thoughts in Ming China, in most situations, remained consistent with the traditional style of ancient Chinese economic thought, that is, most were based on ethics and the 'monarch's rule' (*wang zheng*) with minimal discussion over matters such as value and fair prices that were predominant in Western economic thought at the time.

Regarding the status of merchants, interesting interpretations arose in the prevalent economic thoughts during the Ming period. First, the status of merchants was historically very low in their relationship with the state, and this remained largely unchanged during the Ming dynasty. The first indications were thoughts supporting state-owned commerce that originated in the pre-Qin period. Although the debates between the two factions over the support or opposition to state-owned commerce never ceased during the dynasties before Ming, state-owned commerce always prevailed. The state's monopolistic practices remained dominant in Ming China even though additional opposition began to emerge. Compared to the state, the merchants remained humble. This was reflected in widespread bureaucratic corruption and the necessity for aspiring merchants to somehow gain the support of influential officials in order to conduct business. After the inheritance of previous ideas and the development of theories from thinkers like Sang Hongyang, Liu Yan, and Wang Anshi in the former dynasties, a group of scholars including Qiu Jun, Zhang Juzheng, and others expressed their guarded opposition to state-owned commerce. Nevertheless, several renowned thinkers like Li Zhi and Wang Fuzhi continued to express their preference and support for state-owned commerce. Moreover, even Qiu Jun and Zhang Juzheng had very complicated attitudes towards the state's salt, iron, and wine monopolies. In other words, they expressed at least some support for state monopolization of certain products.

The predominant thoughts supporting state-owned commerce were best exemplified by the salt industry in Ming China. The salt monopoly, from today's perspective, evidently violated the laws of economics. In fact, the Ming court exacerbated the 'violation' by implementing the *kaizhong* method. The motivation may be easy to identify. The main focus of economic thinkers—with government officials as the main body—was to maintain the unity of the empire and the stability of society. Therefore, in order to stabilize the merchant class and maximize the monarchy's interests, the best method was to exploit the merchant class without granting them enough rights. However, the expected effect of this kind of 'use' would easily be offset by the corruption within the Ming bureaucracy if not blocked directly. Han Wen, Li Wen, Pang Shangpeng, Yuan Shizhen, and other relevant officials put forth several considerations regarding the shortcomings in the salt industry. Their concerns actually reflected the position of ordinary merchants in cooperation with the state, and plans were laden with risks and uncertainties. They bore the pressure of potentially being suppressed at any time without notice. The high-level officials occasionally expressed their empathy for merchants; however, the state's interests were always their major concern.

Regarding commercial taxation, the Ming merchants enjoyed different standing during different periods. In early Ming, Emperor Hongwu set very low commercial tax rates and expressed certain disdain for their collection (compared with agricultural tax). Nonetheless, strict punishments to prevent tax evasion were enforced. During the mid-Ming period, appeals for the taxation of merchants where aimed at reducing the burdens placed on peasants and objections to fixed commercial tax rates became the predominant thought. However, the tax evasion also began to run wild during this period. During the late Ming period when suppression of merchants was severe (particularly during Emperor Wanli's late rule), criticism of the heavy commercial taxes being levied became the consensus of scholars, especially those in the Donglin School. However, even with the rapid development of commerce during the late Ming period, theories related to commercial taxes serving as a means to suppress merchants still had faithful supporters among scholars, represented by scholars like Wang Fuzhi.

As a vital part of economic thought in Ming China, the thoughts on foreign trade also reflected the status of merchants. Against the background of the sea ban policy for most of the Ming dynasty, the thoughts on foreign trade in the Ming dynasty failed to move beyond the scope of China's traditional economic thought, but only treated overseas trade as a special problem in some coastal areas without considering the national economy as a whole. Among the two factions of supporting and opposing the sea ban, the supporters of the sea ban policy justified their arguments from the perspectives of 'little benefit to the state' and 'overseas trade leading to pirate harassment'. And the supporters of opening the sea put forward tit-for-tat thoughts, which were from the angles of 'the state and commoners sharing same interests' and 'pirates becoming merchants once trading was allowed'.[1] Nonetheless, these thoughts were with no exception from the perspective of national stability, and did not give real attention to the merchant class, which was completely different from contemporary European countries.

Not only that, for a long time, the Ming central government also regarded merchants who were forced to go abroad to do business as pirates. They were thus under ruthless hunting and cleansing, which also reflected one aspect of the status of merchants. And even worse for scattered merchants in the late Ming period, they had to seek some kind of "protection" under some big maritime merchant group, which was also the product of the smuggling trade system due to the court's stubborn cling to the sea ban policy. However, despite such a harsh policy environment and ideological trend, Chinese merchants still played an important role in the foreign trade of the Ming dynasty overall, as well as in the trading system of the entire world (especially in the Southeast Asia region). It not only actively sought penetration in the tributary system in the early Ming period, but also played an important role in the smuggling trade system in the middle and late Ming periods.

Regarding the traditional ordering of four occupations, the status of merchants has improved to some extent. First of all, beginning with righteousness and profits, one of the most fundamental debates in the history of ancient Chinese economic thought, the traditional thought of 'incompatibility of righteousness and profits' in the previous dynasty, had been partly, if not entirely, replaced by 'righteousness and profits' in the Ming dynasty. These thoughts were further promoted by the fact that some merchants started to help build ancestral temples, or participated in philanthropic activities. Moreover, the rationality of merchants' existence was also thoroughly acknowledged. One of the prominent examples was the unprecedented recognition of the behaviour and role of merchants in usury activities.

And in the debate about luxury and frugality, an unprecedented phenomenon was that the thoughts against luxury forbidding represented by Lu Shen, or equal emphasis on luxury and frugality, began to form a climate of its own. This was unimaginable before the Ming dynasty. In fact, in the Ming dynasty, especially in the middle and late periods,

[1] Chen (1962 [1638], Vol. 270, p. 2850).

merchants became closer to the traditional scholar class in art, books and various forms of luxury consumption, and even sometimes led the trend of the whole society. However, these 'anti-luxury ban' thoughts did not occupy absolute dominance. Some famous scholars at the time, represented by the Yangming School and the Donglin School, severely criticized the extravagant social atmosphere.

Traditionally, the theory of the four occupations put forth by Wang Yangming was regarded as symptoms of the breakdown of the traditional theory of four occupational groups. However, as demonstrated throughout this research, the notion of emphasizing scholars over merchants was deeply rooted in the Chinese subconscious. It was this social reality that catalyzed the change of Confucian attitudes towards merchants that promoted a change in the relationship between scholars and merchants rather than the development of Confucianism itself. The emergence of thoughts suggesting that 'engagement in commerce was a decent way to make a living'[2] and new social phenomena that emerged in the middle and late Ming dynasties like 'the abandonment of Confucianism'[3] were developed because of real issues regarding livelihoods rather than being indicators of fundamental changes in the attitudes towards merchants. In other words, if they could have become officials directly through the imperial examinations, they most certainly would not have prioritized business opportunities.

Moreover, Wang Yangming's new interpretation of the four occupations had been developed and circulated at least during the Tang and Song dynasties. It was not a new theory connected to the middle and late Ming Dynasty. Possible reasons for its reemphazis could have been the rapid development of commerce in the coastal areas of China and merchant-prone areas like Huizhou during the middle and late Ming dynasty. In addition, from the perspective of scholars, merchants were considered to be reliant on officials, and the latter held only conditional appreciation for merchants. Together with thoughts appealing for greater understanding and sympathy for merchants, these all suggest that the status of merchants relative to scholars had not really improved.

[2] Xie (2001 [1624], pp. 90–91).

[3] Shen (1918 [1840], p. 12).

In practice, although some merchants (mainly salt merchants in the Lianghuai region and Shanxi province) benefitted from the implementation of the 'commercial registration' system, upon investigation of the imperial examinations throughout the Ming dynasty and the nationwide merchant community, merchants still did not have even the slightest advantages in the traditional promotion channels that were controlled by the scholar class, and they always faced more discrimination and restrictions than the scholars. Although there was definitely more interaction between scholars and the merchant class, this was essentially the manipulative use of merchants by scholars rather not any heartfelt respect for merchants. Conversely, merchants were obligated to maintain 'special' relationships with scholars, for example, attending their children's marriages and gift-giving. This directly reflected the merchants' lack of independence. Only by relying on officials with certain levels of authority could their property and personal safety be guaranteed.

Compared to peasants, the status of merchants had improved. Although there were still deeply rooted agricultural-based preferences among thinkers, equal emphasis on farmers and merchants as represented by the thoughts of Zhang Juzheng, Hai Rui, and others gradually became mainstream. Moreover, engaging in commerce was recognized by many thinkers as a method of survival that required more advanced skills than those required for agriculture. In contrast, farmers in general were considered to be of lower than average intelligence. In practice, although the restrictions on merchant apparel established by Emperor Hongwu at the beginning of the Ming dynasty were never really abolished at the court level, these bans had never been seriously implemented in practice. Especially in the middle and late periods of the Ming dynasty, the bans were considered vain, and the apparel of merchants was much more luxurious than that of the peasants even though the latter enjoyed higher legal status. In addition, many farmers abandoned farming and opted to join the growing contingent of merchants. Also, many refugees sought to become assistants to merchants and craftsmen, all of which confirm the gradual improvement of the merchants' status relative to farmers. Despite the consistent emphasis on agriculture and peasants, the status of peasants fell below that of the merchants in Ming China, one of the major reasons why many peasants became merchants.

Unfortunately, it is difficult to determine the relative status of merchants and craftsmen. Relevant original literature is very limited. In ancient China, artisanry was regarded as a low-quality occupation, not unlike the condescension frequently faced by merchants. The relative status of the two had rarely caught the attention of scholars since ancient times. It may be inferred that craftsmen usually had permanent workshops that were more easily controlled and managed by the government compared to merchants who were untethered to any specific place; therefore, they were able to garner slightly higher status than merchants compared to the traditional theory of four occupational groups. However, similar to the merchant group, during the wave of commercialization in the middle and late Ming dynasties, the premium work and aesthetic standards of some craftsmen were recognized and appreciated by many people, including scholars. This improved their status to some extent, as evidenced by the complimentary opinions of many scholars. However, like merchants, the scholars' attitudes towards craftsmen were complex. Indeed, admiration and recognition were often accompanied by contempt and disdain.

According to this research, the order of the occupational groups in Ming China should be as follows: Scholars remained indisputably alone in first place followed by artisans and merchants side by side in the second tier. Peasants were placed alone on the last tier. This differs from the traditional ranking. As for the state-merchant relations, it is clear that private merchants were still subject to undeniable suppression. At best, they had proven themselves to be 'useful' for some forms of collaboration with the royals, officials, or powerful groups by providing services beneficial to the state's interests.

8.2 Final Remarks: Ming Merchants and 'The Great Divergence'

Prior to the Age of Discovery, China and Western Europe had similar economic patterns. They were both agriculturally led economies under monarchy. In some ways and some periods, China may have performed even better than Western Europe. For instance, the manufacturing technology of the ships used by Zheng He during the Emperor Yongle years was in fact 'at an advanced level in the world',[4] which can be proved by the fact that 'all the ships of Columbus and da Gama combined, according to a recent account, could have been stored on a single deck

[4] Wu (2004, Vol. 3, p. 686).

of a vessel in the fleet that set sail under Zheng He'[5]; Large quantities of silver from countries such as the Lüsong[6] flowed into China.[7] Meanwhile, under the highly centralized regime, the manor economy was the main form in Western Europe, and this backward mode of production hindered economic development. However, after the Age of Discovery, Western Europe gradually embarked on the path of developing capitalism. Several countries in Western Europe successively became strong in terms of national strength, while contemporary Ming China gradually lagged behind with the gap getting increasingly wider. We may accordingly do a brief comparison here.

First, as elaborated in this book, the ideology of valuing commerce that emerged in the middle and late Ming had never been able to completely defeat the long-standing idea of 'emphasizing agriculture and suppressing commerce', despite some visible improvement. The fundamental relative standing between agriculture and commerce was not shaken, and so was the embarrassing fact that commerce was regarded as a 'branch industry' (*moye*). On the contrary, in Western Europe, mercantilism gradually carve out a niche in the intellectual circle, and the countries' commercial systems also changed in accordance with changes in the ideology.

Second, the relations between the government and the merchants in Ming China and contemporary Europe seem to be quite different. The combination of politics and commercial capital in Western Europe can be regarded as a real cooperative relationship, something not that imaginable in Ming China. The Ming state's attitude towards merchants was clear: taking advantage of them, if not suppressing them. The state did not actively provide the convenience for merchants to obtain higher profits. For example, the *kaizhong* system in the salt business seemed to be the cooperation between the government and merchants to maintain the salt economy of the entire country. However, the court was actually in charge, from production to determining the price range, from issuing salt licences to deciding shipping and selling areas.

We cannot say that there exists no change in this merchant-state relation in Ming China compared with previous eras. While everything was

[5] Strayer (2011, p. 575).

[6] Lüsong at the time was located in current northern part of Philippines.

[7] Du (2017, p. 187).

still intended to be 'controlled by a ubiquitous, efficient and bureaucratic government',[8] the real effect, as stated in this book, often detract from the desired results. It also holds true that the merchants did not have much right to express opinions, let alone bilateral consultations and holding each other up. But at least, they began to have some friends in high places speaking for them, such as Ye Qi. Nevertheless, compared with how merchants were treated at the time, these efforts seem to be inadequate.

In early modern Europe, although the government often plunged into financial crisis due to wars between countries, and the royal family urgently needed to obtain more income from commerce, the difference was that the key way for Western European countries to increase government fiscal revenue was to promote their development of commerce and overseas expansion. The countries were committed to fighting for an advantageous position in international competition, rather than certain 'internal strife' such as blindly controlling and using merchants, or setting layers of supervision and strict control tried to cover all commercial activities.

Third, too many restrictions were put on the maritime merchants by the court, which was very different from the merchants of the same period in Europe. While medieval European merchants might still enjoy some low standing, at least partly thanks to merchants bringing wealth to the country through overseas trade, their status began to rise, which even helped them to influence national economic policies. Looking back at Ming China, the court imposed the strongest ever sea ban policy[9] (except for the Qing China), although Ming maritime merchants actually played a vital role in China's foreign trade (either overtly or covertly), especially in the Southeast Asian trade network, as can be seen from the analysis in this book. While individual merchants made considerable profits in overseas trade booming around the sixteenth century, the state also benefited from it, without adopting predatory expansion.

However, this important role had not been exchanged for the improvement of merchants' status in Ming era. The commercial activities that can generate much-needed fiscal revenue had been rejected by the government. The reason was, as can be seen several places in this book, that

[8] Braudel (1979, p. 131).

[9] Li (1990, pp. 2–3).

the government was more worried about the stability of the rule than the finances, which is also reflected in scholars' economic thought. From their perspectives, only if the people obeyed the restrictions can the border be stable with no external threat. Therefore, these factors must be fully safeguarded before economic development can be considered. The government believed that close ties with other countries could easily make people rebellious and collude with foreign countries to threaten the ruling. At that time, the coast was repeatedly attacked by pirates (although some of them might be mere merchants). Overseas trade without prohibition would inevitably become a hidden danger for the empire. This showed that the court lacked a pioneering and adventurous spirit, compared with the European administration at the time.

And ultimately, in Ming China, unlike in the West that 'liberty concerns the laws that constrain the shopkeeper',[10] it was not the law but the power and the will of some mandarins that determined the fate of merchants. Contrary to many prejudice, these mandarins were often local officials rather than those high-end officials. As we saw in the book, those powerful figures at the court usually show real sympathy for the commoners, including merchants. The daily ruling, however, has to rely on the local officials, whom the merchants had to deal with. The moral standard of local officials was quite different from each other,[11] and how the merchants were treated was accordingly unstable.

These constitute the real dilemma of Chinese merchants in Ming China, which prevent them from being influential in re-shaping the empire, making the Ming China 'el imperio en el que nunca se pone el sol'.[12] The lopsided development of commerce[13] and the highly inadequate participation of merchants in state affairs surely form part of the explanation for the Great Divergence.

[10] McCloskey (2010, p. 11).

[11] In this regard, we have a Chinese saying called, in Chinese, *xiaoren dezhi*. It means 'once some vile characters obtained some power, they were often intoxicated by success and more likely to abuse their power'.

[12] 'el imperio en el que nunca se pone el sol' (in Spanish) was first called out by Charles V (reigns 1516–1556), which means 'the empire on which the sun never sets'.

[13] The thriving commerce and splendid living quality recorded by those European missionaries only existed in limited areas such as Jiangnan region and southeast coastline, and usually excluding rural areas.

Similar to the questions mentioned at the very beginning of this book, Prof. Chen Zhiwu at Yale once put forward an equally classic question, 'why are the Chinese hard-working but not wealthy?'.[14] While this question is more aimed at current individuals, this fits Ming merchants perfectly all right. As we saw in this book, quite a few Ming thinkers believed that 'doing business requires special talents', but it was difficult for the merchants to make the business career bigger and long-lasting. There seems to be a rule that from ancient times to the present, the majority of the merchant families could not be rich for more than three generations.[15] Up till Ming, the state still failed to establish a legal system that guaranteed fair trading and free competition in the market. We saw very few clues in the scholars' economic thought that they even try to make such effort. In some cases, the Ming court was not the founder or defender of the fair-trade system, but rather its biggest destroyer. The additional tax collectors during the Emperor Wanli years of the Ming dynasty might only be the product of some specific period. The phenomenon that many officials and eunuchs who were backed by the royal family used power to control the property of the commoners (including small merchants) and wealthy merchants, however, was more like a normalcy in Ming China.

The keynote of most rulers in ancient China was to 'control and use' merchants,[16] allowing them to chase interests within a certain range, while their political demands must be absolutely suppressed. We did see some pleasant change in Ming China, but the evil legacy was clearly far from wiping out. And if the merchants wanted to make money, especially big money, there was no other way than to fawn the government and make alliances with the officials and the state.

However, it is also biassed for us to lay the blame on the system itself. After all, the way that treats Ming merchants may have its reasonableness

[14] I discussed this interesting question with Prof. Chen Zhiwu during the international conference held in Bad Homburg, Germany in 2019. In the speech given by Prof. Chen during the conference, he mentions another potential answer to this question by comparing with the West: ancient roots of financial divergence (early choice of kin-based family order vs. extra-kin order for inter-temporal risk-sharing). Please also refer to Chen (2008).

[15] 'Wealth fails to pass three generations', or *Fu buguo sandai*, has become an old saying among the people for over thousands of years in China.

[16] Wu (2004, Vol. 3, p. 789).

as well, just as I elaborated in this book. Rousseau specifically pointed out that 'in general the democratic form of government will suit small states, the aristocratic form states of moderate size, and the monarchic form large states'.[17] Montesquieu also believed that 'a despotic authority' might be more reasonable to a huge empire like Ming China,

> A large empire presupposes a despotic authority in the one who governs. Promptness of resolutions must make up for the distance of the places to which they are sent; fear must prevent negligence in the distant governor or magistrate; the law must be in a single person; and it must change constantly, like accidents, which always increase in proportion to the size of the state.[18]

Such a seemingly inevitable system design makes the Ming merchants hard to expand their force and influence like their European mates. Thus, since the Ming merchants were able to increase wealth in the existing social system, they would not insist on subverting the existing system and would try to stabilize and improve their status in the existing system. Even those economic thinkers strongly supporting the merchant class dare not challenge the state-merchant system which was elaborated in this book, although their effort might be the closest to some potential success.

As a final supplement (and summary), the relationship between merchants, market, and monarchy and the relative status of merchants compared with other occupations may also be explained from the perspective of 'entry threshold'. It is easy to understand according to the law of demand and supply that keeping the demand constant, if the supply of labour in one occupation is too high (many people are qualified to do the work in this area), the value will inevitably become less. If we see the problem from this angle, among the four occupations, the scholars are undoubtedly the rarest. After all, as stated in the book, it is extremely hard for scholars to obtain the titles and official positions. It holds true for all dynasties, no exception for Ming China. Perhaps the competition in imperial exams was even more fierce in Ming. However, while engaging in commerce was considered as 'almost no threshold', in Ming China, the merchants who can survive on the markets were generally considered as 'talented' compared with 'dumb farmers'. Likewise, you have to develop

[17] Rousseau (1999 [1762], p. 100).

[18] Montesquieu (1989 [1748], p. 126).

some skills to become an artisan. On the contrary, becoming peasants seems to have some threshold (first you got to have a land to cultivate), but there really exists no technique here (you only need to be diligent). After all, there existed no agricultural mechanization or intellectualization at the time. To make it worse, the result you will get, on a large scale, depends on some external factors such as the precipitation and sunshine, which you cannot predict or control at all. Although it might be true that the empire's emphasis on the agriculture did not change, the dominant force serving as the spokesmen for the monarchy (mainly scholars who were often officials and economic thinkers as well) have countless ties with the merchant and artisan class. As long as these classes did not threaten the stability of the state, the peasants staying at last became the reality under the context of booming commerce in the Ming Empire.

What I would like to emphasize here eventually is that all the above conclusions are based on the research and elaboration within this book. The role and status of merchant and their relationship with the market and the state in early modern China, after all, is a highly complex topic, and thus may not have any deterministic conclusion that everyone would agree with. As we saw in this book, the role and status of Ming merchants appeared to be quite different when they were engaged in various business and dealt with miscellaneous groups of people (or institutes). Nonetheless, mainly from the perspective of economic thought, supplemented with some existing research results in economic history, I am confident that the aforementioned conclusions are closest to the real history.

References

Reference in English

Braudel, F. (1979). *Civilization and capitalism, 15th-18th century, volume II, the wheels of commerce. Translation from the French by Sian Reynolds*. Book Club Associates.

McCloskey, D. N. (2010). *Bourgeois dignity: Why economics can't explain the modern world*. University of Chicago Press.

Montesquieu, C. (1989 [1748]). *The spirit of the laws* (A. M. Cohler, B. C. Miller, and H. S. Stone, Trans.). Cambridge University Press.

Rousseau, J. (1999 [1762]). *The social contract* (C. Betts, Trans.). Oxford University Press.

Strayer, R. W. (2011). *Ways of the world: A brief global history with sources*. Bedford St. Martin's.

Reference in Chinese

Chen, Z. (1962 [1638]). *Compile of memorials to the emperor in the Ming Dynasty (Ming jingshi wenbian)*. Zhonghua Publishing House.
Chen, Z. (2008). *Why Chinese are hardworking but not rich*. Zhongxin Press.
Du, C. (2017). *Who terminated the Ming dynasty*. World Knowledge Press.
Li, J. (1990). *The history of overseas trade in Ming China*. China Social Science Press.
Shen, K. (1918 [1840]). *Luofanlou Wenji*. Liushi Jiaye Tang.
Wu, H. (2004). *Chinese commerce history*. The Finance and Economics Press.
Xie, Z. (2001 [1624]). *Wuza Zu*. Peking: Shanghai Book Store Publishing House.

Bibliography

References in German

Sombart, W. (1913a). *Der Bourgeois*. Duncker & Humblot.

Sombart, W. (1913b). *Luxus und Kapitalismus*. Duncker & Humblot.

Wilhelm, R. (1930). *Chinesische Wirtschaftspsychologie*. Deutsche Wissenschaftliche Buchhandlung.

Reference in English

Andre, F. (2001). Review of the great divergence. *Journal of Asian Studies, 60*(1), 180–182. https://doi.org/10.2307/2659525.

Balazs, E. (1967). *Chinese civilization and bureaucracy: Variations on a theme*. Yale University Press.

Baldanza, K. (2016). *Ming China and Vietnam negotiating borders in early modern Asia*. Cambridge University Press.

Beard, M. (2008). *Pompeii: The life of a Roman town*. Profile Books Ltd.

Bentham, J. (1823 [1780]). *Principles of morals and legislation*. Clarendon Press.

Braudel, F. (1972). *The Mediterranean and the Mediterranean world in the Age of Philip II, Volume I. Translation from the French by Sian Reynolds*. Harper & Row.

Braudel, F. (1979). *Civilization and capitalism, 15th-18th century, volume II, the wheels of commerce. Translation from the French by Sian Reynolds*. Book Club Associates.

T. Hua, *Merchants, Market and Monarchy*,
Palgrave Studies in the History of Economic Thought,
https://doi.org/10.1007/978-3-030-77189-8

Brook, T. (1993). *Praying for power: Buddhism and the formation of gentry society in late-Ming China*. Harvard University Asia Center.

Brook, T. (1999). *The confusions of pleasure: Commerce and culture in Ming China*. University of California Press.

Calder, K. (2012). *The new continentalism: Energy and twenty-first-century Eurasian geopolitics*. Yale University Press.

Chang, C. (1962). *Wang Yang-ming: Idealist philosopher of sixteenth-century China*. St. John's University Press.

Chang, J. L. (1987). History of Chinese economic thought: Overview and recent works. *History of Political Economy, 19*(3), 481–502.

Chen, H. (1911). *The economic principles of confucius and his school*. Columbia University, Longmans, Green & Company, Agents.

Cheng, L., Peach, T., & Wang, F. (2014). *The history of ancient Chinese economic thought*. Routledge.

Cheng, L., Peach, T., & Wang, F. (2019). *The political economy of the Han dynasty and its legacy*. Routledge.

Chou, C., & Edward, H. K. (1974). *An economic history of China*. Center for East Asian Studies, Western Washington University.

Clunas, C. (1991). *Superfluous things: Material culture and social status in early modern China*. Polity Press.

Clunas, C. (1997). *Pictures and visuality in early modern China*. Reaktion Books.

De Botton, A. (2000). *The consolations of philosophy*. Vintage Books.

Deng, K. G. (1997). *Chinese maritime activities and socioeconomic development, c. 2100 BC-1900 AD*. Greenwood Publishing Group.

Deng, K. G. (1999). *The premodern Chinese economy: Structural equilibrium and capitalist sterility*. Routledge.

Deng, K. G. (2000). A critical survey of recent research in Chinese economic history. *Economic History Review, 53*, 1–28.

Elvin, M. (1973). *The pattern of the Chinese past*. Stanford University Press.

Fairbank, J. K. (1983). *The United States and China*. Harvard University Press.

Friebel, G., & Raith, M. (2004). Abuse of authority and hierarchical communication. *RAND Journal of Economics, 35*, 224–244.

Habermas, J. (1989). *The structural transformation of the public sphere* (T. Burger, Trans.). MIT Press.

Haliassos, M., & Tobin, J. (1990). The macroeconomics of government finance. *Handbook of Monetary Economics, 2*, 889–959.

Handlin, J. F. (1983). *Action in late Ming thought: The reorientation of Lü Kun and other scholar-officials*. University of California Press.

Handlin, J. F. (1998). Social hierarchy and merchant philanthropy as perceived in several late-Ming and early-Qing texts. *Journal of the Economic and Social History of the Orient., 41*(3), 417–451.

Haney, L. H. (1911). *History of economic thought: A critical account of the origin and development of the economic theories of the leading thinkers in the leading nations*. Macmillan.

Hansen, V. (1990). *Changing gods in medieval China, 1127–1276*. Princeton University Press.

Harari, Y. N. (2014). *Sapiens: A brief history of humankind*. Penguin Random House.

Hayek, F. A. (1988). *The fatal conceit: The errors of socialism, Collected works of F. A. Hayek* (Vol. I). Routledge.

Hengstmengel, J. (2019). *Divine providence in early modern economic thought*. Routledge.

Ho, P. (1959). *Studies on the population of China, 1368–1953*. Harvard University Press.

Ho, P. (1962). *The ladder of success in imperial China: Aspects of social mobility, 1368–1911*. Columbia University Press.

Horvath, J. (2020). *An introduction to the history of economic thought in Central Europe*. Palgrave Macmillan.

Hsü, I. C. Y. (2000). *The rise of modern China*. Oxford University Press.

Hu, J. (1984). *Chinese economic thought before the seventeenth century*. Foreign Language Press.

Hu, J. (1988). *A concise history of Chinese economic thought*. Foreign Languages Press.

Hua, T. (2019). Underdevelopment of commerce in the history of ancient Chinese economic thoughts: An examination of the status of merchants in Ming China. In *2020 Young Scholar Seminar at ESHET annual conference (European Society for the History of Economic Thought)*.

Huang, R. (1974). *Taxation and governmental finance in sixteenth-century Ming China*. Cambridge University Press.

Hucker, C. (1958). Governmental organization of the Ming dynasty. *Harvard Journal of Asiatic Studies, 21*, 1–66.

Hymes, R. P., & Schirokauer, C. (1993). *Ordering the world: Approaches to state and society in Sung dynasty China*. University of California Press.

Kaur, M., & Isa, M. (2020). *Between the Bay of Bengal and the Java Sea: Trade routes, ancient ports and cultural commonalities in Southeast Asia*. Marshall Cavendish.

Klump, R. (2004). The kingdom of Ponthiamas—A physiocratic model state in Indochina: A note on the international exchange of economic thought and of concepts for economic reforms in the 18th century. In I. Barens, V. Caspari, & B. Schefold (Eds.), *Political events and economic ideas* (pp. 173–183). Elgar.

Le Bon, G. (1896). *The crowd: A study of the popular mind*. The Macmillan.

Li, K. (2010). *The Ming maritime trade policy in transition, 1368 to 1567*. Harrassowitz Verlag.

Li, Z. (2019). *A history of classical Chinese thought. Translated, with a philosophical introduction, by Andrew Lambert*. Routledge.
Lin, H. (2013). Intersecting boundaries: Manuscript, printing, and book culture in late Ming China. *Oriens Extremus, 52*, 263–304.
Liu, Z. (1959). *Reform in Sung China: Wang An-shih (1021–1086) and his new policies*. Harvard University Press.
Loewe, M. (1974). *Crisis and conflict in Han China*. George Allen & Unwin.
Lufrano, R. J. (1997). *Honorable merchants: Commerce and self-cultivation in late imperial China*. University of Hawaii Press.
Ma, D. (2016). *Textiles in the Pacific, 1500–1900*. Routledge.
Ma, Y., & Trautwein, H. (2013). *Thoughts on economic development in China*. Routledge.
Maddison, A. (2007). *Chinese economic performance in the long run: 960–2030 AD*. OECD Development Centre Studies.
Malthus, T. R. (1966 [1798]). *First essay on population 1798*. Palgrave MacMillan.
Mandeville, B. (2017 [1723]). *The Fable of the Bees; or, private vices, public benefits*. Georg Olms Verlag.
Mark, K. (2002). *Salt: A world history*. Walker and Co.
McCloskey, D. N. (2010). *Bourgeois dignity: Why economics can't explain the modern world*. University of Chicago Press.
McCloskey, D. N., & DeMartino, G. F. (2016). *The Oxford handbook of professional economic ethics*. Oxford University Press.
McDermott, J. (2006). *A social history of the Chinese Book*. Hong Kong University Press.
McDermott, J. (2013). *The making of a new rural order in South China*. Hong Kong University Press.
Menudo, J. M. (2020). *The economic thought of Sir James Steuart: First economist of the Scottish enlightenment*. Routledge.
Montesquieu, C. (1989 [1748]). *The spirit of the laws* (A. M. Cohler, B. C. Miller, & H. S. Stone, Trans.). Cambridge University Press.
More, T. (2002 [1516]). *Utopia*. Cambridge University Press.
Mosca, M. (2018). *Power in economic thought*. Palgrave Macmillan.
Needham, J. (2005 [1969]). *The grand titration: Science and society in East and West* (Vol. 1). Routledge.
North, D. C. (1990). *Institutions, Institutional change and economic performance*. Cambridge University Press.
Poettinger, M. (2019). The Medici Pope, Jacob Fugger and the new catholic view on the economy: Johann Eck and the problem of usury. In *International Conference at Forschungskolleg Bad Homburg 2019*.
Polanyi, K. (1944). *The great transformation*. Boston: Beacon Press.
Polanyi, K., & Maclver, R. M. (1944). *The great transformation*. Beacon Press.

Pomeranz, K. (2000). *The great divergence: China, Europe, and the making of the modern world economy*. Princeton University Press.

Reda, A. (2018). *Prophecy, piety, and profits: A conceptual and comparative history of Islamic economic thought*. Palgrave Macmillan.

Reid, A. (1993). *Southeast Asia in the age of commerce 1450–1680* (Vol. 2). Princeton University Press.

Rickett, W. A. (1998). *Guanzi: Political, economic, and philosophical essays from Early China* (Vol. 1). Princeton University Press.

Roncaglia, A. (2006). *The wealth of ideas: A history of economic thought*. Cambridge University Press.

Rothbard, M. N. (2000). *Egalitarianism as a revolt against nature and other essays*. Ludwig von Mises Institute.

Rothbard, M. N. (2006). *Economic thought before Adam Smith*. Edward Elgar.

Rousseau, J. (1999 [1762]). *The social contract* (C. Betts, Trans.). Oxford University Press.

Russell, B. (1922). *The problem of China*. George Allen and Unwin.

Schefold, B. (2000). *Economic interests and cultural determinants in European integration: Conference Proceedings of the 1998 Summer School, Brixen/Bressanone, 31 August-10 September 1998* (No. 21). Europäische Akademie.

Schefold, B. (2014). Marx, Sombart, Weber and the debate about the genesis of modern capitalism. *Journal of Institutional Studies, 6*(2), 10–26.

Schefold, B. (2014). Economics without political economy: Is the discipline undergoing another revolution. *Social Research, 81*(3), 613–636.

Schefold, B. (2016). *Great economic thinkers from antiquity to the historical school: Historical school, old and young*. Routledge.

Schefold, B. (2017). *Great economic thinkers from the classicals to the moderns: Translations from the series Klassiker der Nationalökonomie*. Routledge.

Schefold, B. (2019). A western perspective on the Yantie lun. In L. Cheng, T. Peach, & F. Wang (Eds.), *The political economy of the Han dynasty and its legacy* (pp. 153–174). Routledge.

Schumpeter, J. A. (1954). *A history of economic analysis*. George Allen & Unwin.

Scott, J. C. (2009). *The Art of not being governed: An anarchist history of upland Southeast Asia*. Yale University Press.

Semedo, A. (1655 [1636]). *The history of that great and renowned monarchy of China*. Translated by a person of quality. E. Tyler for John Crook.

Shen, F. (2009). *Cultural flow between China and outside world throughout history*. Foreign Language Press.

Skinner, G. W., & Baker, H. D. (1977). *The city in late imperial China*. Stanford University Press.

Skinner, G. W., & Elvin, M. (1974). *The Chinese city between two worlds*. Stanford University Press.

Smith, A. (1979 [1776]). *The wealth of nations: An inquiry into the nature and causes of the wealth of nations*. Clarendon Press.

Sombart, W. (1967 [1915]). *The quintessence of capitalism: A study of the history and psychology of the modern business man* (M. Epstein, Trans. and Ed.). Howard Fertig.

Stark, W. (2005). *Jeremy Bentham's economic writings: Critical edition based on his printed works and unprinted manuscripts* (Vol. III). Routledge.

Strauss, L. (1998). *Xenophon's socratic discourse: An interpretation of the Oeconomicus*. St. Augustine's Press.

Strayer, R. W. (2011). *Ways of the world: A brief global history with sources*. Bedford St. Martin's.

Subrahmanyam, S. (2012). *The Portuguese empire in Asia 1500–1700: A political and economic history* (2nd ed.). Wiley-Blackwell.

Sun, E., & DeFrancis, J. (1966). *Chinese social history: Translations of selected studies* (Vol. 7). Octagon Books.

Tang, L. (2017). *Merchants and society in modern China: Rise of merchant groups*. Routledge.

Tanimoto, M., & Wong, R. B. (2019). *Public goods provision in the early modern economy: Comparative perspectives from Japan, China, and Europe*. University of California Press.

Twitchett, D., & Mote, F. (1998). *The Cambridge history of China: Volume 8, The Ming dynasty, 1368–1644*. Cambridge University Press.

Vaggi, G. (1987). *The economics of François Quesnay*. Palgrave Macmillan.

Venn, H. (2009). *The missionary life and labours of Francis Xavier taken from his own correspondence: With a sketch of the general results of Roman Catholic missions among the heathen*. Cambridge University Press.

Von Glahn, R. (2004). *The sinister way: The devine and the demonic in Chinese religious culture*. University of California Press.

Von Glahn, R. (2016). *An economic history of China: From antiquity to the nineteenth century*. Cambridge University Press.

Watson, B. (1958). *Ssu-ma Chien: Grand historian of China*. Columbia University Press.

Weber, M. (1951 [1915]). *The religion of China: Confucianism and Taoism*. Free Press.

Weber, M., Runciman, W. G., & Matthews, E. (1978). *Max Weber: Selections in translation*. Cambridge University Press.

Weber, M. (2001 [1904]). *The protestant ethic and the 'spirit' of capitalism*. Penguin.

Weber, M., & Whimster, S. (2004). *The essential Weber: A reader*. Routledge.

Wittfogel, K. (1949). *History of Chinese society: Liao (907–1125)*. Lancaster Press.

Wittfogel, K. (1957). *Oriental despotism: A comparative study of total power*. Yale University Press.

Xiong, V. (2000). *Sui-Tang Chang'an: A study in the urban history of late medieval China*. The University of Michigan Press.
Yu, Y. (2016). *Chinese history and culture* (Vol. 2). Columbia University Press.

Reference in Chinese

Ban, G. (1962 [92]). *Book of Han*. Zhonghua Publishing House.
Chen, B. (2014). *Social transformation and cultural changes in the Ming dynasty*. Chongqing University Press.
Chen, H. (1985 [1521]). *Jishi Jiwen*. Zhonghua Publishing House.
Chen, J. (2010 [1639]). *Bai Shijiao Zhengao*. Normal University Press.
Chen, X. (1986). *Huangming Shifa Lu*. Taiwan Student Press.
Chen, Z. (1962 [1638]). *Compile of memorials to the emperor in the Ming Dynasty (Ming jingshi wenbian)*. Zhonghua Publishing House.
Chen, Z. (2008). *Why Chinese are hardworking but not rich*. Zhongxin Press.
Er, E. (1887). *Zhupi Yuzhi*. Dianshi Zhai.
Du, C. (2017). *Who terminated the Ming dynasty*. World Knowledge Press.
Fan, J. (1998). *The development of commerce in Jiangnan region during Ming-Qing period*. Nanjing University Press.
Fan, Z. (1919 [1052]). *Collected work of Fan Wenzheng (Fan wenzhenggong ji)* (Vol. 1). The Commercial Press.
Fei, H. (1962 [1525]). *Ming Shilu, record of Emperor Zhengde*. Institute of History and Language.
Feng, M. (1979 [1627]). *Stories to awaken the world (Xingshi hengyan)*. People's Literature Publishing House.
Fu, X. (2010 [278]). *Commentary of Fuzi (Fuzi pinzhu)*. Tianjin Ancient Books Publishing House.
Fu, Y. (2007). *The social economy of rural area during Ming-Qing period*. Zhonghua Publishing House.
Fu, Z. (1993). *Jingdezhen pottery notes (Jingdezheng taolu xiangzhu)* (Vol. 8). Bibliographic Literature Press.
Gao, G. (2006 [1578]). *The collected work of Gao Gong (Gaogong quanji)*. Zhongzhou Guji Press.
Gao, P. (1986 [1626]). *Gaozi Yishu*. Taiwan Commercial Press.
Gao, S. (2008). Prices and wages in Beijing during the Wanli period of the Ming dynasty. *Academic Journal of Tsinghua University (Philosophy and Social Sciences), 3*, 45–62.
Gong, T. (2010). Discussion on the changes of craftsmen's status in the literati value system in the middle and late Ming dynasty. *Academic Journal of Shandong University, 1*, 45–48.
Gu, D. (1997 [1571]). *Bingzhu Zhaigao*. Peking Press.
Gu, X. (1997 [1612]). *Xiaoxin Zhai Zhaji*. Qilu Press.

Gu, Y. (1985 [1682]). *Tianxia Junguo Libing Shu*. The Commercial Press.
Gu, Y. (1977 [1690]). *Chronicle of the Ming dynasty (Mingshi Jishi Benmo)*. Zhonghua Publishing House.
Guan, W. (1995). *A study of the political system of the Ming dynasty*. China Social Science Press.
Guan, Z., et al. (1965 [c. 400–100 BC]). *Guanzi*. Taiwan Commercial Press.
Hai, R. (1962 [1587]). *Collected work of Hai Rui* (Vol. 1). Peking: Zhonghua Publishing House House.
Han, B. (1973 [1556]). *Yuanluo Ji*. Taiwan Commercial Press.
Han, D. (1986). *A probe into the social economy in the Ming dynasty*. Renmin Press.
Han, D. (2009). *Studies of cities in the Ming dynasty*. Zhonghua Publishing House.
Han, Y. (1958 [824]). *The collected work of Han Changli*. The Commercial Press.
He, M. (1985 [1536]). *Yudong Xulu Zhaichao Neiwai Pian*. Zhonghua Publishing House.
He, Q. (2015 [1631]). *The collected work of Jingshan (Jingshan Quanji)*. Fukien Renmin Press.
He, X. (1960 [1579]). *Collected work of He Xinyin (He Xinyin Ji)* (Vol. 3). Zhonghua Publishing House House.
Hiroshi, F. (1984). Research on Xin'an merchants. *Research on Chinese Socio-Economic History, 3*, 51–54.
Hu, J. (1998 [1965]). *History of Chinese economic thoughts* (Vol. 1–3). Shanghai University of Finance and Economics Press.
Hua, Q. (2002). *General history of China*. Shanghai Ancient Books Publishing House.
Hua, T., & Wang, R. (2014). *The years of studying abroad*. China Tourism Press.
Huan, K. (1992 [c. 66–49BC]). *Discourses on salt and iron (Yantie Lun)*. Zhonghua Publishing House.
Huang, H. (2019). *Tea village livelihood: The space and social changes of a tea village in Fujian Province*. Guangming Daily Press.
Huang, K. (2000 [1634]). *Shuma Ji*. Peking Press.
Huang, W. (1983 [1551]). *Ming Daobian* (Vol. 4). Zhonghua Publishing House.
Huang, Z. (2011 [1662]). *Mingyi Daifang Lu*. Yuelu Publishing House.
Huang, Z. (1975 [1695]). *Songyuan Xue'an*. Heluo Tushu Press.
Ji, W. (2013 [1943]). *History of late Ming thought*. Zhonghua Publishing House.
Jiang, J. (1990). *History of Chinese commerce and economics thoughts*. China Financial and Economic Publishing House.
Jiang, Y. (2000 [1605]). *Xuetao Xiaoshuo*. Shanghai Ancient Books Publishing House.

Jiao, S. (2011). *History of ancient Chinese book collection*. China International Broadcasting Press.

Li, D. (1962 [1509]). *Ming Shilu, record of Emperor Hongzhi*. Institute of History and Language.

Li, D. (2004). *A study of imperial power in Ming Dynasty*. China Social Science Press.

Li, D. (2013). Suppressing before emphasizing the merchants. *Modern History Institute Collected Papers, 82*, 1–53.

Li, J. (1990). *The history of overseas trade in Ming China*. China Social Science Press.

Li, J. (1995). *The history of overseas trade in ancient China*. Guangxi Renmin Press.

Li, M. (1991 [1529]). *Kongtong Ji*. Shanghai Ancient Books Publishing House.

Li, W. (1997 [1626]). *Dami Shanfang Ji*. Qilu Press.

Li, W. (2000 [1647]). *Liaozhai Ji*. Peking Press.

Li, X. (1997 [1594]). *Dongdai Shanfang Shilu*. The Phoenix Press.

Li, Z. (2000 [1602]). *Li Zhi Wenji*. China Social Science Literature Press.

Li, Z. (2001 [1602]). *Fen Shu*. Yuanfang Press.

Liang, J. (2019). *Lectures on history of Western economic thought*. Fudan University Press.

Lin, X. (2015 [1565]). *Lin Ciya Xiansheng Wenji*. Xiamen University Press.

Liu, D. (2010 [1636]). *Guide of landscape and articles in the capital city (Dijing Jingwu Lue)*. Shanghai Ancient Books Publishing House.

Liu, J. (1962 [1491]). *Ming Shilu, record of Emperor Chenghua*. Institute of History and Language.

Liu, M. (2012). The export of porcelain under the sea ban policy in early Ming China. *Archaeological Studies, 4*, 84–91.

Liu, Q. (2000). *Usury capital of Ming-Qing period*. China Social Science Literature Press.

Liu, Q. (2015). *The maritime merchant empire: The official-merchant relations and the origin of the Zheng group*. Zhejiang University Press.

Liu, W. (2002 [1397]). *The Ming Code*. Shanghai Ancient Books Publishing House.

Lu, C. (1993 [1551]). *Lu Ziyu Ji*. Shanghai Ancient Books Publishing House.

Lu, F. (1992). *The collection of Chinese painting and calligraphy*. Shanghai Shuhua Press.

Lu, J. (1985 [1552]). *Jianjia Tang Zazhu Zhaichao*. Zhonghua Publishing House.

Lu, S. (1987 [1544]). *Yanshan Waiji*. Shanghai Ancient Books Publishing House.

Lu, S. (1993 [1544]). *Jintai Jiwen*. Shanghai Ancient Books Publishing House.

Lü, K. (2008 [1618]). *Lü Kun Quanji*. Zhonghua Publishing House.

Luo, Z. (2006). *A study of the mental state of scholars in the Late Ming dynasty*. Nankai University Press.
Ma, Y. (1985 [1571]). *Discussion on agriculture (Nong Shuo)*. Zhonghua Publishing House House.
Matsuura, A. (2016). *The research on overseas trade in Qing China*. Tianjin Renmin Press.
Qian, M. (2012 [1952]). *The political gains and losses in Chinese history*. Jiuzhou Press.
Qian, Y. (2009). *Shentan Di Renjie*. China Social Science Press.
Qiu, J. (1986 [1487]). *Daxue Yanyi Bu*. Taiwan Commercial Press.
Semedo, A. (1655 [1636]). *The history of that great and renowned monarchy of China*. Translated by a person of quality. E. Tyler for John Crook.
Shang, Y. (2009 [338BC]). *Shang Jun Shu*. Zhonghua Publishing House.
Shen, B. (1980 [1597]). *Wanshu anthology (Wanshu Zaji)* (Vol. 1). Peking Ancient Books Publishing House.
Shen, D. (2007 [1642]). *Wanli Yehuo Bian* (Vol. 26). Zhonghua Publishing House House.
Shen, K. (1918 [1840]). *Luofanlou Wenji*. Liushi Jiaye Tang.
Shen, M. (1996). *History (Lishi)* (Vol. 1 and 3). Shanghai Education Press.
Shen, S. (1989[1587]). *Ming Huidian*. Zhonghua Publishing House.
Shi, J. (2017). *Robbing the people: Eight officials famous for accumulating wealth in Chinese history*. Zhongxin Press.
Shi, Q. (1996 [1605]). *Salt Laws in Lianghuai (Lianghuai Yanfa Zhi)*. Qilu Press.
Sima, G. (1919 [1086]). *Wenguo Wenzhenggong Ji* (Vol. 23). The Commercial Press.
Sima, G. (2013 [1084]). *Zizhi Tongjian*. Zhonghua Publishing House.
Sima, Q. (1959 [86BC]). *Records of the grand historian*. Zhonghua Publishing House.
Song, L. (1976 [1369]). *History of Yuan*. Zhonghua Publishing House.
Song, Y. (2010 [1637]). *Tiangong Kaiwu*. Shanghai: Shanghai Ancient Books Publishing House.
Sun, H. (2001). *History of Chinese refugees, volume of ancient China*. Anhui People Press.
Sun, S. (2009). *Matteo Ricci and Xu Guangqi*. China International Broadcasting Press.
Sun, W., & Sun, Z. (2002). *Introduction to international finance*. Tongji University Press.
Tang, S. (1922 [1560]). *Jingchuan Xiansheng Wenji*. The Commercial Press.
Wan, Y. (2004). *Court history of the Qing dynasty*. Baihua Wenyi Press.
Wang, A. (1961 [1086]). *Wang Linchuan Ji* (Vol. 39). World Publishing House.

Wang, D. (2015). *Advanced lecture notes on the history of economic thought*. Shanghai Renmin Press.
Wang, F. (1956 [1692]). *Nightmare (E Meng)*. Zhonghua Publishing House.
Wang, F. (1975 [1692]). *Discussion on Zizhi Tongjian (Du Tongjian Lun)*. Zhonghua Publishing House.
Wang, S. (1997 [1598]). *Guangzhi Yi* (Vol. 2). Zhonghua Publishing House.
Wang, S. (1986 [1590]). *Yanzhou Xugao*. Taiwan Commercial Press.
Wang, X. (1984 [1936]). *Chinese commerce history*. Shanghai Bookstore Publishing House.
Wang, Y. (1978 [1525]). *Chuanxi Lu*. Shanghai: Shanghai Ancient Books Publishing House.
Wang, Y. (1983 [1759]). *Liunan Suibi*. Zhonghua Publishing House.
Wang, Z. (1996). *Huizhou merchants and Huaiyang social changes in the Ming and Qing dynasties*. Sanlian Press.
Wen, G., et al. (2001). *The local history of Shanghai*. Shanghai Education Press.
Wen, P. (2001). *The Western history*. Baihua Wenyi Press.
Wen, T. (1962 [1630]). *Ming Shilu, record of Emperor Wanli*. Institute of History and Language.
Wu, H. (2004). *Chinese commerce history*. The Finance and Economics Press.
Wu, K. (1929 [1504]). *Paoweng Jiacang Ji*. The Commercial Press.
Wu, X. (2012). *Mighty for two thousand years (Haodang Liangqian Nian)*. Zhongxin Press.
Xie, G. (1980). *Selected social and economic historical materials of Ming dynasty*. Fujian Renmin Press.
Xie, J. (1962 [1411]). *Ming Shilu, record of Emperor Hongwu*. Institute of History and Language.
Xie, K. (1966 [1693]). *Lianghuai Yanfa Zhi*. Taiwan Student Press.
Xie, Z. (1959 [1624]). *Wuza Zu*. Zhonghua Publishing House.
Xie, Z. (2001 [1624]). *Wuza Zu*. Peking: Shanghai Book Store Publishing House.
Xu, M. (1998). A probe into the issue of merchants' household registration in the Ming dynasty. *Study on Chinese History, 3*, 1–16.
Xu, G. (1979 [1633]). *Nongzheng Quanshu* (Vol. 2). Shanghai Ancient Books Publishing House.
Xu, G. (1984 [1633]). *Xu Guangqi Ji*. Shanghai Ancient Books Publishing House.
Xu, G. (2000 [1596]). *Xu Wenmugong Ji*. Peking Press.
Xu, H. (1983 [1281]). *Luzhai posthumous writings*. Taipei Commercial Press.
Xu, H. (2011). *Study of Ming history in China in the 20th century*. Taiwan University Press.
Xu, J. (2009 [1583]). *Shaohu Xiansheng Wenji*. Qilu Press.
Yan, C. (1993 [1574]. *Shuyu Zhouzi Lu*. Peking: Zhonghua Publishing House.

Yan, J. (1996 [1596]). *Yan Jun Ji*. China Social Science Press.
Yang, S. (1962 [1424]). *Ming Shilu, record of Emperor Yongle*. Institute of History and Language.
Ye, S. (2003). *History of ancient Chinese economic thoughts*. Fudan University Press.
Ye, X. (1994 [1627]). *Cangxia Cao Quanji*. Peking Press.
Ye, Y. (1985[1604]). *Zhechai Jishi*. Zhonghua Publishing House.
Yin, S. (2000 [1631]). *Mingshi Qie*. Peking Press.
Yu, R. (1986[1620]). *Manuscript of ministry of ritual (Libu Zhigao)*. Taiwan Commercial Press.
Yu, S. (1980 [1608]). *Gushan Bizhu*. Jiangsu Renmin Press.
Yu, Y. (1987). *Religious ethics and merchant spirit in modern China*. Linking Publishing.
Yu, Y. (2004). *Confucian ethics and merchant spirit*. Guangxi Normal University Press.
Yuan, H. (2010 [1610]). *Pinghua Zhaiji* (Vol. 3). Shanghai Ancient Books Publishing House.
Zang, R. (2009). *Posthouses and postal service in ancient China*. China International Broadcasting Press.
Zhang, D. (2010 [1684]). *Memory of dreams in Tao'an (Tao'an Mengyi)*. Zhonghua Publishing House House.
Zhang, G. (2000 [1646]). *Zhang Zhongmingong Yiji*. Peking Press.
Zhang, H. (1985[1593]). *Songchuang Mengyu*. Zhonghua Publishing House.
Zhang, J. (1937 [1582]). *Zhang Wenzhonggong Quanji*. The Commercial Press.
Zhang, L. (2000 [1598]). *Jialong Shuchao*. Shanghai Ancient Books Publishing House.
Zhang, R. (1962 [1577]). *Ming Shilu, record of Emperor Jiajing*. Institute of History and Language.
Zhang, T. (1974 [1739]). *The history of Ming*. Institute of History and Language.
Zhang, X. (2002 [1636]). *Records of sights in the West Garden (Xiyuan Wenjian Lu)* (Vol. 32). Shanghai Ancient Books Publishing House.
Zhang, Z. (1999). *Political system of the Ming dynasty*. Wunan Book Press.
Zhao, N. (2000 [1627]). *Zhao Zhongyigong Wenji* (Vol. 4). Peking Press.
Zhou, G. (2004 [c. 400–100 BC]). *Zhouli*. Shanghai Ancient Books Publishing House.
Zhou, Q. (1987 [1626]). *The research on Eastern and Western Trade (Dongxiyang Kao)*. Shanghai Ancient Books Publishing House.
Zhou, X. (1985 [1586]). *Jinglin Xuji*. Zhonghua Publishing House.
Zhu, G. (2012 [1632]). *Yongchuang Xiaopin* (Vol. 9). Shanghai Ancient Books Publishing House.

Zhu, Q. (1957). *Li Zhi: Pioneer of anti-feudalism in China in the 16th century*. Hubei People Press.
Zhu, R. (1986). The social status of merchants in the Song dynasty and its historical role. *History Research, No., 2*, 127–143.
Zhu, T. (2002 [1529]). *Yanzheng Zhi*. Shanghai Ancient Books Publishing House.
Zhu, Y. (1986 [1398]). *Ming Taizu Wenji*. Taiwan Commercial Press.

Index

T. Hua, *Merchants, Market and Monarchy*,
Palgrave Studies in the History of Economic Thought,
https://doi.org/10.1007/978-3-030-77189-8

The manufacturer's authorised representative in the EU is Springer Nature Customer Service Centre GmbH, Europaplatz 3, 69115 Heidelberg, Germany. If you have any concerns regarding our products, please contact ProductSafety@springernature.com

Printed and bound by CPI Group (UK) Ltd, Croydon, CR0 4YY
30/09/2026
02225455-0013